MIGRANTS

*Exploring the Colors
of my Family History*

Also by **Roger Mendoza**

Non-Fiction
My Little Cowboy

Fiction:
Purging Purgatory: A Ghost Story

MIGRANTS

Exploring the Colors of my Family History

ROGER MENDOZA

Published by Romen Graphics
www.RomenGraphics.com
Book website: www.LaFamiliaMendoza.com

No part of this publication may be reproduced, stored in a retrieval system, or transmitted, in any form, or by any means, electronic, mechanical, photocopying, recording, or otherwise, without the prior consent of the author or publisher (except for the inclusion of brief quotations in a review).

While the author and publisher have used their best efforts in preparing this book, they make no representations or warranties with respect to the accuracy or completeness of the contents of this book. Additionally, the author and publisher have removed all specific birthdates for all relatives who were still living at the time this book was published.

Cover design by Roger Mendoza

Copyright © 2020 Roger Mendoza
All rights reserved.

ISBN-13: 978-1-938962-30-1 (hardcover)
ISBN-13: 978-1-938962-29-5 (paperback)

Library of Congress Control Number: 2020916013

To my mother – Carmen.
She called me to this life and nurtured and cared for me.

Acknowledgments

I have been inspired to write the story of my family's history by many people throughout the years. I am so thankful for all of the experiences - both positive and negative that added so much diversity to my life. Of course, I'm grateful to my mother, Carmen Garcia Mendoza, who inspired me to learn about my past. She spoke on camera about her family as well as about my father's family. My father, Enrique Mendoza, offered precious anecdotes and stories from his early days in Mexico. Both of them told me fascinating stories that piqued my interest. This prompted me to want to record everything I could find about their past.

I'm grateful to my cousin Mary Lou Gomez-Rettie for editing this manuscript and correcting or filling in some information that she had heard from her mother, Matilde Escobedo, and from other family members. Her help was incredibly appreciated.

Thanks to my sisters, Irma, Mary Carmen, and Margaret for editing the manuscript and making the manuscript shine.

My cousin Olga Gomez Espinosa told me stories about her mother, Matilde Escobedo, and other family members. She sent me detailed emails with recollections about her mother.

My cousin Yolanda Mendoza Rodriguez told me stories and let me copy her family pictures.

My cousin Joe Mendoza helped me with some last-minute fact checking on his father, Jesus.

My brother Richard facilitated a trip to South Texas in 2007 that included him, my sister, Minnie, her husband, Eddie Alejandro, and me. I video-recorded interviews from my aunts and uncles (Margarita Elva Mendoza Trevino, Marcolfa Escobedo, and Anselmo Longoria Jr. ("Chemo"). Each of them talked about their family history on camera.

My cousin, Anselmo Longoria, Jr. ("Chemo"), one of my mother's favorite cousins, gave hours of detailed information about his family's early life in McAllen. Additionally, he allowed me to scan his countless photograph albums that preserved loving memories of his long life. Chemo sent me a letter a few weeks later with a very detailed map of the Longoria's and Mendoza's homes from circa 1930.

I thank my brothers and sisters who provided their recollections of La Familia Mendoza history from so long ago. My four older siblings: Henry, Minnie, Irma, and Richard shared their recollections, stories, and photographs from the time when my grandparents, Encarnacion and Margarita, lived. The rest of my siblings: Mary Carmen, Rose Mary, Ramie, Bobby, and Margaret shared their stories, precious photographs, and other puzzle pieces from our past.

There are too many to list, but I want to thank all those relatives and friends who offered little tidbits of information that helped me to add some spice to these stories.

CONTENTS

Introduction ... 1
1 - Estefana up to 1910 ... 6
2 - Encarnacion & Margarita up to 1910 ... 14
3 - Encarnacion & Margarita 1910 to 1919 ... 20
4 - Estefana 1910 to 1919 ... 29
5 - Estefana & Carmen 1920 to 1928 ... 34
6 - Encarnacion & Margarita 1920 to 1924 ... 40
7 - Encarnacion & Margarita 1925 to 1927 ... 48
8 - Mendoza's Reunited 1927 to 1928 ... 55
9 - McAllen 1928 to 1929 ... 62
10 - Anselmo the Hero 9/1929 ... 69
11 - Budding Romance 1929 ... 76
12 - The Store - 1930 ... 85
13 - The Census - 4/1930 to 8/1930 ... 88
14 - Mamacita Danced - 9/1930 to 11/1930 ... 97
15 - Mendoza Shakeup - 11/1930 to 12/1930 ... 106
16 - Making Moves - 1/1931 to 3/1931 ... 113
17 - We Need Money - 5/1931 to 10/1931 ... 125
18 - One Door Closes - 10/1931 to 12/1931 ... 137
19 - A New Loteria Tent - 1932 ... 144
20 - Two Become One - 1/1932 to 7/1932 ... 150
21 - Goodbye, McAllen - 8/1932 to 9/1932 ... 169
22 - San Antonio - 9/1932 to 12/1934 ... 177
23 - Family Life - 1/1935 to 10/1936 ... 188

24 - Sacrifices - 11/1936 196
25 - More Family - 4/1937 to 12/1939 203
26 - Old Soul - 4/1940 to 12/1941 210
27 - New Home - 1/1942 to 5/1945 221
28 - Living 6/1945 to 2/1947 233
29 - It's Time - 4/1947 to 12/1948 241
30 - The Pace of Life - 2/1949 to 12/1953 252
31 - Peace at Last - 1/1954 to 9/1954 262
32 - Aftermath - 1954 272
33 - Rebuilding - 1954 to 1955 279
34 - The Recorder - 1955 to 1956 292
35 - Day in the Life - 1956 304
36 - Memorial - 1956 313
37 - Ghost of Plutarco - 1957 320
38 - Family United - 1958 327
39 - Future 336

Meet the Family 344
About the Author 374
Notes 375

Introduction

On January 5, 1983, Enrique Mendoza (73) and his wife, Carmen Garcia Mendoza (69), sat with their eighth son, Rogelio Mendoza (27), in the living room of 139 Aganier Avenue in San Antonio, Texas. Rogelio recorded the interview on his recently purchased J.C. Penney VHS Video Recorder. The recorder had a huge, bulky camera that sat on a tripod across from his parents.

During the interview, Enrique and Carmen talked about their lives growing up. They went on to tell about how they met, married, and raised their children. Carmen offered accounts of events that had happened to her from when she was eleven and older. Her earlier memories, for some reason, were lost to her. The memories that she shared were full of color and imagery. She knew quite a bit about Enrique's family too. Carmen had learned so much from her closeness to her husband's family. Carmen loved to chat with them over coffee and cake. She had spent years with Enrique's family discussing the lives of her "comadres" (Enrique's sisters, sisters-in-law, and cousins). Carmen was close to them all and knew many deep-down secrets that they had discussed with her. She rarely revealed any of those confidences while we were recording the interviews. Her memory was sharp and refined. Enrique told a few stories about his life growing up in Mexico and the tidbits of his life. His mind was not as sharp as Carmen's. However, he used practical methods to record his life experiences. He loved taking pictures, taking 8mm films, making audio recordings, and saving important documentation from his life. Enrique kept papers and photographs that had belonged to his parents. Carmen and Enrique had both amassed a considerable collection of pictures, family documents, and mementos from decades of living. Most of those have been digitized and used in recording the family history.

I likely inherited my father's knack for recording the family's history through movies, pictures, and books. My memory is certainly not as sharp as my mother's. I had interviewed them many times before 1982 and afterward, too. I took meticulous notes and recorded the interviews with them on my various cameras throughout the years. My parents were very supportive of my passion for preserving their history.

I lived in Southern California and usually had two weeks off from work each Christmas and would take my recording equipment and picture camera home to San Antonio to take pictures and conduct my interviews. I also had a darkroom where I processed the film I had taken and made prints from them. In that darkroom, which used to be my closet, I processed thousands of negatives and prints. My parents let me borrow the treasure trove of their photographs and negatives. I used my Yashica SLR film camera (that I had bought from my brother, Henry, for $25) to photograph their pictures and used their negatives to generate prints. When the cost of film scanners dropped to an "affordable" price, I bought one. It was a professional scanner that cost $1,700. With that scanner, I was able to scan the hundreds of film and slides from my parent's collection of photos.

As time went on, my parents and other family members helped me collect more information about my family. In 2007, my brother, Richard, and I both lived in Colorado. He also was interested in preserving our family history. He suggested that we should vacation in San Antonio at the same time and go to South Texas to

Migrants: Exploring the Colors of my Family History

interview our cousin Chemo Longoria (Carmen's cousin), Aunt Margarita Elva Mendoza (Enrique's sister), and Aunt Marcolfa Escobedo (Carmen's sister). Soon after, Richard and I drove to San Antonio in my Honda Pilot. A day or two later, Richard, along with our sister, Minnie, and her husband, Eddie, drove down to McAllen, Texas, where Cousin Chemo Longoria lived. It was a leisurely visit, and we stayed there for a couple of days. Chemo graciously answered all of our questions about our family's past in front of the camera. He and his wife Mary Alice brought out a dozen or so family albums full of pictures, letters, and other precious memories. Chemo was kind enough to allow me to digitally capture quite a bit of his collection. During breakfast the next morning, he drew a map on a napkin where his parents had lived in 1930. My parents had lived on that property too. He later sent me a letter with a more detailed map drawn professionally on a sheet of paper.

Next, we traveled to the border town, Roma, Texas, where Aunt Margarita Elva lived. She used to have a large clothing/material store that was on the first floor of her house. Customers from both sides of the border frequented her store. By 2007, Aunt Margarita Elva had long before retired. We visited together for a few hours while my camera recorded her. She shared heart-warming stories of her early life, her parents, and her brothers and sisters. She left nothing out. She talked lovingly about them as well as her husband and children. With a twinkle in her eye, she shared a story of how she, as a young girl of about ten years of age, would deliver her brother Enrique's love letters to Carmen during their courtship.

Our next stop was Progresso, Texas, to visit Aunt Marcolfa (Carmen's sister). Again, I set up the camera as mostly, Minnie, Eddie, and Richard asked questions. Marcolfa shared her memories from long ago. She was about four years old when she lived with her family in McAllen, and she couldn't remember much about her mother, Estefana. Marcolfa was six years old when her mother died. But she told stories about what she'd learned about her from her older sisters. Surrounding her were loving pictures of her mother, Estefana, Maria Luisa (her older sister), and of course, her children.

Much of the information gathered to prepare these family biographies came from documents and pictures handed down from parents and grandparents. This information was crucial in creating the family biographies and histories for this book. Additionally, census records, newspapers, and a plethora of historical documents added voluminous amounts of information about each of the family members. Additionally, Ancestry.com provided numerous tools to assimilate this information into a coherent, integrated fashion. The use of Ancestry.com, a sophisticated family tree management system, provided an easy way to organize all of the family tree information. To add a refined dimension to this data, Ancestry.com integrated seamlessly with its AncestryDNA databases and provided a tool to automatically find members in the tree who shared DNA with others. Of course, AncestryDNA folks have indicated that their tools are not foolproof. In any case, both Ancestry.com and AncestryDNA.com helped me resolve the mystery of my mother's father.

Enrique and Carmen's lives, as well as their relatives, continue to speak through the stories expressed in this book.

Photographs, documents, stories, and recordings have helped to produce a robust and rich history of my parent's families. Currently, the "La Familia Mendoza" archives contain thousands of photographs, documents, films, videos, and audio recordings about my family.

In writing this book, I have made every effort to capture the history of my family accurately. There are very few events that I write about in my family's past that are not crystal clear because of conflicting recollections or missing records. In those rare instances, I write about the events as they likely happened, and then I'll present the alternate timeline of events as a note. Regardless, the events recorded from different sources in the "La Familia Mendoza" archives, help to weave a rich story of life from the late

1800s to 1959.

The roots of my family's history begin in Spain and France. However, the narrative of my family's colorful history begins in Mexico.

1 - Estefana up to 1910

Matamoros, Tamaulipas, is in the Northeast corner of the beautiful country of Mexico. Seventeen miles further east at the Gulf of Mexico was the long-gone port city of Bagdad. Up until 1865, Matamoros benefitted significantly from the export of cotton to Europe through the Bagdad port. At that time, Matamoros was a thriving city of 30,000 inhabitants with a robust economy.

After the end of the American Civil War, the economy of Bagdad/Matamoros began to falter. Another twenty years of destructive hurricanes followed by a major one in 1889 had transformed the once-prosperous Bagdad port into a pristine sandy beach. Gone was the thriving agricultural economy of Matamoros, along with half the population who left to more profitable regions to the north. In the aftermath of the violent destruction of the hurricane that befell the residents, the townspeople would have been wanting for something better.

In March of 1892, Estefana Longoria was born in Matamoros, Tamaulipas, Mexico. Her parents, Alejandro Longoria and Estefana Martinez, were indeed elated to welcome their newest baby girl. Baby Estefana had two brothers: Guillermo (8) and Benjamin (2) and two sisters: Luisa (6) and Matilde (4). Excitement must have filled the air in the household of seven. Her father probably would have wanted another boy to help with the farm work. Her mother,

Migrants: Exploring the Colors of my Family History

on the other hand, celebrated another daughter that she could dote over as she had done with her other two daughters. Over the next few years, the children would each learn to read and write as they came of school age. Although, Guillermo would undoubtedly have had a head start on them.

By December of 1899, Estefana was seven. She had fair skin and was taller than the other children in her school. Her hair was light brown, not black like many of the other children from her small town in Tamaulipas, Mexico. Her eyes were brown with flecks of lightness, almost blue, or maybe an ashen gray with hints of brown. She was no longer the baby of the family. Now Estefana (7) had two younger siblings: Anselmo (5) and Alejandro Jr. (3) and four older siblings: Guillermo (15), Luisa (13), Matilde (11) and Benjamin (9).

Luisa had completed school and helped her mother with the sewing, cooking, and other such duties. Luisa was proficient at needlework. Her mother had likely taught Luisa how to sew and attend to other household duties that she would use later in life when she got married.

Estefana must have felt safe in her small, loving world. Her mother and older siblings would, no doubt, have insulated her from the harshness of life.

Her father, Alejandro Longoria, would likely have had a different view about his family's well-being. It was getting more challenging to provide for his family. The economy of Matamoros was nowhere near where it had been when he was younger.

He had considered moving from Matamoros to Brownsville, Texas, in the United States. Matamoros was across the Rio Grande River[1] from her sister city of Brownsville, Texas. Across the border, he would be able to give his family a better life, and the citizens of both countries traveled easily between the two cities. The Brownsville Herald, the newspaper from the United States, was distributed in Matamoros. The paper talked about cheap farmland in Brownsville. Alejandro probably imagined that on the farm he could plant crops, raise chickens, keep goats, and so much more. In his eyes, the United States offered him a chance to raise his family in a land of opportunity and safety.

About January 1, 1900, the Longoria family moved to Brownsville, Texas. Alejandro surmised that he could bring his family back to Matamoros if things didn't go well here. The family moved into a house in the rural area adjacent to the city center of Brownsville. The population of Brownsville in 1900 was 6,305.[2]

The Longoria family had begun a new life in the United States in the first few days of the emerging century. Alejandro and his eldest son, Guillermo, worked the land of their new home.

At eight years old, Estefana was too young to know why they moved to the United States. At that age, she probably would have happily played with her doll and clothed it with a pretty dress that her mother might have made for it. She would have enjoyed hand-me-downs from her two older sisters. She was still her mother's baby girl. Also, she must have enjoyed playtime with her two younger brothers, Anselmo (6) and Alejandro Jr. (4).

Six months later, the 1900 United States Census started.[3] When the census taker came to Alejandro's house on June 11, 1900, he supplied the required information for the census taker for each family member. When the census taker wrote Estefana's name, he mistakenly put the brother's, Benjamin (10), statistics on the same line. Benjamin's name was missing from the 1900 census.

Benjamin's birth[4] and baptismal[5] certificates ensured that Benjamin would not be a forgotten member of the family. One tragic note regarding the 1900 census revealed that Estefana Martinez had nine children, of which only seven were alive. Although in those times it was not uncommon to lose a child either during or shortly after childbirth, it was none-the-less tragic, especially for the mother.

The census also showed that the second oldest child, Luisa,

could read and write, and that her occupation was needlework, a skill probably learned from her mother. Perhaps that was another source of income for the family.

Guillermo, the eldest child, and his father were both listed as day-laborers (a hint that they were the breadwinners for the family).

In all, Alejandro (41) and his wife Estefana Martinez (33) had four boys: Guillermo (16), Benjamin (10), Anselmo (6), and Alejandro Jr. (4). And they had three daughters: Luisa (14) and Matilde (13), and Estefana (8). The older children and their parents were literate in Spanish, and none of them could speak English.

Life seemed to be good for the Longoria family. Alejandro and Estefana welcomed another baby boy, Cristobal, on January 18, 1901. The family had now grown to eight children.

Unfortunately, tragedy struck two years later. In 1903, in Monterrey, Nuevo Leon, Mexico, Alejandro's father-in-law, Esteban Martinez, reported the tragic death of Alejandro and Estefana Martinez Longoria's son Benjamin. On the death certificate Esteban stated that at 4:00 a.m., on the morning of November 19, 1903, twelve-year-old Benjamin died.[6] Benjamin's mother, Estefana Martinez, would most likely have been visiting her parents in her childhood town of Monterrey. Perhaps, Matilde (15) and Cristobal (1-1/2) had gone with her to Monterrey. Cristobal would have been too young to leave behind. The family would have felt the pain of losing a young son and brother.

Each week the local newspaper, The Brownsville Herald, published a list of "Uncalled for" letters in the post office. In 1905, two letters addressed to Alejandro Longoria were held in the Brownsville, Texas post office for pickup - one from October 14[7] and the second from October 28.[8] It's unclear if they were intended for nine-year-old Alejandro Jr., or to his father.

The next month, another letter was waiting for 19-year-old Señorita Luisa Longoria on November 18, 1905.[9] Another hint that this letter came from Luisa's mother in Mexico as it appears, she often traveled there to visit her parents.

On March 25, 1907,[10] a letter addressed to 13-year-old Anselmo Longoria was listed in the paper.

Who sent those letters to the Longoria family? Both of the parents could read and write. One possibility is that Estefana Martinez, their mother would likely have stayed with her family in Monterrey. She had just lost her son, Benjamin, at the end of 1903. In any case, circumstances had cast a terrible and tragic shadow over the Longoria family. Not only had Estefana Martinez lost her 12-year-old boy, but it appeared that the move to Brownsville, Texas, had begun to splinter the family.

By mid-1909, 25-year-old Guillermo had met the love of his life, Juana Anaya (17). Estefana was also 17 years old. Estefana was a reserved but very independent young lady. She was a beautiful, small-framed woman who stood 5'7" tall. She would undoubtedly have caught the eye of some young man, just as Juana Anaya had.

On July 13, 1909, the Brownsville Herald newspaper published a list of "Uncalled for" letters.[11] "Mrs. Estefana Longoria de Garcia" was listed under the "Ladies" heading. Under the Gentlemen's title was recorded: "Manuel Garcia." This letter from 1909 was the last one addressed to the Longoria's published in the Brownsville Herald. Years later, on the census form from 1930, she stated that she was first married at age 15 (that would be about 1907 as she was born about 1892). Years later, her death certificate said that her husband was "Manuel Garcia." Had Estefana been married to Manuel Garcia in 1909? No marriage certificate was found for Estefana Longoria and Manuel Garcia.

By 1910, life was good for the Longoria family. The preparations were underway for the marriage of Guillermo and Juana. They were undoubtedly thrilled beyond words with their upcoming union.

On February 19, 1910, Guillermo and Juana were married.[12] The whole family was bursting with excitement. The days were a comfortable 74 degrees F, and the nights were a chilly 55 degrees F.

Then, the unthinkable happened. On March 23, 1910, Luisa Longoria passed away at the age of 23. She would no longer be doing her needlework, of which she had been so proud (and which may have contributed to the family income).

Luisa had used strychnine to end her life. It was a devastating blow to the family. For several excruciating hours that it took for Luisa to die, her family would not have been able to bring her back from the brink of death. Her father, if he were there, would have been speechless, his eyes wide with grief as he watched his daughter writhing in pain. Her mother, if she were there, would have cried as she pleaded with God to save her daughter's life. Estefana would have quietly stood in shock, trying to hold back her tears as Luisa's body fought the poison. And all of Luisa's siblings would have felt their hearts ripped from their hollow chests as they stood helpless to stop their sister from leaving her problems behind. Guillermo, in particular with his wife, had instantly gone from sheer happiness, in his new wondrous married life, to devastation. The guilt and the horror that her family felt must have been tremendously overwhelming.[13]

It was 18-year old Estefana, who reported the death of her sister to the authorities. Perhaps she'd learned English well enough to recount the terrible details to the record-taker. Ten years before, she only knew how to speak Spanish. She may have attended school for a couple of years after arriving in the United States. Perhaps she had friends who spoke English. In any case, she was able to muster up enough strength to tell the record-taker that her beloved sister had committed suicide. The document revealed Luisa's parent's names had been written in a different handwriting style than the rest of the document. A handwriting expert would have noted the downward slant of the scrawl for the name of the father, Alejandro Longoria. The slant indicated disdain for Alejandro. The mother's name, Estefana Martinez, was written almost perfectly horizontal. The writing of the birthplace of Mexico progressed happily upward. On the righthand side of the form, the doctor recorded the cause of death in large blotchy, technical handwriting (which was nowhere near as delicate as the handwriting on the rest of the document): "Suicide with Strychnine."

The family had splintered into tragic pieces after Luisa's death. Her mother, Estefana Martinez, left for Mexico (if she wasn't already there) and left her husband, Alejandro Longoria Sr. behind in Brownsville.

The 1910 United States Census[14] had some errors. Guillermo (25), his wife, Juana Anaya (18), his brother, Alejandro Jr. (13), and his sister, Estefana (17), were still living on the family farm established by his father in Brownsville, Texas. The two brothers were laborers at that time. It incorrectly stated the details for Alejandro Jr. and Estefana. Guillermo was probably still in shock from Luisa's death when he attempted to explain to the census taker the members of his household. His sister, Luisa, had just died, and the rest of his family was gone. He probably felt the burden of the world on his shoulders as he talked to the census taker. He misreported that his brother Alejandro Jr. was 27 and that his sister "Estefanita" was his three-year-old daughter. Guillermo was probably nervous as the census taker asked him, "Didn't you tell me that you just got married? How could you have a three-year-old daughter?"

Guillermo might have said, "Oh, I was married before."

Is that the reason that the census taker had written that Guillermo had been married twice on the census form? Also, the census taker wrote an oddly shaped "3" for Estefanita's age, as if he wrote it with uncertainty. Of course, it's possible that Guillermo had a daughter named Estefanita, but unlikely.

The horror of the death of his sister, Luisa, would undoubtedly have continued to weigh heavily on the family's hearts. It's a mystery why Estefana might have been married at the time and also living with her brother Guillermo. Perhaps, a record yet to be found would answer that question. In any case, life continued for the Longoria's, despite the catastrophic assault on their family.

Growing up in Brownsville, Alejandro Jr. worked with Guillermo to provide for the new family. Their sister, Estefana, was sure to have continued to milk the goats or cows, collect the eggs, and feed the animals. Certainly, Estefana, along with her sister-in-law, Juana, would have taken care of cleaning the clothes, cooking, and other household chores. Many years later, Estefana's daughter, Carmen, said that her mother was skilled at cooking, caring for the chickens, cows, goats, and other sources of food for her family. These tragic events had taught her to develop an empathetic and compassionate character.

Estefana Martinez and her daughter Matilde were not recorded on the United States Census from 1910 in Brownsville or the surrounding communities. It's entirely plausible that they both went back to Monterrey to stay with the parents of Estefana Martinez.

Alejandro Longoria Sr. had stayed behind and continued to work the fields. (Alejandro Sr. would later move in with his son, Anselmo in Pharr, Texas).

The missing pieces of the Longoria family tale continued with Estefana Longoria, daughter of Alejandro Longoria Sr. and Estefana Martinez Longoria. Was Estefana Longoria now Mrs. Estefana Longoria de Garcia, wife of Manuel Garcia (as was indicated on the Brownsville Herald Newspaper from July 13, 1907)?

Years later, Anselmo Longoria Jr. ("Chemo"), said that his father Anselmo was attending school in Brownsville. Perhaps, Cristobal (9) was also in school. Even though the Longoria family had fractured, the two youngest boys may have been able to receive a formal education. This must have come at a great sacrifice for a family that depended on the income of farm labor.

2 - Encarnacion & Margarita up to 1910

The Republic of Texas had declared its independence on March 2, 1836, from Mexico, and it became its own country. After nine years as an independent republic, on December 29, 1845, the Republic of Texas agreed to become part of the United States of America. It was annexed into the United States and admitted into the union. Of course, Mexico never acknowledged Texas's independence and thus began the Mexican American War from 1846 to 1848. After the United States won the war, they paid Mexico 15 million dollars for the lands that would later become Arizona, California, New Mexico, Nevada, Utah, portions of Colorado, and Wyoming. Mexico also gave up its claims to Texas.

At some point, there were flags of six different countries flown over Texas: Spain, France, Mexico, Republic of Texas, Confederate States of America, and the United States of America.

It would make sense that many descendants of early Texas would have bits and pieces of DNA from more than one of those countries. Two such families are the Ybarbo and the De La Garza families.

Juan de la Garza was born about 1843 in the state of Nuevo Leon, Mexico. By 1880, he was living in Floresville, Texas, in Wilson County with his wife, Margarita Lopez. They had five children: Eugenio (10), Virginia (9), Juan (5), Margarita (2), and

Migrants: Exploring the Colors of my Family History

Salomon (3 months).[1] Sometime after 1880, after Salomon was born, Margarita Lopez and her daughter, Margarita, disappeared from Juan's life. It is assumed that they died. Soon after, Juan met Mariana Ybarbo.

In 1890, Mariana Ybarbo (41), a 5'4" tall, brown-eyed woman, was from a wealthy family that owned vast swathes of land in West Louisiana and East Texas. She owned over 2,000 acres of land in the town of Nacogdoches in East Texas. Her brother, Vital (b. 1848), was a confederate soldier. Her great-great-grandfather was Antonio Gil Ybarbo (b. 1729, d. 1809).[2]

Mariana's siblings Regina Ybarbo (5), Teresa Ybarbo (46), and Ben Ybarbo (47) were born in Texas. Her brother, Vital (57), and her mother, Alafonsa Flores Ybarbo (69), were born in Louisiana. Alafonsa Flores Ybarbo was a descendant of French immigrants on her mother's side.

By 1899, Juan de la Garza and Marianna Ybarbo had three children, Clarita (6), Guadalupe (2), and Margarita (4). [His second daughter by the same name]. It's unclear what happened to Guadalupe and Clarita because the only record that remains of them is a picture postcard. On the back of the postcard was written, "Here I put the names of my children, the older is named Clarita; the one in the middle is a boy who is named Guadalupe, and the other girl is Margarita."[3] Margarita de la Garza was born on February 22, 1885, in Floresville, Texas.

By 1900, many of Margarita's half-siblings: Virginia (29), Juan Jr. (25), and Salomon (20) had moved to General Terán, Nuevo Leon, Mexico. By that time, Margarita's half-brother, Eugenio (30), had been married to Florinda Maldonado (27) for nine years, and they lived in or near Seguin, Texas.

Margarita was about 15 years old when a famous Mexican composer, Fernando Medina, composed a song for her. Perhaps it was for her "Quinceañera." That is the celebration of a young girl's coming of age 15th birthday. Years later, the composition played as a beautiful, whimsical melody. Imagine what it was like for Margarita to have her very own song composed for her.[4]

By 1902, Juan de la Garza and his wife, Mariana Ybarbo, and their daughter, Margarita (15), had moved to General Terán. Juan died about two years later.

On April 25, 1906, a baby who was named Virgilio was born. It was a sad story in which Margarita (21) took the baby as her own because the parents had either died or were unable to care for the infant. In those days, it was a scandalous affair for a young, unmarried woman to adopt a baby. Of course, her mother, Mariana Ybarbo, would have helped her raise Virgilio.

Margarita was living in General Terán. She was an energetic, attractive woman, 5'4" in height, dark hair, a somewhat dark complexion. A small, fashionable mole adorned her upper lip. She likely enjoyed the life of a daughter who had a wealthy mother. However, Margarita benefitted immeasurably from the richness of the love of her extended family on both her parent's sides. Her relatives on the De La Garza side of the family were living all around her - in General Terán, and scattered throughout Texas. Likewise, the Ybarbo relatives lived in some of those same places, too, but many more lived in East Texas around Nacogdoches.

Sometime between 1906 and 1907, Margarita met Encarnacion Mendoza, the young man that she would eventually marry. Perhaps, she had met Encarnacion in Monterrey when she and her mother visited family there. Alternatively, they could have met in General Terán when Encarnacion traveled there to sell his bakery products or to operate the Loteria.

Encarnacion was born on March 25, 1882. Various legal documents stated other birth years, like 1879, 1880, and 1882. However, most of the documents agree that he was born on March 25. He was born in Monterrey. Some of the later records indicated that he was born in General Terán, which is a small town about 44 miles from Monterrey. In any case, he was most likely born on

March 25, 1882, in Monterrey, Nuevo León, Mexico.[5]

His parents were Jesus Ramirez Mendoza and Maria Guadalupe Garcia. They lived in the state of Nuevo Leon in Monterrey. Years later, Encarnacion's son, Enrique, couldn't remember much about his grandfather, Jesus, except that he worked as a train conductor of sorts. Enrique said that his grandfather was rarely home, and that was the reason he didn't know much about him. Encarnacion remembered his grandmother Guadalupe affectionately and visited her often in Monterrey during the summer. He enjoyed the large bowl that she kept filled with candy. Enrique also noted that his father, Encarnacion, had a sister named Maria Mendoza.

"She had a beautiful singing voice," Enrique later said.

In 1906, Encarnacion was living in Monterrey. He was a handsome, single 24-year-old, and 5'2" tall. Encarnacion was a very energetic young man. He had dark, olive skin, brown eyes, and black hair.

He was a "commerciante" [merchant] with his own business located on Veracruz Street, No. 4, in the heart of Monterrey. His parents likely supported him financially and with good parental inspiration. As a self-starter, he was most certainly utilizing his natural entrepreneurial skills. He was very self-assured and very successful in his endeavors. In a business journal from 1907, Encarnacion had recorded listings of items purchased for the Loteria, such as crystal vases, crystal cups, and other prizes.[6]

In his business journal, Encarnacion also included recipes for various Mexican pastries like "Polvorones, Pastel, Reposteria, Panque, Cucas, Ojarasca, and Moyette." He likely operated a Loteria, which was a game very similar to bingo, where people won prizes by filling out a "bingo" card with numbers or symbols called out by Encarnacion. He was quite successful in this business.

By June of 1907, the business must have been going very well for him. Encarnacion filed paperwork to acquire more property on his same street, No. 24 and No. 25 on Veracruz Street.[7] It's unknown if he was successful with this transaction. It's most likely that he was not able to obtain that property because he left Monterrey shortly after that. Perhaps after meeting the love of his life.

Margarita and her mother, Mariana Ybarbo, were living in the Zaragosa neighborhood of General Terán. Margarita's half-brother, Salomon de la Garza, was living nearby. Margarita must have been thrilled when she got the news that her half-brother, Juan, and his wife, Juana Saenz, had given birth to a son named Manuel ("Méme") Garza on February 13, 1907. Margarita was extremely close to her half-siblings and other relatives, both those near her in Mexico and those in Texas. Méme's birth date on his baptismal certificate stated his birth year was 1907[8], and his U.S. draft card, many years later, noted that his birth year as 1908[9].

On April 4, 1908, in the Nuevo Leon, Mexico, Civil Registration Marriages Journal, there was an entry for a license for the marriage of Encarnacion Mendoza (24) and Margarita de la Garza (20). The license, recorded at Montemorelos, Nuevo Leon, Mexico, stated that a notice would be published so that if anyone objected to the marriage, they could respond to the civil court. The license showed that Encarnacion's parents (Jesus Mendoza Ramirez and Maria Guadalupe Garcia) were both deceased and that Mariana Ybarbo was a widow (her deceased husband was Juan de la Garza). Years later, according to Encarnacion's son, Enrique, his grandparents Jesus and Maria Guadalupe were still alive when he was a child. It appears that the marriage record incorrectly lists Jesus and Maria Guadalupe as deceased.[10]

By April 28, 1908, no one had responded in the negative to the marriage license that Encarnacion and Margarita had filed. On that day, Encarnacion Mendoza married Margarita Garza in the city of Montemorelos. According to the license, Margarita was a previous resident of Wilson, Texas. The record also stated that Encarnacion was from Monterrey. As stated earlier, Mariana and her daughter were born in Texas - Mariana in Nacogdoches about 1848, and Margarita in Wilson County in 1885.

Encarnacion welcomed Virgilio as his son and officially recognized him as Virgilio Mendoza. Soon after, Encarnacion, his wife Margarita, and Virgilio moved to General Terán, which was less than 12 miles away.

There is no reference to the Monterrey businesses after Encarnacion Mendoza moved to General Terán. He did, however, keep the many business friends that he had in Monterrey like bank managers and other business associates. It would make sense that Encarnacion had sold his interests in the Monterrey business and poured his resources into a new business in General Terán. But now he would move powerfully forward in his business venture with his wife, who would work cooperatively with him towards greater success. Moreover, they would both find love in each other that grounded them in a beautiful, spiritual union.

A few months later, Margarita was pregnant with their first child. The happy couple indeed rejoiced as they began their family together in their new home in General Terán.

On March 20, 1909, Encarnacion and Margarita had their first baby, Jose Enrique Mendoza. The beautiful couple could not have foreseen what would happen next to them. Their baby died. The heart-wrenching event would have been devastating to them. Starting a family was not going to be quite as natural or comfortable as they might have expected. However, Margarita and Encarnacion would have the support of close family members and their parents.

3 - Encarnacion & Margarita 1910 to 1919

By June 19, 1910, Encarnacion (28)[1], a pregnant Margarita (23)[2], Mariana Ybarbo (61)[3], and Juan Saenz (8)[4] traveled from their house in General Terán to Seguin, Texas. Young Juan Saenz was the son of Margarita's brother Juan Garza and his wife, Juana Saenz. It appeared that Margarita had wanted her son, Enrique, to be born in the United States.

Mariana's hair had grayed, but she was as energetic as ever. The group continued to Seguin and stayed at Eugenio de la Garza's house. Eugenio, Margarita's half-brother, was married to Florinda Maldonado. When they arrived, Florinda might have said to Margarita, "My goodness! You're ready to have your baby at any moment. Margarita was pregnant with her second child.

On July 8, 1910, Margarita gave birth to a beautiful baby boy (their second child) and named him Enrique.[5] A mid-wife delivered him. The mid-wife was a black woman, much beloved by the de la Garza family. The midwife joked with Margarita and Encarnacion, "When you for Mexico, for me, the baby." She meant that when the family left, they should leave baby Enrique with her. Years later, when Enrique recounted the story about what the midwife had said, he laughed with glee. His mother had told him that story.

A few weeks later, Encarnacion, Margarita, Mariana, Enrique, and Juan Saenz traveled back to their home in General Terán.

Happiness returned to the family. Encarnacion was thrilled with his new boy. Margarita felt a sigh of relief as she experienced the joy of motherhood.

On November 22, 1910, Enrique Mendoza was baptized as Jose Enrique Mendoza at their church, *Nuestra Señora de la Soledad*, in General Terán, Nuevo Leon, Mexico.[6] According to United States law, Enrique was considered a U.S. citizen. Perhaps, Margarita in her wisdom, believed that someday, they might all return to the United States.

On July 13, 1911, Miguel Garza, a relative of Margarita, registered the Texas birth of Enrique Mendoza in the Mexican birth registry in General Terán, Nuevo Leon, Mexico.[7] The registry showed Enrique's birthplace as Texas. Perhaps the registration was necessary for Enrique to ensure that he could live in Mexico as other Mexican citizens could. There's no way to know for sure why Miguel Garza registered the birth of Enrique, except that it would make sense to have an official Mexican government birth record to comply with Mexican law. The Mexican Revolution was in full swing at that time.

On December 9, 1911, Encarnacion and Margarita had their third child at 6:00 p.m.[8] He was born in the Hidalgo section of General Terán. They named him Encarnacion Jr. Later his nickname would become Canacho.

How wonderful Encarnacion and Margarita must have felt that their family was growing. Encarnacion was thrilled to have two boys (three including Virgilio). Margarita was thankful to God for the beautiful gifts that he had bestowed upon her family.

On February 10, 1913, Encarnacion and Margarita had their fourth child at 5 p.m.[9] They named him Heriberto (nicknamed Beto). Encarnacion registered his son's birthdate with the local authorities in General Terán. Years later, Heriberto would put January 26, 1913, on his draft card.

On November 6, 1913, the Spokane Chronicle of Washington

State reported that rebels took the Mexican cities of Montemorelos and General Terán (and other cities). The newspaper reported that the rebels burned and looted indiscriminately throughout the towns. By the next day, the rebels were "repelled" and the Federal troops "reoccupied" the towns. However, the rebels had done much damage to the city.[10]

On March 25, 1914, Encarnacion and Margarita had their fifth child at 3:30 p.m. They named her Consuelo Guadalupe Mendoza.[11] She died three months later on June 29, 1914.[12]

On April 15, 1916, Encarnacion and Margarita had their sixth child, Jesus Mendoza (nicknamed Chuy), at 12:00 midnight.[13] Later, Jesus would enter April 2, 1916, as his birthdate on his U.S. draft card.[14]

At the start of 1917, Encarnacion and Margarita's growing family lived in General Terán. Encarnacion owned a meat market, a general store, a theater, and a bakery. Encarnacion (35), and his wife, Margarita (31), had five children: Virgilio (10), Enrique (6), Encarnacion Jr. (5), Heriberto (3), and Jesus (1).

By January of 1917, Margarita found that she was expecting her next child. That was good news to her, she loved children. Perhaps she worried about the revolution and how it might affect her family.

By February of 1917, the revolution continued unabated in Mexico. The president of Mexico at that time was Venustiano Carranza. Fortunately, the tiny town of General Terán, with only a few hundred people, was far enough away from the violence to be affected adversely by it (aside from the occasional rebels that would pass through the town). It was "protected" by the forces of Carranza.[15]

Encarnacion was well known as a kind and considerate man. Years later, his son, Enrique, said, "Encarnacion was once the mayor of General Terán and very influential in the town."

Enrique went on to describe his father's businesses and some stories that he remembered. In addition to his well-established businesses, Encarnacion ran a Loteria. The Loteria was a game of chance similar to bingo where customers played for prizes. At times, it stood operating next to his other businesses in General Teran. At other times, he took the Loteria to the nearby towns.

One day, some men on horseback arrived in town looking for supplies. They were rebels loaded with weapons, ready and willing to use them if necessary. The insurgents were precisely in search of places like Encarnacion's retail establishments.

Several horseback riders rode up to the town center, where Encarnacion's retail establishments predominantly stood. It would have been a frightening spectacle to see large numbers of soldiers with guns, riding up thunderously. Enrique and his siblings were playing outside the home, perhaps not aware of the danger.

Encarnacion had urged his children to go inside. Some ran and hid in a place where they could watch, while the younger ones might have run inside the house. Encarnacion talked with the rebel men. The family story claimed that it was Pancho Villa (Mexican revolutionary) who rode up with his men and demanded supplies from Encarnacion. The exchange was peaceful, and Encarnacion provided supplies (beans, rice, and other staples) to the rebels. Eventually, the insurgents left without harming anyone in the town.

An article of the time almost matches Enrique's account of the above incident. The difference was that instead of Pancho Villa, it had been Pedro Gonzalez and the Felicistas who visited the Mendoza's. The rebels were followers of General Felix Diaz (nephew of Porfirio), an enemy of Pancho Villa and then President, Venustiano Carranza.[16] General Felix Diaz was the leader of the National Reorganizer Army (Ejercito Reorganizador Nacional). On February 4, 1917, Sunday, Page 3 of The Laredo Weekly Times reported another incursion of General Terán by the rebels:[17]

DEFEATED CARRANCISTAS THEN TOOK GENERAL TERAN, BUT FELICISTAS ONLY STAYED LONG ENOUGH TO GET SUPPLIES.

While in Possession of Small Town, They Incidentally Captured Horses, Arms, and Ammunition.

According to information by an American arriving yesterday afternoon, the Felicistas under the leadership of Pedro Gonzales who crossed the Rio Grande into Mexico at a point not far from Laredo on New Year's night, won a victory at the little town of General Terán on last Monday, when they attacked and defeated the garrison of Carranza soldiers there and then entered the place until they departed at their own pleasure.

The American says that the Felicistas appeared on the outskirts of General Terán and were immediately engaged by the Carrancistas. A lively battle ensued for a while, and then the defenders of the town were repulsed with heavy losses, being driven back into the nearby country. The Felicistas then entered General Terán, replenished their supplies of provisions, captured a number of horses and a number of arms and ammunition belonging to the Carrancistas and spent several hours leisurely in the town mingling with the people, whom they treated most cordially and showed no intention of harming in any way. When the Felicistas assaulted General Terán, says the American, they had orders not to destroy the railroads or damage public property, and these orders were strictly adhered to in every respect.

After spending several hours in the town, the Felicistas unceremoniously took their departure, and a short time after that, the Carrancistas who had fled returned to the place, finding the people of the place safe and unharmed by the invaders and speaking of them in laudatory terms. It appears that everywhere the Felicistas under Pedro Gonzales have appeared, they have not resorted to the usual tactics of Mexican soldiers of looting, murdering and committing indignities on women and children, but on the other hand, go as soldiers into a place rather than bandits or raiders. The town of General Terán is seventy kilometers of Monterrey on the railroad line in the direction of Victoria and has only a few hundred population.

It is entirely plausible that Encarnacion's generosity towards the Felicistas would have appeared to the Carranzistas as supporting the enemy. That was a problem for successful tradespeople like Encarnacion that chose non-violent methods to suppress violence.

"Either you're with us, or you're against us," each side might say.

Encarnacion was not inclined to take sides. Encarnacion was a savvy businessman who was an influential member of his small town. It's highly likely that, in this case, he would have wanted to provide provisions to a potentially hostile and dangerous rebel army so that they could be on their way and cause no harm to his town.

As the article from the Laredo Weekly Times showed, Encarnacion made the right decision - at least in the eyes of rational folk. The city was utterly defenseless, and Encarnacion's only option would have been to act with kindness, generosity, and compassion to protect his family and his city.

Pancho Villa might have similarly visited General Terán at

another time. Encarnacion would have provided beans and rice to those rebels too. In any case, the opposition would have viewed his generosity as willfully supporting the enemy.

Another newspaper article reported a similar incident in General Terán. On April 29, 1917, Sunday, Page 10 of the Laredo Weekly Times reported another incursion of General Terán by the rebels:[18]

SOUNDS LIKE A CHAPLIN PLAY

The Capture of Town of General Terán, Mexico, by Rebels, Furnishes Good Plot for a Comedy.

There are some great soldiers down in Mexico, as is illustrated by the following story brought to the border by a passenger who arrived from Monterrey yesterday afternoon.

On Sunday night, a party of eight revolutionists of the Felipe Rodriguez affiliation entered the little town of General Terán, between Monterrey and Victoria, at midnight, went to the church there, and began ringing the bells. Immediately the Carranza garrison, which consisted of fifteen or twenty men, lined up and surrendered to the rebels, presumably believing that there was a big rebel force attacking the town. The revolutionists disarmed the Carrancistas, took their rifles, ammunition, and food supplies, and on the next morning, unceremoniously took their departure. The Carrancistas could have captured the handful of rebels if they had exercised their heads instead of their feet.

After each of these "incursions," everyday life returned to General Terán.

On August 6, 1917, Encarnacion and Margarita welcomed their seventh child, Jose Armando Mendoza.[19] He was baptized on January 19, 1918.[20]

On May 6, 1918, Margarita Garza de Mendoza got a *Declaration of Alien About to Depart the United States*.[21] On the form, she indicated that she planned to buy clothes and visit with her family in Seguin, Texas for three weeks. On May 14, 1918, Margarita presented the "Declaration" form along with a letter from Romulo Elizondo (inviting her to Seguin) to the border agent (at the United States border).

Margarita was admitted into the United States via the footbridge on her way to Seguin, Texas.[22] Her mother-in-law, Guadalupe Mendoza, a 56-year-old widow, accompanied Margarita.[23] At that time, Guadalupe was living in Monterrey.

On June 5, 1918, Jose Armando Mendoza (10 months) died.[24] On the Mexican Civil Registration Deaths journal, it stated that Sr. Julian Jaso, a married laborer, reported the death. Jose Armando had died at midnight the previous day from a high fever. Encarnacion and Margarita had identified the body.

The death of their son was another devastating blow to Encarnacion and Margarita. Margarita was about six months pregnant at the time. Had Margarita traveled with her ten-month-old infant to Seguin, Texas? The border crossing hadn't indicated that Margarita was traveling with an infant. Had Margarita left the infant behind when she went to Seguin, perhaps to give birth to her next baby there? In any case, she had returned home to General Terán when she and Encarnacion identified their son's body. It must have been particularly rough for Margarita since she needed to preserve her strength for the upcoming birth of her next child.

For both Encarnacion and Margarita, this was the third child that they had lost (Jose Enrique in 1909, Consuelo Guadalupe in 1914, and Jose Armando in 1918). They drew strength from each other to move forward through the pain, not only for themselves but for their four living children: Enrique (8), Canacho (7), Heriberto (5), Jesus (2).

On August 2, 1918, Encarnacion and Margarita welcomed their eighth child at 8:00 p.m.[25] They named her Maria Consuelo Mendoza. Shortly after that, in September of 1918, 8-year-old Enrique started school.

On September 25, 1919, Encarnacion and Margarita welcomed their ninth child, Margarita Elva Mendoza.[26] Her baptismal certificate (dated January 8, 1921) from Nuestra Señora de la Soledad Catholic Church stated that she was eight months old when she was baptized.[27] These types of discrepancies were common in these sorts of records. Perhaps the document should have stated that she was 13 months old. Her Godparents were Gaspar Cantú Garza (b. 1879) and his wife Juliana (b. 1879). Gaspar Cantú Garza was a close relative of Margarita through her father. A few years later, Gaspar Cantú Garza would be heavily involved in the management of Encarnacion's and Margarita's properties.

There is an unusual handwritten notation on one of the corners of Margarita Elva's birth record that stated: "Matrimony was in San Antonio, Texas on December 21, 1908; the birth date was September 23, 1919." Could this notation have suggested that her parents, Encarnacion and Margarita, had been married in San Antonio, Texas, instead of in Montemorelos as the Marriage record stated? It's not likely, but it could be a hint that years later, Margarita Elva might have suggested that to the record keeper.

Now with six children, Encarnacion was successfully operating his business, and Margarita was busy maintaining the household and was deeply involved with the Catholic church (Nuestra Señora de la Soledad). They had survived rebel incursions into their town, the loss of three young children, but they forged ahead.

4 - Estefana 1910 to 1919

At the end of 1910, Estefana Longoria lived with her brother, Guillermo Longoria, and his wife, Juana Anaya, in Brownsville, Texas in Cameron County. Estefana's brother, Alejandro, lived there too, based on the United States census of 1910.[1] They lived on the farm that was originally established by their father, Alejandro Longoria Sr.

On September 16, 1912, Estefana gave birth to her first child in Brownsville, Texas.[2] She named her daughter Maria Luisa after her dear sister that ended her own life tragically two years earlier. This might have meant that Estefana had her first child at her father's farm in Brownsville. Her mother, Estefana Martinez, appeared to have been separated from the family and was probably not there for the birth of her first granddaughter.

As for the father of Maria Luisa, there was no marriage certificate found. However, Estefana may have been married to Manuel Garcia when Maria Luisa was born. A clue came from the Brownsville Herald, showing that there was a letter addressed to Mrs. Estefana Longoria Garcia and another to Manuel Garcia, both on July 13, 1909.[3] If she was indeed married to Manuel Garcia, it's unknown what happened to him after Maria Luisa was born.

A few months later, in late 1912, Guillermo and his wife moved to Nueces County near Robstown, Texas. By 1913, Guillermo and his wife, Juana, welcomed their first baby boy, Alberto. Alberto was the first of four children they had between 1913 and 1919. Guillermo worked on a farm and found that Robstown, Nueces County, Texas, was a place that he and his growing family could stay for a long time.

By 1914, Estefana returned to live with her brother Guillermo in Robstown. On September 19, 1914, she gave birth to a second daughter and named her Maria del Carmen ("Carmen"). The birth certificate listed Canuto Garcia as the father of Carmen. Two months later, Carmen's baptismal certificate also listed Canuto Garcia as her father.

Years later, Carmen said that she never knew her father. She said that her mother, Estefana, had told her that her father had gone off to war and never returned. What her mother told her would have been plausible, given that World War I occurred between 1914 and 1918.

Many years later, in an interview in 1983 with Carmen, she said that she was born in a little ranch just outside of Robstown. She recalled the name "Blon" or "Blun." Could she have meant Bluntzer, which is halfway between Robstown and San Patricio in Texas?

In a subsequent interview in 1984, Carmen said, "I never met my father. And I never met Mary's [Maria Luisa] father either."

Carmen went on to say that her cousin, Andrea Contreras (daughter of Pablo Contreras and Cecilia Escobedo),[4] had told her that Carmen and her sister, Maria Luisa, had different fathers. And that Andrea's mother, Cecilia Escobedo Contreras, had told Andrea that it was true. Carmen said that Cecilia would undoubtedly know, but that she really shouldn't have shared Estefana's secret.

"I hope that God forgives her for sharing Estefana's private business," Carmen had said during that interview. It seemed that Carmen was disappointed that Cecilia had not honored her mother's secret.

In any case, there was a Canuto Garcia who lived in San Patricio County on Bluntzer Road. He lived very close to where Estefana's daughter, Carmen, was born. Robstown was 14 miles from the town of Bluntzer and 17 miles from San Patricio. Even so, Canuto had been married to Manuela Garcia since October 18, 1908,[5] and they had two boys that were roughly the same age as Maria Luisa and Carmen. At the time, Estefana was probably still living with her brother's family in the nearby town of Robstown, Texas, in 1914.

Just because this Canuto Garcia lived nearby to Estefana does not prove that Canuto Garcia from Bluntzer was Carmen's father. There was another piece of the puzzle that might have confirmed whether or not the Canuto Garcia from Bluntzer was the father of Carmen Garcia. And that could be shown with DNA.

Several descendants of Canuto Garcia from Bluntzer shared segments of DNA with the descendants of Carmen Garcia. There is an extremely high probability Canuto Garcia was from Bluntzer and was Carmen Garcia's father. According to his naturalization papers, he was 5'5", 110 pounds, medium complexion, black hair, and blue eyes.

By the beginning of 1915, an almost 23-year-old Estefana had two children, Maria Luisa was two years old, and Carmen Garcia was four months old. Neither child would be able to remember her father who had been absent from their lives, as both children were much too young.

Guillermo Longoria and his wife had two more children: Virginia in 1915, Theresa in 1916. They were still living in Robstown, Texas.

By mid-1917, Estefana Longoria had two children, Maria Luisa Garcia and Carmen Garcia, and were likely still living with Guillermo.

The future brightened for Estefana when she met a very kind man whom she had become very close too. Crisanto Escobedo was 5'2-1/2" tall with a dark complexion, black hair, and brown eyes. He was born on October 27, 1890, in Mexico. He was from La

Ascension, Aramberri, Nuevo Leon, Mexico, and he had lived for a while with his sister, Cecilia Escobedo, and her husband, Pablo Contreras, in Matamoros, Tamaulipas, Mexico. That was the same city where Estefana Longoria's family had lived until 1900. Crisanto Escobedo's sister was the same Cecilia Escobedo whose daughter, Andrea, would years later tell Carmen that she and her sister, Maria Luisa, had different fathers.

Crisanto Escobedo, his sister, and her husband had moved to San Benito, early in 1914. Perhaps Crisanto and Estefana had met in Brownsville. San Benito was just 20 miles away from Brownsville. Before 1912, Estefana lived with her brother, Guillermo, on the farm in Brownsville. Or it's also possible that Estefana had met Crisanto as children in Matamoros, Tamaulipas, Mexico (Estefana's home until 1900).

On August 29, 1917, Estefana Longoria (25) had crossed the border into the United States at the Brownsville port of entry accompanied by her husband, Crisanto Escobedo (26),[6] and her brother-in-law Pablo Contreras. They likely were married in Mexico.

As 1917 drew to a close, Estefana (25), Crisanto Escobedo (27), and their two children, Maria Luisa (5) and Carmen (3), were living in San Benito. Crisanto had many family members there, his parents and some siblings. Now, Estefana had the loving family that she'd always wanted.

Estefana's brothers, Anselmo (23) and Alejandro (20), and her father, Alejandro Sr., were all living in Pharr, Texas.[7] Both Alejandro and his brother, Anselmo, worked as carpenters. Anselmo's youngest brother, Cristobal (16), probably lived with them too. Guillermo and his family had settled down in their farm in Robstown. It's unclear where Estefana's sister, Matilde Longoria, was living.

On November 19, 1918, Anselmo Longoria married Ofelia Montalvo.[8] They lived in Pharr, Texas, for a short while and then moved to McAllen, Texas. On October 9, 1919, Anselmo and his wife Ofelia gave birth to their first child, Anselmo Jr. ("Chemo"). He was baptized on November 26, 1919, at Sacred Heart Church in McAllen, Texas).[9]

Another tragic death happened in the Longoria family. Years later, in an interview, Matilde Escobedo (Estefana's daughter) said, "My Tia Matilde [Longoria] was already dead by the time I was born. Tia Matilde had been forbidden by my Longoria grandparents to marry her "novio" (sweetheart). She killed herself rather than live without her novio."

Estefana Martinez was likely dead around this time. [Her granddaughter, Carmen Garcia (Estefana Longoria's daughter), suggested that she had died early on.]

By the end of 1919, Estefana was the only surviving daughter of Alejandro and Estefana Martinez Longoria. The women of the Longoria family were strong-willed and independent. They were all loved and cherished.

5 - Estefana & Carmen 1920 to 1928

The 1920 United States census[1] showed that Guillermo (35), his wife Juana Anaya (28), and their four children: Alberto (7), Virginia (5), Teresa (4), Leandro, (7 months) rented a house on a farm in [Bluntzer,] Nueces County, Texas. Guillermo worked as a farmer. Juana's father, Sebastian Anaya (68), lived next door with his two sons: Manuel (27), widowed, and Miguel (18). A few of the other neighbors listed on the census originated from France, Germany, England, and Scotland, they were the owners of the ranches where Guillermo lived. A majority of his neighbors (including his family) were renters from Mexico with children born in Texas.

On January 14, 1922, Estefana (29) gave birth to her and Crisanto's first child, Matilde Escobedo.[2]

Years later, Carmen said, "[My sister] Matilde was born in *El Banco Rancho* in Brownsville, Texas."

In 2000, Matilde confided to her family, "My parents named me Matilde after my mother's sister. . . . I looked exactly like my father, Crisanto."[3]

From the years 1922 through 1927, Estefana's family (Estefana, Crisanto, Maria Luisa, Carmen, and Matilde) moved and settled in Rancho Las Prietas near Brownsville, Texas.

Matilde later said, "My father [Crisanto] worked as a foreman on the [farm] in Brownsville. We lived in a farmhouse provided by the landowner. Maria Luisa and Carmen had to help my father in the [fields]."

Carmen later said that the farm had a large farmhouse that had been vacant for many years. They lived there for free because the owners wanted someone to take care of the house and fields. It belonged to a very wealthy family. It had a large balcony and had two large bedrooms, a roomy "sala" [living room], and a large kitchen. There was an enormous windmill that stood a short distance from the house.

Carmen smiled and said, "At one time, when the owners lived there, it [the windmill] had pumped water into the house, but it had stopped working long before [my family moved in there]."

Carmen also said that her mother was the happiest there with her husband, her children, and their beautiful home. It was spacious and very comfortable. Her husband, Crisanto (31), was quite resourceful and had provided well for them during the early days of their marriage.

"He grew ejote [green beans], calabacita [squash], cotton, and slaughtered marranos [pigs], he made chorizo [sausage], and dried meats and much more," Carmen recalled fondly.

They had one cow that Carmen loved to milk. They had several chickens. They always had eggs and enjoyed a cooked chicken every so often. She said her mother was quite skilled at killing the chickens. Her mother had a technique where she would grab the chicken by the throat and quickly break its neck (to cause as little pain as possible).

Carmen remembered the first time that her mother had asked her to kill one of the chickens for supper. Carmen chased after the chickens as they ran screaming from her. When she finally caught one of them, she found that she didn't have the strength to kill the chicken quickly. She got hold of one the chickens by the throat and succeeded in choking the chicken – but not enough to kill them.

She said, "poor chicken. It would still run around the yard." She had told her mother, "I can't do it. All I do is choke it."

Her mother caught the chicken, grabbed it by the neck, and killed it with one swift twist of the neck. Estefana continued with what she had been doing and left Carmen to prepare the chicken for cooking.

Years later in an interview, after she had talked about her time on the farm, she said, "I've never killed a chicken."

In 1923, Anselmo Sr. moved his family from Pharr, Texas, to some property he had purchased in McAllen, Texas. McAllen was only three miles away from Pharr. He was prospering in his construction and lumber businesses and could afford to buy property for his growing family.

In 1924, Anselmo M. Longoria (Architect) began the construction of Sacred Heart Church.[4] The church, located at 306 South 15th Street in McAllen, was established in 1911 by the Oblates of Mary Immaculate as a small wooden chapel. Sadly, on October 21, 1924, it had been utterly destroyed in a fire. Anselmo Longoria designed and eventually built the new church that would last well into the future.

By 1925, Carmen (11) had already missed more than a year of school and returned to the fourth grade. She was embarrassed to be there because she was so much older than the other kids in her class. She soon quit and never returned to school after that. Instead, she helped her mother with household chores.

On November 4, 1925, Estefana gave birth to her fourth girl, Marcolfa Escobedo.[5]

In 1926, Anselmo Sr. established *Phoenix Lumber Company*. He started it with his father-in-law (Evaristo Montalvo). Anselmo later bought out his father-in-law and partner and became the sole owner of the business.[6]

In September 1927, Anselmo's son, Chemo (8), was sent off to boarding school[7] in Monterrey.

When Estefana was expecting her next child, Carmen took on

many more duties washing the clothes, cleaning the house, and more. On December 28, 1927, Estefana gave birth to her fifth child, her only boy, Alejandro ("Alex") Escobedo.[8] Estefana was undoubtedly happy to close out the year with a beautiful baby boy. She must have mused about her baby boy, that perhaps when he is older, he might feel outnumbered by his four older sisters. Then again, he might feel pampered by his older sisters. For Crisanto, it must have been bittersweet, since his mother, Anastacia Valdez, had passed away in Mexico three weeks before.[9]

After Alejandro Escobedo was born, Estefana continued with the housework and raising five children. During this time, Carmen (13) and Maria Luisa (15) were teenagers who would have to help with household chores, the younger siblings, and work in the fields.

Carmen later said, "When a boy was born, they would shoot 21 shots."

Alejandro's birth record stated that he was born in Brownsville. The family was living in Rancho Las Prietas in the southern part of Brownsville, next to the border.

Years later, Matilde's daughters had asked her about their mother.

Matilde said, "My mother was a strong woman. I recall her taking us out on a "chalupa" [boat] in a Brownsville "resaca" [lagoon] close to our house. She was minding the oars. Maria Luisa, Carmen, Marcolfa, Alex, and I were passengers [in the boat]. It was a hot summer afternoon, so she decided to take us around the [lagoon]. Unfortunately, the [boat] sprung a leak, and it started to fill up with water. My mother had to push hard on the oars to get us back to shore. Somehow, she managed to get us all safely [to] shore. We were very scared because none [of] us could swim except for my mother. I remember my mother as always having a smile on her face."

About 1928, Crisanto (38), Estefana (36), Maria Luisa (16), Carmen (14), Matilde (6), Marcolfa (3), and Alejandro (1) moved to San Benito to a small house. It had a kitchen and a bedroom and was attached to a restaurant. A significant change in their circumstances must have happened for them to leave the farmhouse and move into a tiny house. It may also have been that Crisanto began to experience problems with his health.

Carmen said that she knew Matilde's father, Crisanto, very well. He was a very kind and loving man, she said. "He was just like Matilde."

Over the next two years, Estefana and Crisanto's family of five children continued, struggling at times to keep food on the table. They were still living in San Benito, Texas. Crisanto's sister, Cecilia,[10] was living nearby with her husband and seven children. Estefana's children had undoubtedly spent time and played with Cecilia's children.

On one auspicious occasion, Cecilia's daughter, Andrea, had told Carmen that she and Maria Luisa had two different fathers. At the time, Carmen didn't believe her. But Andrea insisted that her mother, Cecilia, had told her. Andrea went on to say that Estefana had confided that to Cecilia, Andrea's mother. Carmen was bothered that her Aunt Cecilia had revealed a taboo secret such as this. Carmen said that she never said anything about that to her mother.

About ten years later, after the disclosure of this family secret, a car struck Andrea's mother, Cecilia, on March 17, 1948. She died a few weeks later (April 27, 1948).[11] Recalling what seemed like a betrayal of her mother, Carmen said, "Maybe God punished her for telling [that secret]. May she rest in peace."

About this time, Estefana had a baby and had named her Isabelita Escobedo.

Carmen later said with a sigh, "The baby lived very, very briefly. The cord was wrapped around her neck."

The loss of this child was a sad event for the family. However, Estefana certainly felt the love of her family. She persevered through life with the strength of a saint. Estefana was a formidable inspiration and had a determination that flowed throughout her family.

Carmen loved to help her mother with the housework. She especially enjoyed spending time with her friends and going to the movies.

"In those days, silent movies still played at the theater, and there was a piano player," Carmen happily recounted. Carmen knew the man that played the piano, who was either a relative or a close family friend.

"When there was a lot of action on the screen, the piano player would play faster and faster," Carmen said as she smiled at the memory.

By the end of 1928, life was relatively calm for Estefana, her husband, Crisanto, and her five children. They were living in San Benito, raising their young children, and eking out a living.

6 - Encarnacion & Margarita 1920 to 1924

By the beginning of 1920, Encarnacion and Margarita were quite busy with the Loteria and their businesses in the town of General Terán, Nuevo Leon, Mexico. It was Margarita's habit to donate to their church generously and to support her community. Both Encarnacion and Margarita were very much involved with the Catholic Church. They went to church at Nuestra Señora de la Soledad not far from their home in General Terán. Afterward, they would often congregate on the porch outside of the church and visit with their extended family like her cousin Carmen Villagomes de Garcia or her niece Ricarda Garcia de Garza. The latter served as their church's treasurer.

Both Encarnacion and Margarita were well respected in the community and were well known for their generous and loving nature. No doubt, her loving mother, Mariana Ybarbo, who lived near Encarnacion and Margarita's family, would accompany them to church.

In July of 1920, Pancho Villa notified interim president Adolfo de la Huerta that he was ready to negotiate a peace settlement and retire.[1] Soon after, Villa was granted a 25,000-acre hacienda outside Hidalgo del Parral in Chihuahua, about 470 miles from General Terán. Two hundred of his men also got land, and fifty or so had become his bodyguards.[2] The death of the previous president,

Venustiano Carranza and Pancho Villa's surrender in July 1920 essentially ended the Mexican Revolution.

Encarnacion had had some close encounters with Pancho Villa when he had passed through the small town of General Terán. Thankfully, Encarnacion and Margarita's home was hundreds of miles from Villa's hacienda. Besides, Pancho Villa and his dangerous rebels had little need to visit General Terán (except if he were traveling through on their way to another town). Now that the Mexican Revolution was essentially over, perhaps the violence that had assaulted the Mexican people would begin to subside.

Encarnacion would undoubtedly be relieved that the revolution was over. Encarnacion continued to work hard for his growing family. He was running his businesses successfully and traveled on occasion with the Loteria. When he was at home, he would set up his tent with his crystal vases and pitchers and other prizes outside of the building that housed his businesses. He ran a bakery, a meat market, a theater, and his Loteria. He worried less about the rebels who had visited his town and more about how to increase his revenue.

No one would have expected what would have happened next.

A severe storm hit General Terán as the following news clipping from "The Marengo Republic News" in Illinois on May 1, 1922, reported:[3]

> **Mexico City, May 1.** - Forty houses have been leveled to the ground, one person killed and 30 injured by a tornado which struck the town of General Terán in the State of Nuevo Leon, according to advice received here this afternoon. Other neighboring towns suffered damage.

The storm would most certainly have damaged Encarnacion's businesses, including his Loteria, that was set in a tent. Thankfully his family had come through safely, although it would have been a terrifying experience for them. Encarnacion and Manuel Garcia (a relative on Margarita's side of the family) became business partners in the business shortly after the storm.

There must have been some significant damage to his business because a month later, on July 2, 1922, Encarnacion and his partner bought a 5-1/2 KW generator for 1,500 pesos. They purchased it from Petz Hermanos Garage for the business. Encarnacion would be ready for the next storm.

On June 17, 1921, Encarnacion and Margarita's tenth child was born. Rube de la Luz was born at 10:00 a.m.[4] Her father reported the birth, and they wrote her name down as Rubi[5] de la Luz Mendoza. Her birth record indicated that her father, Encarnacion Mendoza, was 40, and her mother, Margarita de la Garza, was 36. Her paternal grandparents were Jesus Mendoza and Guadalupe Garcia (both deceased). Her maternal grandparents were Juan de la Garza (deceased) and Mariana Ybarbo (living) It was a blessing for Encarnacion and Margarita Mendoza to welcome another child.

The Mendoza family was living comfortably. Encarnacion was able to provide quite well for his family because his businesses were very profitable. And with his business partner, he could continue his upward climb of success.

It must have been a magical leap into the new world when commercial radio began transmission in Mexico. The radio transmissions were too far away from General Terán, but Encarnacion would most certainly have heard about the wireless wonder.

Encarnacion would have eventually heard that on July 20, 1923, General Pancho Villa, at 45 years of age, had been assassinated. This sort of news traveled fast between the towns in Mexico (mostly by travelers). Many people thought that President Alvaro Obregón, an enemy of Villa, was responsible for Pancho Villa's death. Encarnacion had once given food and supplies to Pancho

Villa - not because he supported the rebels cause necessarily, but to de-escalate an armed political conflict. Dread must have lingered in his heart at the thought that President Obregón or others might threaten the semblance of peace that had come to his little town. Perhaps he had hoped the next president would be better for Mexico.

On September 6, 1923, Plutarco Elias Calles declared his candidacy for the presidency.[6] Would Encarnacion know that he was a well-educated atheist, one who hated the Catholic Church? The Church had condemned him because he was born to an unwed mother and was the son of an alcoholic father who'd abandoned him as a child. His mother's brother raised him, and Plutarco took the surname Calles to spare him the shame. Encarnacion would most likely have not known any of that. He wouldn't have known what Plutarco Elias Calles (or his son, Aco) had in store for Encarnacion and his family (and for all of Mexico).

Among the businesses that Encarnacion had, he and his business partner Manuel Garcia (a relative of Margarita) had started repairs to the local theater that Encarnacion owned. The roof required replacement, so they purchased the building materials to put a new roof on the theater and stored them in a tent on a vacant lot across from the business. Twelve-year-old Enrique, Encarnacion's son, and Enrique's fourteen-year-old cousin Méme Garza volunteered to stand guard over the material. Méme was the son of Margarita's brother, Juan Garza and Juanita Saenz. Inside the tent, they had just enough room for Enrique and Méme to hide inside. They stayed up all night with wooden sticks to use as weapons to ward off a troublesome interloper that might want to take some of their property. Méme was a couple of years older than Enrique. They were the best of friends, though. Enrique was the studious type who liked school very much, he even played a part in a student stage play. Méme wasn't too excited about school. He'd play hooky from school and eventually dropped out.

Encarnacion was content, Margarita was expecting, and they both were happy as they waited for their next child.

On September 25, 1923, Margarita gave birth to her eleventh child, Maria Leslie del Roble Mendoza. Margarita was certainly joyful as she held her tiny new baby.[7]

On November 2, 1923, Eugenio de la Garza (53), son of Juan de la Garza and Margarita Lopez, half-brother of Margarita Garza Mendoza died in Seguin, Texas of Pulmonary Tuberculosis.[8] His son, Benjamin De La Garza (29), reported the death. Margarita was close to her half-brother, Eugenio, and his wife, Florinda. Back in 1910, Margarita had traveled to Seguin and had given birth to her son, Enrique, in their home.

By the end of 1923, the Mendoza family included: Encarnacion (41), Margarita (38), Virgilio (17), Enrique (13), Canacho (12), Heriberto (10), Jesus (7), Maria Consuelo (5), Margarita Elva (4), Rube (2), Leslie (3 months), and Margarita's mother, Mariana Ybarbo (75).

By the beginning of 1924, Encarnacion continued his business enterprise with his partner, Manuel Garcia (Margarita's relative). His businesses were at 24 Calle Juarez, General Terán, Nuevo Leon, Mexico. The businesses were doing very well. Encarnacion continued to have his Loteria tent on the edge of his property. His neighbor, Teodoro Elizondo, complained that Encarnacion's tent was on his property and was interfering with his own business. Teodoro wanted the tent removed from his property. The Loteria would have been quite noisy with the people playing, laughing, and cheering as they played.

Encarnacion was well connected to the business and government community. According to the family, Encarnacion himself had been mayor of General Terán.

In April of 1924, Encarnacion visited with Mr. Arturo Garcia, the Municipal President of General Terán, and told him about a problem that he was having with his neighbor, Teodoro Elizondo.

Encarnacion hoped to find a peaceful and fair resolution that would be in his favor. Soon after that meeting, Mr. Arturo Garcia wrote this letter to Mr. Teodoro Elizondo:[9]

Monterrey, N. L., April 5, 1924.
Mr. A. García
Municipal President of
General Terán, N. L.

Very dear and fine friend:

Mr. Encarnación Mendoza, a neighbor of that place, has been talking with me about the matter that you know regarding him placing his outside market [on your property]. And I have come to know that you have decided not to give him your permission.

And that because you are an official that respects the provisions aimed at the improvement of the city that you have been entrusted, I beg of you to reconsider and consider Mr. Mendoza's request since he is a credit to [the Municipality], under which he has complied with each and every one of the provisions emanating from that residence, and is willing to pay the rent for his small establishment that will be the same amount that is charged to the other people who are in the market.

As such, I urge you to grant the guarantees requested by Mr. Mendoza, terminating any personal incident; and without another particular, I repeat myself, as always, your affectionate, attentive friend and S. S.

Arturo Garcia

* * *

Teodoro relented and gave Encarnacion permission to continue to use his (Teodoro's) small piece of land, albeit at a discounted rental amount.[10] Things continued going very well for Encarnacion and Margarita, their family, and their businesses.

In April 1924, Méme, Enrique's cousin, traveled to Texas. Enrique would have been sad to see his close companion leave.[11]

On June 30, 1924, Enrique, a few days from his fourteenth birthday, graduated from sixth grade at "Escuela Oficial Para Niño's" in General Terán.[12]

In July of 1924, the town must have been abuzz with the news that Plutarco Elias Calles had won the presidential election. He'd won over 84% of the votes.[13] Encarnacion and most of his neighbors might have felt that Mexico had just elected a president who would bring about the much-needed change to his town. The future seemed hopeful for Encarnacion and his family.

Cousin Yolanda Mendoza Rodriguez recounted a childhood story that her father, Jesús Mendoza, had told her: One time, Canacho (13), Heriberto[14] (11), and Jesús (8), played hooky from school and went off swimming. They took off their clothes and got in the water. Soon after, Canacho and Heriberto saw their father, Encarnacion, quickly approaching. Canacho and Heriberto tried unsuccessfully to get Jesus's attention, who was out too far swimming. Encarnacion hadn't noticed Canacho and Heriberto run away with their clothes. Jesus saw his father and knew that he was in trouble. He walked home in shame alongside his father. Margarita wondered in shock at Encarnacion as she saw her naked eight-year-old boy run past her into the house.

On August 8, 1924, Maria Leslie del Roble Mendoza was baptized at "Nuestra Señora de la Soledad" in their hometown of General Terán, Nuevo Leon, Mexico.[15]

Plutarco Elias Calles assumed the office of the president of Mexico on December 1, 1924. His predecessor, President Alvaro

Obregon, had been quite influential in getting Calles elected. The president went to work immediately to implement his plans.[16]

Encarnacion would most certainly have had worry and dread about the political changes that might affect his family and businesses. Without political stability, there could be limited economic stability. The future of the country and his family were in the hands of the new president.

7 - Encarnacion & Margarita 1925 to 1927

Encarnacion and his business partner, Manuel Garcia, (Margarita's relative) had been running their business as co-owners since 1922. As was often the case for families in business together, there was only a verbal agreement between them concerning the ownership of the business. Encarnacion owned the building.

They needed to organize their business and keep better records to survive a highly regulated, corrupt business environment. They formalized their business in a contract as follows:[1]

February 25, 1925 - Teatro Salon Juarez

Contract to record joint ownership of "Teatro Salon Juarez" by Encarnacion Mendoza (45 years) and Manuel Garcia (55 years) since August 10, 1922. They will share equally in the profit/losses of the business. Either one of them can sell to the other for half of the cost of the business. Since the company is now legal, the taxes for the business are due each August (10% in public "timbre," and for every 1000 pesos, there is a fee of 4.00 pesos).

Encarnacion Mendoza and Manuel Garcia's business have 4,000 pesos in capital.

The address of the business, *Mendoza and Garcia*, was Calle Juarez, No. 12.

They have been making improvements to the business and expect to continue. And that the construction will be completed within six months. Encarnacion owns the land and does not expect any rent unless he sells the building to his partner. If that happens, he wants $10 per month rent for the property.

On March 25, 1925, Encarnacion celebrated his 43rd birthday. Although some official records showed him as older and other times younger, by 1918, Encarnacion had settled on a birthday of March 25, 1882, when he registered for a birth certificate.[2] March 25 was a happy day for him and his family, none the less.

Encarnacion had spent his birthday at home without his wife. Margarita had taken their son, Enrique, to Monterrey to find an academy so that he could learn the business skills that would help him to earn a living. She had always been a forward thinker. She had noticed that her son was very good at business finances.

She wanted Enrique to study in Monterrey because there were terrific business schools there. She and her mother, Mariana Ybarbo, had occasionally visited Monterrey since moving to General Terán back in 1904.

When Margarita and Enrique arrived in Monterrey, they stopped at a convent to ask them for a recommendation on the best business school for her son. It's interesting to note that Margarita chose a Catholic Convent of nuns to recommend a school for her son. Of course, she had always been deeply religious. The nuns recommended a business school (Academia Comercio) named Zaragoza Academia in the heart of Monterrey. Although, the nuns suggested that it would be better if Enrique were to study to become a priest.

Margarita responded sternly, "No!"

By that time, Margarita was likely well aware of the direction that the government was going concerning its apparent anti-clerical views. In that political climate, it would be unwise for anyone to pursue the priesthood. She thanked them and more than likely donated to the convent.

On March 27, 1925, Enrique started at Zaragoza Academia. Margarita had left her son safely nestled at the boarding school.

President Plutarco Elias Calles had begun to improve the infrastructure of the country. He worked to improve health and hygiene. He invited foreign companies like Ford, Bayer, DuPont, Hoechst, and others to build factories and plants in Mexico. There were infrastructure, railroad, and road improvements. Corruption became intertwined with the government agencies that managed these improvements.[3]

By the middle of 1926, Enrique had completed his first year at Zaragoza Academy. He took on a part-time job as a bookkeeper with Mr. Sabine, a shopkeeper who was near the academy. At the time, Enrique was enjoying his independence living at apartment No. 303, in Monterrey not far from the academy. At fifteen years old, he was on his own and earning a little bit of money. Even so, Enrique still received some financial assistance from his parents. He focused on his studies and ignored most everything else.

Back home in General Terán, Encarnacion saw that the political climate seemed to be coalescing into a murky sea of change. Encarnacion and his wife, Margarita, had heard inklings of an anti-clerical campaign that had leaked out of the secretive and tightly controlled government circles.

Encarnacion and Margarita were optimistic that they would be able to withstand the political climate. However, as the government imposed aggressive, sweeping changes to Mexico, the rebellious portion of the population became more active. Rebels seemed to frequent General Terán more often. Encarnacion owned several major businesses and often did business with them.

In an interview in 2007, Encarnacion's youngest daughter,

Margarita Elva, said that as a child, she had seen rebel men ride up on horseback to their home in General Terán. She remembered that they had unkempt, stringy, long hair, not unlike some of the troublesome young men of modern times. She was referring to the men she'd seen on the news who trafficked in crime in her hometown of Roma, Texas, just yards away from the Mexican border. She remembered her father talking with them peacefully, selling (or giving) them what they wanted, and then sending them on their way.

By the mid-1926, five million Mexicans were vaccinated against smallpox, to reduce the deaths by this disease. The Mexican government created the new Department of Public Health. The president went to work and implemented stricter health-related laws that directly impacted Encarnacion Mendoza and Manuel Garcia's business. Inspectors would zealously pay close attention to their meat market and bakery. On the surface, it seemed like a good thing to improve the sanitary requirements of the markets which sold to the public. However, the inspectors expected bribes to produce reports in the merchant's favor. Businesses who failed compliance were either closed down or fined. Extreme measures for "problematic" merchants sometimes included physical violence.[4]

Encarnacion had met Plutarco and had developed an amicable relationship with him. As they got to know each other, they became good friends. Plutarco would often visit his son, Aco, in General Terán. Aco, too, had become close to Encarnacion.

In an interview, Enrique said, "My father and Plutarco Elias Calles had a good relationship. He liked my father very much. But the people behind him [Calles supporters] were bad. They turned Plutarco against my father."

Encarnacion and Margarita, no doubt, were alarmed as the changes initiated by President Calles negatively impacted them. Next, the president ramped up an anti-clerical campaign. To

Encarnacion's family, not only was the government impacting his business, but it was also attacking their faith.

On July 2, 1926, President Calles had enacted "Calles Law." With that law, the government had ordered the closure of all monasteries and convents, the government seizure of numerous church buildings, and the expulsion of more than 200 foreign nuns and priests. On July 31, 1926, The Bishops issued a pastoral letter threatening to suspend masses immediately. It stated in no uncertain terms that beginning August 1, 1926, there would be no baptisms, no marriages, and no church services.[5] Violence soon erupted among the population throughout Mexico in support of the Roman Catholic church. It was called the Cristero Rebellion which would last for three years and resulted in countless deaths and extensive destruction of property.[6]

Encarnacion and Margarita would have been fearful and maybe angry at the assault from the president. Encarnacion would have most certainly expressed his views publicly, perhaps to his customers and business acquaintances. His family was Catholic and deeply religious.

At this time, the president's son, Plutarco Elias Calles Jr. ("Aco"), was living in General Terán. As the son of the president, he had easily acquired vast acres of land with large citrus orchards. The orchards most certainly, now owned by a politically influential family, would have had a considerable impact on the small town of General Terán. President Plutarco Elias Calles enjoyed spending time in General Terán at Aco's ranch.[7]

Encarnacion would have talked often with Aco and also with his father (President Plutarco Elias Calles). It's likely that Encarnacion discovered that he and the Calles family had polar opposite views regarding religion. In light of the political climate, their relationship soured.

By December 15, 1926,[8] Encarnacion and his family had fled from their home in General Terán to Weslaco, Texas. Something extremely threatening must have happened between Encarnacion and the Calles family to explain why Encarnacion's family left so abruptly. Perhaps, their friendship had been irrecoverably damaged. Also, it's understandable that passionate supporters of Plutarco might have routinely threatened Encarnacion and his family.

Encarnacion's family promptly packed their belongings and fled across the border to Donna, Texas. Margarita had relatives there as well as throughout Texas. Many were from her father's side of the family (Juan de la Garza).

Encarnacion was quite a planner, so he had likely organized his family's exit for weeks (if not months) before. He'd made arrangements for Gaspar Cantú Garza (related through Margarita) to take care of his businesses and rent his home. He probably had made arrangements with Margarita's relatives in Donna, Texas too. Mariana Ybarbo, Margarita's mother, likely went with them and arranged for her siblings to take care of her property while she was gone.

In an interview with Margarita Elva Mendoza (daughter of Encarnacion Mendoza), she said that her father had come across the border and then, soon after, deported back to Mexico. Later, Margarita Elva Mendoza noted that her mother snuck him back across the border. Could March 2, 1927, be the date he went across the border legally with a non-quota immigration visa obtained from Monterrey, Nuevo Leon, Mexico, as stated on Encarnacion's September 23, 1936, application?

Margarita had wanted to bring her son, Enrique (16), with them, but Encarnacion must have assured her that their son would be safe in Monterrey. He likely told her that Monterrey's strong military presence heavily fortified the city.

Encarnacion would most certainly have sent his son a letter advising that the family would be going to Donna, Texas, to stay with the family there. He would have told him that Enrique's uncle, Gaspar Cantú Garza, would also help him if he ran into any problems.

Encarnacion (47) likely traveled to Monterrey with his nephew (Hernan Cordova) to visit his son, Enrique, at the end of February 1927.[9] While he was in Monterrey, he also got an immigrant visa from the Mexican Consulate. He crossed back into the U.S. on March 2, 1927, to rejoin the rest of his family in Donna, Texas.[10]

Encarnacion wasted no time and set up a bakery in nearby Weslaco, Texas. Of course, Encarnacion also had the Loteria and his family with him. Encarnacion and Margarita were quite resourceful. No doubt they'd brought enough from General Terán to aid them in setting up the bakery.

Encarnacion worked the Loteria in Weslaco and many of the small towns in the Texas Rio Grande Valley, such as San Juan, Alamo, Donna, Weslaco, La Feria, Laredo, Cotulla, and La Villa. Their business was very profitable at the time. They bought the merchandise to use as prizes for the Loteria and sold it at a good profit.

Encarnacion and Margarita

8 - Mendoza's Reunited 1927 to 1928

Enrique was most certainly enjoying his life in Monterrey. He was living alone in his apartment and earning some money to enjoy some of the excitement of the big city of Monterrey. Life moved much more quickly there than in the tiny town of General Terán, which was 62 miles away to the southeast. His friends drove back to General Terán and from Monterrey occasionally. Dressed in their fancy three-piece suits and smoking their cigarettes, no one would likely have mistaken them for rebels. Those insurgents were unkempt and lived roughly, most often on the dusty trails on their horses attacking government soldiers.

Enrique (on the right) and friend on the road from Monterrey to General Terán:

***

Enrique soon developed a talent for bookkeeping. He had become proficient at balancing his journals - keeping the "centavos" even between the left side and the right side of his balance sheets. After school, he worked for Mr. Sabine, a local businessman.

As Enrique's final examinations approached, he found himself short on money. He hadn't earned enough to pay all of his expenses. Perhaps his clothing and cigarettes and, of course, food would have depleted his allowance quicker than a sixteen-year-old would have wanted.

Enrique had written a letter to his father asking for money. The message back from his father was to get the cash from Gaspar Cantú Garza. Encarnacion had left Gaspar to collect the rent on his property and his house and evidently to provide Enrique money, should he need it.

Enrique wasted no time in typing a letter to his uncle, Gaspar Cantú Garza, asking for the cash. The letter he'd clacked away on his typewriter from his small apartment at No. 303 in Monterrey.[1]:

Enrique Mendoza
Section 303
Monterrey, N. L.

May 12, 1927.
Mr. Gaspar Cantú Garza
General Terán, N. L.

Dear Uncle:
On the occasion of my next exams, which will be the 21st day of the current month [May 21, 1927], which my father had already indicated, I am pleased to beg you to send me 125.00 pesos; Well,

I wrote to Papa asking for the money, and he said that he had already arranged with you. Uncle, I would beg you in the most attentive way to do me the favor of sending the money to me by mail, in case Papa has already spoken with you. Well, of course, as you may understand, I have many expenses, and as I had not asked you [before] for anything because I did not know that Papa had asked you to take care of this.

At the same time, I cordially invite both you and Jesus and your family members to attend my exams,

   Yours always,

your nephew who appreciates you,

Enrique

Presumably, Gaspar Cantú Garza sent the money to Enrique soon after.

On May 21, 1927, at the age of 17, Enrique graduated from the Academia de Comercio "Gral. Zaragoza." He proudly accepted his certificate and carefully protected it in his tiny apartment at No. 303, Monterrey, Nuevo Leon, Mexico. He liked living there on his own.

In June 1927, a few days after his graduation, Enrique received a telegram that said that his mother was gravely ill and that he should come home to Weslaco, Texas, right away.

Margarita was worried that her son might become a victim of the volatile revolution that was taking place in Mexico. She must have known that people were dying every day because of the Cristero Rebellion. Was she worried sick or sick and worried?

In any case, Enrique prepared for his trip home to go to his mother. Enrique told his boss that he'd return in one or two weeks. Of course, his boss understood. Enrique gathered his belongings into a suitcase. He didn't have much. Enrique carefully packed his diploma. The 16" by 20" certificate had his picture prominently displayed on the left side with his name plainly under it. He was very proud of his newfound skill in accounting and was excited to finally show the diploma to his mother and, of course, to the rest of this family. He bought a ticket on the next train headed to Weslaco, Texas. He didn't know that a train in another part of the country had been blown-up using dynamite two months before. [In April 1927, there were over 100 killed when the Cristeros used dynamite to destroy a Mexico City-Guadalajara train].[2]

During the train trip, there was a severe rainstorm. The train barely made it to the next train station. The passengers were told that they could return to Monterrey for free, or they could stay in the station and wait for the storm to subside. Enrique chose to sleep that night on the train station floor and wait for the next train. The next morning, he boarded the train, and a few hours later arrived near the U.S. border. He was given directions to the U.S. Port of Entry.

When he got there, he saw a sign for a grocery store. He didn't understand any English at the time, and he laughed at the idea that there was a store that sold "groceras" (English translation: "insults"). He later learned what a grocery store sold.

When he got to the U.S. Immigration and Naturalization Services, he didn't have his passport with him when the clerk asked for it. Without any proof of U.S. citizenship, Enrique told him that he was from General Terán. He paid $8 and got a passport with his picture (showing Mexican Citizenship) and continued on his way into Weslaco, Texas.

He arrived at Weslaco, where his mother and family were waiting for him. Enrique later said that she got well quickly after that. Enrique's parents told him that he would not be returning to his tiny apartment at No. 303, Monterrey, Nuevo Leon, Mexico.

Encarnacion had established the bakery in Weslaco, Texas, and owned a Ford Model T. He didn't know how to drive; however, Enrique and his brother Canacho did know. It was a finicky car, and so often, it was almost impossible to start with its hand crank that was at the front of the vehicle. Years later, Enrique recounted the story about the difficulty of starting the Model T. They would often start the engine by pushing the automobile instead of using the "hand-crank" starter. However, if someone lifted the rear wheel before cranking, the crank would turn much easier. Before cranking the engine, he would yell, "Levanta la pata!" ("Pick up its leg!").

After the rear wheel was off the ground, he would put all of his weight into turning the crank. One time as a friend cranked the engine, the handle kicked back and gashed his leg pretty badly. The friend fell back as blood oozed from his leg. Enrique drove his friend to the gas station.

In broken English, the friend asked the gas station attendant, "Hey Mister, give me one shot of gasoline."

The puzzled attendant gave him the gasoline. The injured friend poured the gas on his open wound and shrieked in pain.

A short while after arriving in Weslaco, Enrique filed the proper paperwork with the United States Immigration & Naturalization Service to prove his U.S. citizenship. He was refunded the $8 he'd paid when he entered the U.S. and given his U.S. credentials.

In 1927, Margarita got Enrique a job at the "Tienda de Abarrotes" (a wholesale store) that had been in business for about a year and desperately needed a bookkeeper. He worked as their bookkeeper on the second floor of an office building located near downtown Donna, Texas. The salesforce, all men, traveled throughout the region and had many clients. Enrique said, "The business was very profitable and had yearly sales above millions of dollars."

On December 10, 1927, Encarnacion received a tax bill for his business in General Terán. It included an unpaid balance for 8.34 pesos for 1926 and 10.45 pesos for 1927. With the surcharges and other fees, the total balance owed was 27.75 pesos. E. Ramirez "El R. De R. Del E." [El Recaudacion de Rentas del Estado] signed the document.[3] Were these the taxes that had increased due to the presidents increased taxation? The long arm of the Mexican government had reached across the border and into the United States.

About this time, Encarnacion had moved his family to downtown McAllen, Texas.

On March 20, 1928, Encarnacion crossed the border alone from Mexico into the U.S. at Roma, Texas.[4] He told the border agent that his residence was McAllen, Texas. Could Encarnacion have gone to Mexico to pay his overdue tax bill? The following week, on Saturday, March 31, 1928, Encarnacion obtained an Annual Occupation City Tax license for the City of Rio Grande. He was operating the Loteria in various cities around south Texas and was careful about following the local tax laws. He had likely returned to General Terán earlier in the month and perhaps had a chat with Aco (son of President Plutarco Elias Calles).

In April 1928, Encarnacion received a letter hastily written in pencil from Gaspar Cantú Garza.[5] Gaspar scribbled his words with urgency and with a seemingly desperate tone. After reading the letter, it was apparent that Gaspar had talked to Aco. Perhaps, Aco had angrily complained to Gaspar about Encarnacion or worse yet, maybe some sort of legal action was taken against Encarnacion's business or property interests in General Terán.

The handwritten letter was scrawled alarmingly across the page from edge to edge. It was conspicuously absent of punctuation marks as Gaspar pleaded multiple times with Encarnacion to return home to General Terán.

Gaspar wrote, "The best solution is to come [back], do not waste time . . . you can get with Calles [Plutarco Elias Calles Jr., ("Aco")] to work the Loteria in the surrounding towns."

Why had Aco "prevented" Encarnacion from conducting his

Loteria business?

Gaspar went on to say that Encarnacion could even move back into his home. Although, if he moved back, he would lose the rent from the tenant who was currently renting it, and that it was badly in need of repair. Gaspar frantically urged Encarnacion to move back to "defend" his property.

"Time is running out!" wrote Gaspar.

What must Encarnacion have thought as he read that letter? Why was the house in such a state of disrepair after about one year? There is much more left to discover about the story of how Encarnacion's home in General Terán would have fallen into such disrepair. Had there been a violent episode in their home before they left General Terán? It certainly wouldn't have been outside the realm of possibility. The Mexican government would most certainly not have liked that Encarnacion had, years, before aided the anti-centralist government rebels such as Pancho Villa. Had the government damaged their home or had the current tenant failed to maintain the house.

No matter what the situation, Encarnacion must have had a good reason not to return to General Terán to "defend" his property. He more than likely wrote Gaspar a letter asking Gaspar to calm down and continue to take care of the property. Perhaps Encarnacion had asked Gaspar to make preparations to sell all of Encarnacion's property in General Terán.

9 - McAllen 1928 to 1929

Encarnacion Mendoza did not drive. Perhaps, he'd never learned how to drive. It wouldn't have been that unusual at the time. Encarnacion had grown up in Mexico, either riding a horse or using a horse-drawn cart. Fortunately, Virgilio, Enrique, and Canacho did learn to drive.

On June 20, 1928, Encarnacion bought a used 1923 Ford ("Model T" or "Model TT") truck for $175.[1] He had put $31 down and financed the balance of $144 over twelve months through Ford Motor company. The Model TT was the commercial version of the Model T that came with a longer 12" wheelbase and sturdier frame and rear axle. It had a 4-Cylinder engine and had a maximum speed of 20 MPH. The truck had a stake bed that made it convenient to transport the two-by-four lumber, tent, and other items used for the Loteria.

Encarnacion paid the truck off twelve months later. With the new vehicle, there would be ample room in the truck's bed to hold two tents for the Loteria. He had everything he needed to expand his business. He had a large, reliable truck, the proper tax license, the tent, and its supporting framework, the game cards, the Loteria basket with the numbers, and plenty of prizes. Life had given them a new start in the United States.

Encarnacion had found a lumberyard called, *Phoenix Lumber*

Migrants: Exploring the Colors of my Family History

Company, where he could buy lumber and other hardware for his Loteria tent. It was located not far from downtown McAllen. It was run by a nice and personable gentleman named Anselmo Longoria. He liked shopping there because Anselmo gave him a good discount.

On September 1, 1928, in the Mexican section of McAllen, Texas, Canacho (18) was fooling around and caught the attention of the local law enforcement.[2] It's unclear precisely what Canacho had done or if he had done anything at all. He was picked up by the police and immediately taken to the border. He was not a U.S. Citizen at the time.

Canacho was given a choice to be deported back to Mexico or to go back to Mexico voluntarily. He chose the latter. He told the border agent that he had been in the United States since December 15, 1926. That date is the same day that the rest of his family arrived in the United States. Is it possible that Canacho had driven the truck loaded with the family's belongings (and the family) into the U.S. back on December 15, 1926? Only Enrique, Canacho, and Virgilio knew how to operate the family truck, and at that time, Enrique was in school in Monterrey. Canacho was likely driving the family into the United States on December 15, 1926.

On September 4, 1928, Canacho entered the United States legally through Hidalgo, Texas, and went back home to McAllen, Texas.[3] The Mendoza family was once again whole. The family separation must have been jarring to Encarnacion and Margarita. They needed to take action to begin to integrate into the United States legally.

On September 25, 1928, Encarnacion obtained a registration certificate with the Mexican Consulate in Hidalgo, Texas.[4] In it, he stated that he was 49 years of age and married. His occupation was Merchant. He was 5'1" in height with medium-dark complexion, brown eyes, and had black hair. It stated that he was born in General Terán, Nuevo Leon, Mexico and that he had last entered the United States on March 2, 1927, and had lived in McAllen,

Texas, since that date.

Years later, his daughter Margarita Elva said that her mother had smuggled her father across the border into the U.S., and then later, the U.S. sent him back to Mexico. Margarita Elva had also said that when he came back into the U.S., "They fixed all the papers."

Her recollection seemed to have elements that were more similar to Canacho's experience in 1928 than her father's. In any case, it appears that Encarnacion came into the U.S. without a documented border crossing for him on or about December 15, 1926. Then on March 2, 1927, Canacho traveled into the U.S. with his entry recorded in a border crossing record. In the 1920s, it was highly likely that the U.S. border personnel might have missed some of the border crossings. Perhaps, Encarnacion had initially (in 1926) come across hidden in a boat, as his daughter, Margarita Elva had later recounted.

By 1928, Enrique worked for Cantu & Sons, as a bookkeeper in McAllen. He started at $2, then $5 the second week, and then $10 by the third week. Later, Enrique was earning a whopping $50 per month. He started from scratch to get the books in order. Enrique also did inventory. He was also doing the books for "Tienda de Abarrotes" in downtown McAllen while working for Cantu & Sons.

Margarita was very active as a volunteer with the Red Cross. During this time, the Red Cross had set up hundreds of health centers and child welfare stations staffed by Red Cross doctors, social workers, and nurses. She was always generous and often gave food to the area public schools.

Enrique soon had three jobs. He worked for Cantu & Sons for $50/month doing bookkeeping. Enrique worked one night a week for Penner's bakery ("Panaderia Penner's"), which paid him $5 to $6 per week. He also worked part-time as a bookkeeper for "Tienda de Abarrotes" and was making $5 to $6 per week (another time, Enrique said he made $8 per week).

On November 30, 1928, President Plutarco Elias Calles's

presidency ended. This news would have been exciting for Encarnacion and his family - at least for Encarnacion and his wife, Margarita.

"Would it be safe to return to the country that they had both called home for so long?" they might have thought.

They might also felt that they were happy to continue to build a life in the United States.

In 1929, Mariana Ybarbo was living comfortably with her daughter Margarita and her family. At 81, Mariana felt safe when she was with her daughter. She, too, had fled the religious persecution and the political unrest in Mexico that had plagued so many Mexican citizens.

Mariana was born in the United States in East Texas in 1858, to a long line of wealthy and notable Ybarbo's. Her brother, Vital Ybarbo (b. 1843, d. 1922), had served with the Confederate States Army, who fought against the United States forces during the U.S. Civil War. He owned 160 acres in Nacogdoches, Texas. Mariana owned 2,300 acres in Palestine, Texas, in Anderson County.

Vital Ybarbo was an attorney and had filed suit back in 1901 to resolve an ownership dispute regarding Mariana's land property.

By December 11, 1902, Vital (acting as her attorney), her brother Benjamin Ybarbo and her husband Juan de la Garza transferred the property through a quitclaim deed to P. L. Bradford.[5]

In all likelihood, the lawless acquisition of land by opportunists was responsible for the loss of the 2,302 acres throughout Texas. It's unclear if any of the people listed on the quitclaim deed received any compensation for the land.

However, in 1929, Mariana's daughter, Margarita, believed that her mother still owned that land (in Nacogdoches, Texas). Certainly, Margarita would have seen it when she was a young girl living there with her parents, Mariana Ybarbo and Juan de la Garza. However, soon after, on December 11, 1902, Juan, Mariana, and their daughter moved to General Terán.[6] Perhaps they had received a respectable sum of money for the 2,302 acres after all.

By April 26, 1904, Juan de la Garza, Mariana's husband, was dead, and Mariana appeared to be living quite comfortably in General Terán. Mariana's younger brothers Vital and Benjamin had died in 1922 and 1923, respectively.

In 1929, she was living with her daughter, Margarita's family. Both Margarita and Encarnacion welcomed Mariana as part of their family. Encarnacion knew how much Margarita loved her mother. Margarita firmly believed that she should care for her aging mother.

Mariana lived comfortably with the Mendoza family and most certainly considered herself wealthy. She had money of her own and owned property in General Terán and also East Texas (at least so she thought). She had relatives in East Texas and Nacogdoches who owned tens of thousands of acres. Those relatives had stayed there and thwarted others who might have wanted their lands. Mariana was generous with Margarita's family and was undoubtedly pleased that Encarnacion's Loteria business had become successful in the United States.

During that time, Encarnacion, with the help of his sons and hired help, earned quite a bit from the Loteria. Encarnacion often ran two Loteria's simultaneously in nearby tents. Encarnacion would manage one Loteria, and one of his son's would manage the other. The two Loterias were often in competition with each other, making within $10 or $15 of each other. Each Loteria could easily make $100 to $150 (which was quite a bit of profit for them). Thanks to their hard work, Encarnacion's family lived quite a comfortable life.

On June 3, 1929, Encarnacion made his last payment for his truck. The business was going very well for him, and he was fortunate to have paid it off within a single year. He relied heavily on that truck for the Loteria.

Sometime around this time, Encarnacion had expressed interest in moving into one of Anselmo's houses right off of Houston Avenue. By this time, Anselmo had become a trusted family friend of Encarnacion and Margarita. Anselmo had told him that he had the perfect house for Encarnacion's family with an adjoining lot for the Loteria tent. The house and lot were right across from the lumberyard. Of course, Encarnacion and Margarita discussed Anselmo's offer, and they both decided that it was ideal for them. They set about making plans for another move to the house that Anselmo had offered to rent them.

On June 7, 1929, Mariana filed her Last Will and Testament ("Will"). She stated that after the money from her estate paid off her obligations, the remaining money, furniture, and property (no matter where it was, she had stated) should go to her daughter, Margarita. She said that Margarita could do as she pleases with her inheritance. Anselmo Longoria was a witness and signee of Mariana's Will. Margarita loved her mother dearly and cared for her in her old age. They had lived together in the U.S. in East Texas, then in Mexico, and later returning to Central Texas - their homeland.

A glimmer of hope came their way when, on June 21, 1929, the Cristero Rebellion in Mexico ended when the church's self-imposed ban on religious services ended.[7] The Calles Law, during the rule of atheist President Plutarco Elías Calles, eventually led to the Cristero Rebellion that lasted from 1926 to 1929. However, the anti-clerical laws remained in the Mexican Constitution of 1917.[8]

Mariana and her daughter, Margarita, welcomed this news. Both of them were deeply religious and had been heart-broken when their Church in General Terán had closed their doors to parishioners when the Cristero Rebellion began. Both Encarnacion and Margarita might have wanted to return someday to Mexico, but it was probably still too dangerous.

In McAllen, however, they both attended and loved the Sacred Heart Catholic Church that was close to their new home. It was a beautiful church.

About July 1929, Encarnacion and his family moved from downtown McAllen to 802 15th Street house about a hundred feet or so from Anselmo Longoria's house. Anselmo owned this home, along with several homes along 10th Avenue (later renamed Houston Avenue). His property extended from 15th Street to 16th Street. Anselmo's construction business ("Phoenix Lumber Company") was across the street from his residential property. Anselmo's office building sat right next to the lumberyard.

By September 4, 1929, the Great Depression[9] had started in the United States. Perhaps, the little town of McAllen was far enough from the financial woes of the depression that it might not affect them. The Longoria family and the Mendoza family celebrated more than their share of good fortune. Anselmo Longoria's Phoenix Lumber Company was doing well, and so was the Mendoza's Loteria business. Both families worked hard to advance their family's wellbeing.

Anselmo Longoria was resourceful and was used to living an entrepreneurial life that was the result of his productive engineering skills. His siblings were not well off. His brother, Guillermo, struggled as a farmer in San Patricio, and his brothers, Alejandro and Cristobal, would eventually work in some capacity with Anselmo. His sister, Estefana, was not as fortunate.

10 - Anselmo the Hero 9/1929

Anselmo Longoria was born in Los Cuates, Matamoros, Tamaulipas, Mexico, on April 21, 1894.¹ He was baptized Catholic on November 22, 1894, at The Immaculate Conception Church in Brownsville, Texas. Anselmo was the sixth child born to Alejandro De La Garza Longoria and Estefana Martinez.

In 1900, his family moved across the border to Brownsville, Texas, the sister city of Matamoros. At five years old, the move hardly mattered to him as long as he was with his family. At six, he attended Brownsville Public School. His native language might have been an obstacle for him, at first. He would quickly assimilate into the culture to feed his hungry mind. He learned English. He most certainly had the kind of brain that could quickly integrate complex thought into a plethora of new, creative ideas.

At the age of sixteen, Anselmo left school to help with family expenses. He was earning a living working with his cousin, Francisco G. Longoria, a building contractor. Unsurprisingly, Anselmo learned the trade quickly. He possessed an engineering mind that was quite adept at building on his prior education. As an apprentice, he had learned the particulars of residential and commercial construction.

By 1917, he was working at one of the largest construction companies in South Texas, M. R. Nelson Construction Co. Then,

Mr. Nelson promoted him to General Foreman, some of the workers objected. No way would they work for a Mexican, some had complained. Mr. Nelson brought his workers in line when he threatened to fire the objectors. It couldn't have been easy for Anselmo, but, fortunately, he had learned how to bear the indignity. Anselmo focused on the business. Nothing was going to stand in the way of his work, not even racism. He had been honing his skills for years. He was finally in a position to go to a whole new level in his goal of becoming a premier architect.

On December 19, 1918, Anselmo (24) married Ofelia Montalvo (18). It was a match made in heaven. Ofelia at 5'2" in height had found her true love: a thin 5'11" tall, dark-skinned forward-thinking man with black hair and brown eyes. They bought a home in Pharr, Texas, and they soon began their family. Their first son, Anselmo Jr. ("Chemo"), was born in October of 1919. In 1921, his family was blessed with their first daughter, Delia, followed by another daughter, Elida, in 1923.

Although he was quite successful at the M.R. Nelson Construction Company ("M.R. Nelson"), he wanted much more than they could offer. He went to Chicago, Illinois, and attended Chicago Technical College and graduated as an architect (about 1922 or so).

By 1923, he had left his job at M.R. Nelson to start his own construction business. He struggled, as new business owners often do and soon designed and built commercial and residential buildings in South Texas.

In 1924, he started his lumber and construction business and partnered with his father-in-law, Evaristo Montalvo, and named it *Phoenix Lumber Company*. It was located across the street from his new residence in McAllen, Texas, at the corner of 10th Avenue (later renamed Houston Avenue) and 15th Street. Anselmo's construction company was in a building that overlooked the lumberyard. Soon after that, Anselmo was able to buy out his father-in-law's interests in the business. Anselmo had the house where they had lived in Pharr, Texas, moved to the lot adjacent to his home in McAllen.

On October 24, 1924, a fire destroyed Sacred Heart Church located at 306 15th Street, not far from Anselmo's home in McAllen. Anselmo won the contract to rebuild the church. The old church was a relatively small wooden structure that had succumbed to a fire caused by an electrical short.[2]

In 1925, Anselmo and Ofelia welcomed their fourth child, a baby girl named after her mother, Ofelia.

After nearly two years, the new church, dedicated on April 11, 1926, was a crowning achievement for Anselmo. Anselmo was undoubtedly proud of the magnificent church, as were the other 3,000 parishioners.

The McAllen Daily Press published the following article about Anselmo Longoria and his business on November 20, 1926:[3]

PHOENIX YARD BOOSTS BUILDING

A. M. Longoria, [the] building contractor of the Phoenix Lumber Company, has done more than sixty thousand dollar's worth of building in McAllen since last April and is now building the Nassar Building on Main Street.

The [Sacred Heart] Catholic Church, erected at a cost of $40,000, the T. Allan Building, costing $3,000 are among some of the structures Contractor Longoria has added to McAllen, while the Gutierrez and Austin building at Mission which cost $20,000 has attracted the attention of those interested to building of the better type.

Contractor Longoria makes his own plans, having planned all of the above-mentioned buildings except the Catholic Church.

Mr. Longoria built the C. G. de la Garza building at Mission three years ago. And a year ago, when it was necessary for heavy charges of dynamite to be used in tearing out foundations of the old Valley Electric plant there, the strength of the structure was thoroughly tested and was not damaged in the least.

Large stocks of building material are carried at the *Phoenix Lumber Company* for use in carrying on the development program in McAllen and vicinity.

Anselmo had borrowed about $2,000 to fund his business. He used his McAllen property as collateral. The company had improved, and he started a business in Mexico, manufacturing a product he called Mansional. It was very similar to what would later be called sheetrock or drywall. He had then obtained patents in Canada and Mexico and had a patent-pending in the United States. The business was located in Monterrey and was named "Mansional Mexico."

The Longoria's rejoiced with the birth of their fifth child, a baby boy, Heron, in 1928.

By the end of 1928, Anselmo owned *Phoenix Lumber Company* outright. He continued with the construction company and owned several houses between 15th and 16th Streets (right across from his lumberyard). In McAllen's financial market, everything seemed ordinary. Life continued as if everything was okay.

Anselmo's duplex home was located at 1515 10th Avenue (later renamed Houston Street) in McAllen, Texas. It was a large house with two main sections separated by an opening from front to back between them. On one side was a large living room, a kitchen, a bedroom, a bathroom, and another bedroom. On the other side were Anselmo's office, a bedroom, and a kitchen exclusively used for ironing.

Anselmo also owned the house behind his, and the house he had moved from Phar. The property was quite large and was like a compound. There was also a large flat plot of land that he had converted to a small miniature golf course. Anselmo was doing quite well financially.

In late 1929, Anselmo tried unsuccessfully to start a construction business in Monterrey. His son, Anselmo Jr. "Chemo" detailed it in the *Biography of Anselmo Longoria, Sr.*[4] from March 27, 1990;

"In 1929 he went to Monterrey, Nuevo Leon, Mexico and set up a factory to build doors, windows, and cabinets and also to design and build houses and commercial buildings with his new system. He had a hard time making a go of the door and window factory as the Mexican builders do not use wood windows, and the only thing they use made out of lumber are some of the doors. He struggled with this factory for a couple of years and finally ended selling all the woodworking equipment."

Chemo goes on to say that his father, Anselmo, had "invented a new system of building [construction], which he called *The Polyganol System*. In this system, all the rooms and building were irregular. He claimed they would give you more area and space."

Anselmo forged ahead with his passion for the construction industry to find efficient ways to build homes. These setbacks never deterred Anselmo from his reaching his goal of establishing his businesses.

Polygonal system. Invented by Anselmo Longoria, Sr.

* * *

Anselmo traveled back and forth between his company in Monterrey, Mexico and *Phoenix Lumber Company* in McAllen, Texas. Anselmo was working hard in his businesses and expected great things for him and his family.

In San Benito, his sister, Estefana, was struggling. Her husband, Crisanto, had fallen ill. She could not bear to lose the man who had been so kind and loving to her. She loved him dearly. On September 14, 1929, Estefana's husband, Crisanto Escobedo, succumbed to pneumonia and passed away.

"I was six years old when my father was buried in San Benito. His brothers and sisters [Matilde's aunts and uncles] bought him a beautiful headstone to mark his grave," Matilde Escobedo said in January 2000.

A grieving Estefana was in trouble. She had five children and no means to support them. Things weren't going well for Estefana and her five children. Their family was living in a room that was part of a restaurant. They would have to move. They had no money.

News that his sister Estefana's was in serious trouble shocked Anselmo. His heart most certainly broke for his sister, who he affectionately called Anita, short for Estafanita.

He wasted no time in readying the house that stood a hundred feet or so behind his. He knew it would be perfect for his sister. He rushed to San Benito and brought her sister's shattered family back to McAllen, Texas. He moved them into the house that Estefana could call her very own. He loved his sister dearly and would do anything to keep her safe. Estefana's daughter, Maria Luisa went to work for the Longoria's on Anselmo's miniature golf course. Anselmo also paid for Maria Luisa to go to business school.

"Maria Luisa began her studies at a business college. She learned to write in beautiful handwriting," Matilde Escobedo later said. "Carmen didn't want to go to business school and opted for babysitting [Uncle] Anselmo's children."

Carmen, Estefana and Maria Luisa eventually took a job at a

nearby grocery store. The balance to Estefana's family was somewhat restored. Although, a new family dynamic would come into play for the families located on Anselmo's spacious property. Anselmo had saved his sister, and she was certainly grateful to him. Estefana and her family could heal with the love of her brother.

Note: Matilde Escobedo, daughter of Estefana, remembered the events of this time a little differently than her sister Carmen. Matilde said that her father, Crisanto, was still alive when Anselmo saved her family from poverty. She said that Crisanto stayed behind in San Benito and worked the fields and died a short while later. The rest of Carmen and Matilde's stories are the same. Crisanto had died on September 14, 1929. And Estefana's family was living in McAllen, Texas, two weeks later.

By the end of September 1929, Estefana (37), her five children: Maria Luisa (17), Carmen (15), Matilde (7), Marcolfa (4), and Alejandro (2) were living at 1515 Rear 10th Avenue. In the primary residence lived Anselmo (35), and his pregnant wife, Ofelia (29), and their children: Anselmo Jr. "Chemo" (10), Delia (8), Maria Elida (6), Ofelia (4), and Heron (2).

Anselmo introduced his sister Estefana to Encarnacion and Margarita, who lived across the alley from Anselmo's house. Encarnacion (47) and Margarita (44) lived with their nine children: Virgilio (19), Enrique (18), Canacho (17), Heriberto (16), Jesus (13), Consuelo (12), Margarita Elva (9), Ruby Luz (8), and Leslie (7).

Margarita's mother, Mariana Ybarbo (81), and Guadalupe Mendoza (19) "adopted" daughter of Encarnacion and Margarita, also lived with Encarnacion and Margarita.

Meanwhile, Estefana's daughter, Carmen, noticed a serious young man who lived in a house just beyond the fence behind Anselmo's house.

"I saw a skinny boy," Carmen said in a 1983 interview.

That "skinny boy" noticed her too.

11 - Budding Romance 1929

On September 19, 1929, Carmen had turned fifteen. It was a bittersweet birthday for her. Her stepfather, Crisanto Escobedo, whom she loved dearly, had just died. When her uncle, Anselmo, had moved them to McAllen, she felt a renewed hope. Her uncle had swooped in and saved her family.

Their new house was much bigger than the room where they had lived in San Benito. The latter, a restaurant storeroom, was too small for their family. The new house was perfect, Carmen thought. However, she missed her friend, Antonia, from San Benito as well as her Escobedo cousins like Andrea, her aunt Cecilia, and other relatives of her stepfather. In any case, Carmen was thankful that she and her family were safe at last. She soon made a new friend in McAllen, Leonor Padaz.[1]

Leonor lived at 810 15th Street in the house directly behind the house where Carmen lived. Leonor had several brothers, including a brother that was about a year older than Carmen. Carmen was still in shock from her stepfather's death and the sudden move to McAllen. Her new friend, Leonor, brought a ray of sunshine into her life. Leonor, like Carmen, seemed to be wise beyond her years. When her mother allowed it, Carmen and Leonor would go to the cinema a few blocks away.

Carmen later said, "In those days, a piano player sat off to one side playing music that was artistically matched to the movie."

It was the perfect diversion for her. The movie show would cost a nickel, and she enjoyed going to the movies with her best friend.

Indeed, her mother, Estefana, would have approved of the expense because it was for her hardworking daughter. Carmen loved her mother as well as the rest of her siblings. She was particularly close to her young toddler brother, Alejandro, who was almost two years old.

By October of 1929, Enrique was nineteen years old and continued to earn money doing bookkeeping and helping his father with the Loteria. Enrique loved working as an accountant doing the bookkeeping for a business, where he was able to sit behind a desk with an adding machine and a pile of journals. Enrique was good at it. When he needed an expensive piece of equipment to support his bookkeeping, he would almost always purchase it on credit. On October 22, 1929, Enrique bought a Remington portable typewriter on a payment plan for $65. He put $10 cash down payment and promised to pay $5 per month until it was paid off.

Enrique was an experienced accountant and bookkeeper. He'd learned to type when he was at the *Zaragoza Academia* in Monterrey. When he was there, he had typed a letter to his Uncle Gaspar Cantú Garza. In that letter, there were only one or two words that had been corrected by typeover. He meticulously inserted (by hand) the accent marks on the words that required them. He had formatted the letter professionally. The placement of the text on the page with a strict left margin and the sentences narrowly hugging the right margin showed that he was a well-educated, detail-oriented person who was focused on his future. He had written the letter on May 12, 1927, when he was about to graduate. Enrique was undoubtedly motivated to pursue a job that would coincide with his desire to become a successful business person. He was meticulous as would be expected from a skilled bookkeeper.

On October 29, 1929, the United States Stock Market crashed.[2]

To Anselmo, this seemed like a distant catastrophe that likely would not affect him or his town.

On November 1, 1929, Anselmo Longoria's company, *Phoenix Lumber Company*, won a construction project to build a new four-story building for Roosevelt Elementary School.[3] It was a major win for Anselmo and one that would generate a substantial profit for him. The school was not far from Anselmo's home. Both his children and the Mendoza children attended that school.

Anselmo's niece, Carmen, was most certainly proud of her uncle, who had rescued her family. She loved visiting Anselmo's house. It made her feel safe when she was near him. Her aunt, Ofelia, was welcoming too. Sometimes Carmen would relax on the swing on their porch after a long day of household chores. Perhaps she wished for a life where her family would live comfortably and happily. Years before, Carmen's family had lived in a house that belonged to a wealthy family in "Rancho Las Prietas" near Brownsville. She had learned what it felt like to have a better life. Now she believed that the wealthiest man in her world had saved her family. And, Anselmo had given them another chance to achieve their dreams.

On the afternoon of November 18, 1929, Carmen was relaxing on the porch of Anselmo's house. She saw a petite, young girl running towards her. The little girl was smiling and giggling as she came close to Carmen. It was one of the Mendoza children. Ten-year-old Margarita Elva walked up to Carmen, took an envelope from inside her blouse, and handed it to Carmen. Margarita Elva had carefully hidden it there earlier when her brother, Enrique, had promised her a nickel if she delivered the letter to Carmen.

Years later,[4] Margarita Elva said, "I put the letter inside my shirt, and there was nothing to hold the letter. I was a young child with nothing there." She giggled. "It was funny." She'd assured her brother that she would not lose the letter as she climbed the fence that stood between their house and the Longoria house.

Margarita Elva would have told her in her innocent voice, "My brother, Enrique, asked me to give you this letter."

"Gracias," Carmen likely said as she took the letter and then watched Margarita Elva scurry away and climb the back fence with ease and run into her house.

Margarita Elva would have then reported to her brother that the letter was delivered and then received her payment.

Carmen read the letter that came from the skinny boy that she'd seen on the day that her family moved there.[5]

McAllen, Texas
November 18, 1929

Ms. Carmen Garcia
City

Dear Carmen,

Although this is the first time I am writing to you by letter, I do this with the object of learning the following:

You understand perfectly well that I love you; for this reason, I am writing this so that you reply and tell me what you think about this. Don't believe that I know that you are going to say "yes"; because I cannot read your mind. I only await your answer, which I hope you tell me as soon as you find it convenient to do so. I do not also know if you have a commitment to someone. If so, do me the favor of telling me right away and forgive me if I bothered you with this letter.

Without more, I await your answer. Affectionately, Enrique

* * *

Carmen smiled as she read the letter. It was written like an important, formal business letter. She was impressed. She carefully stowed it away in a safe place.

When she next saw her friend, Leonor, she told her all about Enrique. She may have even let her read the letter from Enrique.

Leonor told her, "Why do you like him? He's too skinny."

Carmen had hesitated to answer his letter. Another boy, Pépe Vela, had also sent her a similar letter, just as Enrique had. Carmen had been flattered when she got Pépe's letter. Years later, she said, "Pépe was simpatico."

She'd seen Pépe before and didn't care for him. She'd seen him loitering on the street corner, not doing much of anything. She thought that Pépe would never amount to much in life.

Carmen adjusted to her new life in McAllen. She was devoted to her mother and siblings. She had hopes of enjoying a bit of normalcy in her life.

While she was at her Uncle Anselmo's house, Carmen had met Margarita Garza Mendoza, Enrique's mother. Margarita was good friends with Anselmo's wife, Ofelia. Ofelia and Margarita would spend time chatting about their latest sewing projects and going on about each of their families. It could have been there where Carmen heard Ofelia say, "The Mendoza boys are so good and well-behaved."

Carmen's mother, Estefana, would also have been social with Ofelia and Margarita on occasion. But, Estefana was more reserved than the other two. She was not shy, but rather a very private person. She was a person who might have had secrets of her own and not the type to share them. Just like her brother, Anselmo, she was thoughtful, resourceful, and practical. She was not overly emotional.

Later, Carmen told her sister, Maria Luisa, about the letter. Maria Luisa, not unlike her mother, would have told Carmen to simply answer Enrique one way or the other. Maria Luisa certainly was the type to move forward and definitively deal with matters as they surfaced. Perhaps, she felt a little sympathetic towards Enrique too.

Carmen continued to visit with her new best friend, Leonor Padaz. Leonor urged Carmen to steer clear of Enrique. Leonor didn't care much for Enrique.

Perhaps, Carmen had avoided him for a while longer because of Leonor's influence. "He's too skinny," Leonor had said.

Maria Luisa scolded Carmen, "Answer him!"

During an interview with Carmen and Enrique in 1983:

Enrique said that he wrote Carmen a letter, and she wouldn't write back to him. He was quite animated when he said that. Perhaps, Enrique was replaying his frustration from that time. He said that he couldn't understand why she wouldn't answer him. During the interview, he turned to Carmen and giggled as he said, "Answer me!"

In the interview, Carmen had been sitting quietly beside Enrique as he complained about the incident that had happened fifty-four years before and laughed. Then she turned back to the camera and said that her sister had scolded her and shouted at her, "Answer him!" She started to say something more about why she didn't answer Enrique, and then he interrupted her, "You should have just answered me!"

In that instant, Carmen looked annoyed at him. She turned back to the camera and said, "You see? He's been like this all his life. Exigente – Demanding his own way." She went on to say, "He was someone that liked to win. It wasn't so much that he liked me. He just wanted to win me." She smiled wryly and winked after she said that.

Sometime late in November of 1929, Carmen had a change in heart and wrote back to Enrique and consented to be his girlfriend. She probably told him about what Leonor had said about him. Carmen was the type of person who was open and honest and not afraid to articulate what she thought about things.
On December 4, 1929, in a 2nd letter, Enrique was happy to get a letter from Carmen.[6]

McAllen, Texas
December 4, 1929

Ms. Carmen Garcia

Unforgettable, Dear Carmen,
You can't imagine how happy I was to receive your letter, that which corresponds to my love, for what I am very content, and I am at a loss for words to tell you how much I love you.
For a long time, I felt feelings for you, and I would have told you sooner, but because of your company with a certain girl, I had decided not to, because you know very well how she is, I don't want to tell you that she is not a good girl, but I say that she is not a good friend. So, if you appreciate my love, such as you said in your letter, I ask that you don't go out to walk with her, as you promised. I've never spoken so seriously to any woman that I love as I do to you, and you already know it will be a sad day for me when we move from the house if we do not resolve to live near the house where you live.

On Sunday, I want to talk to you for the first time as a couple. I'm going to do everything possible to not go out, in case you have a chance to be on the side. If you want, and you have no objection to talking for a while before Sunday, you can tell Lupe[7] the place where we can meet. You are probably surprised by the length of this letter. What do you expect from someone with so much love in me, and who loves you and wants to see you?

Enrique

On December 24, 1929, Enrique gave Carmen a gift.[8] He'd carefully thought about what to give her and most certainly had consulted his mother.

Carmen was flattered when she received the gift. It was talcum powder and perfume. Years later, in an interview, she said jokingly, "Enrique must have thought that I was smelly for giving me that talcum powder and perfume."

Carmen and Leonor often walked past Enrique's house, on the way to the cinema. Enrique rushed up to Carmen. Carmen likely slowed down and let Leonor walk up ahead. It's not clear exactly what Enrique had told her, but it may have been the time when he asked her to stop hanging around with Leonor. He most certainly would have been annoyed that Leonor had encouraged Carmen to steer clear of him. Carmen would not have liked that Enrique didn't want her to see Leonor. Maybe she had told him, perhaps a little too frankly, that Leonor was her friend, and she would never think of hurting her. She, most likely, turned and walked away, leaving Enrique standing there, wondering what he had said to upset her.

At the time, Enrique had been working several bookkeeping jobs.

His heavy workload helped him to take his mind off of why Carmen had been upset with him - at least for a little while. What he didn't know is that an important business opportunity was about to present itself to him.

About this same time in 1929, Anselmo had tried unsuccessfully to start a construction business in Monterrey and sold it after two years.[9] This failure would have had some financial consequences for him and his family. Fortunately, he still had the construction business and the lumberyard in McAllen to support his family.

Anselmo and Ofelia welcomed their sixth child, a baby boy, Jose Eduardo.

On January 12, 1930, Enrique was issued a United States citizen identification card.[10] It had his picture and described him as having a dark complexion, black hair, brown hair, and 5'7" height. On the back of the card, it said, "This card presented to any immigrant inspector at the port where issued will entitle the person named and described on the reverse side hereof, who resides at McAllen, Texas, to admission to the United States upon proper identification issued at Hidalgo, Texas, 1-12-1930."

12 - The Store - 1930

An older man in his mid 80's (about 84 or 85) by the name of Mr. Garza (no relation to his family) came by Enrique's house one day and talked with him and his mother, Margarita. The old man told them that he had a store that had been long shuttered. He wanted Enrique to become his partner and re-open the store. The store sold fabric and shoes. The man said that he was too old to work the store, and his daughter, Rebecca Garza, had no interest in the store. His daughter was studying to be a nurse. The old man was desperate and broke down crying as he told them his sad story.

At first, Enrique didn't want to do it. He was already making a good living doing bookkeeping for "Tienda de Abarotes" and "Cantu & Sons." The man continued to tell his story. Enrique's mother encouraged Enrique to help the man and take over the business. With a great deal of reluctance, Enrique agreed to work with the old man. The old man wanted to have very little to do with the operation of the store. Mr. Garza insisted that the company should be in Enrique's name. Enrique objected, but the man stood firm on that issue.

When Mr. Garza showed him the store, Enrique was astonished. The store had rows of shoes on display that had long gone out of style. The women's shoes in the inventory were no longer fashionable.

"They were very pointy," Enrique later said.

Enrique knew that the stock would be impossible to sell at a profit. He thought that perhaps he and his mother could donate some of it to needy people in Mexico.

Enrique was still working several bookkeeping jobs. He was doing bookkeeping for Cantu & Sons (a wholesale warehouse) as well as for one or two other accounts. And on the weekends, he would help his father at the Loteria.

He soon began the long process of bringing the store to an operating level. This meant long days of purchasing inventory, setting up retail displays, and getting the financial accounting in order. He opened a checking account and registered the name of the business as "Enrique Mendoza and Company." Enrique had the sole authority to write checks for that account. He named the store: "Bueno, Bonito, Barato." His siblings helped him to organize the dusty store, and he went to work on the accounting end of the store.

Enrique worked with the dedication and enthusiasm required to get the store operating. He took inventory and assessed the assets and liabilities of the business. He made the appropriate entries into an initial set of accounting journals. The creditors agreed to give the new business credit to buy modern clothing, fabric, and shoes. His suppliers included A.B. Frank, Strauss Frank, and others. He arranged to pay Mr. Garza $15 per month rent for the building and paid himself a weekly salary of $7 per week. He stopped working for Cantu & Sons. Everything was running smoothly.

One of the suppliers, Strauss Frank, gave him a great deal on the price of a popular crepe fabric that his store sold. He purchased the items from the supplier for 49 cents for a yard of fabric and sold it for 59 cents per yard. J. C. Penney's bought a similar fabric for 59 cents per yard from another supplier and sold it for 64 cents per yard. His suppliers gave him a generous line of credit. Each of the creditors offered him up to 90 days to repay. But Enrique always paid them within 30 days. He always kept a balance of at least $1,000 in the business bank account. Soon, the store had clients from all over - even from across the border. The business had regained its footing, and the store was once again up and running.

At the time, Mr. Garza's wife called Enrique "Mi Quiqo" (pronounced: Kee-Ko). Enrique's family usually called him "Quique" (pronounced: Kee-Ke). Mrs. Garza liked him very much and suggested to Enrique that he marry her daughter, Rebecca. She told him that Rebecca was studying to be a nurse. Enrique's eyes must have looked at her incredulously as he said, "I already have a girlfriend." Mrs. Garza was not pleased. She most certainly narrowed her eyes at him in disappointment. Mrs. Garza went a little cold towards him after that.

Enrique's younger sister, Margarita Elva, was about ten years old at the time and worked at the store. Enrique believed that this is where she learned the retail business. In an interview in 2007, Margarita Elva (88) agreed. At Enrique's store, she had learned about sales, inventory, and other skills when she worked at Bueno, Bonito, Barato. At the time of the interview, she had long retired from running her fabric store in Roma, Texas. But it was obvious that her training and work experience at Bueno, Bonito, Barato were extremely beneficial to her (future) success at her fabric store.

Enrique was determined to make the business successful. The store would often stay open until 1:00 a.m. The business was off to a good start with all of the work and inventory he had invested.

He decided to stop working at all of his other jobs and focus on the store. Enrique said goodbye to his office at Tienda de Abarotes on the second story of the building located in downtown McAllen. He had a private office there in which he had done the bookkeeping for them. He gave that up so that he could build the store, "Bueno, Bonita, Barato" into a massive success.

13 - The Census - 4/1930 to 8/1930

Enrique was busy working hard at the store and hadn't had much time to write Carmen. By this time, though, he felt more comfortable talking with her when he saw her outside, usually on Sunday, when she was at home.

On Sunday, April 6, 1930, Enrique saw Maria Luisa working at Anselmo's miniature golf course. She liked taking care of that quaint little golf course. Her uncle Anselmo paid her a few dollars to keep the field in good shape. Enrique took a deep breath and walked up to Maria Luisa and asked about Carmen.

"Carmen is busy," she most likely said. She wouldn't have offered much more than that to him.

The following Tuesday, he wrote his 3rd letter to Carmen. It had been four months since his last letter to her.[1]

McAllen, Texas
April 8, 1930

Ms. Carmen Garcia

Unforgettable Carmen:
   Without any [fault of] yours, I refer to [what you told Luisa]. I offer you this about the meeting:

Luisa said on Sunday that you had a reason that you did not want to play with me, I have no objection to write you, and I only hope that in the future we do not have the slightest displeasure.

Let me know if you have saved me a corner; well, ever since Luisa told me that [you could not see me on Sunday], I spend each moment thinking about you, and I would like to have the pleasure to talk with you and tell you "How much I love you." So answer me and tell me where we can talk. Well, I need to ask you something important concerning our relationship.

Accept my most sincere affection from one who loves you and adores you.

Enrique

It was very fortuitous that Anselmo Longoria's family and the Mendoza family had become successful entrepreneurs. As entrepreneurs, the families avoided the financial woes of the Great Depression that had started in 1929. They celebrated their share of good fortune. Anselmo Longoria's *Phoenix Lumber Company* was doing well, and so was Encarnacion's Loteria business. Both families worked hard to advance their family's lives.

Historical Note:[2] The United States deported many Mexicans in Texas to Mexico during the Great Depression. There were large-scale deportation of immigrants, particularly from rural areas. Hostility to immigrant workers grew as jobs became scarce. Mexicans were offered free trainrides back to Mexico. Some went back to Mexico voluntarily. Some were tricked into leaving. And some, who looked Mexican were also deported. Bank foreclosures drove many Mexicans from their lands.

On Thursday, April 10, 1930, a census taker came by Anselmo and Ofelia's home, then Estefana's home, and a little later to Encarnacion's home[3] to record the 1930 census.

The census showed that Anselmo owned his home and that it had a value of $8,000. His household was listed as Anselmo (35), Ofelia (30) [wife], and children: Maria E., Maria O., Heron, Jose M. Anselmo Jr., and Delia. [Note: The ages recorded in the census for the children were incorrect].

The census next showed that Estefana's family resided at 1515 Rear 10th Avenue. The house in which Estefana's family lived, owned by Anselmo, was valued at $1,800. Estefana's household included Estefana (37) [widow], and children: Maria Luisa (18), Carmen (15), Matilde (8), Marcolfa (4), Alejandro (2). All were born in Texas except for Estefana. She was born in Matamoros, Tamaulipas, Mexico. Additionally, the census noted the occupation of Maria Luisa as "Overseer of Golf Course."

Next, Encarnacion's family rented a house at "802 15th Street." The house, also owned by Anselmo, was worth $1,500. The census listed Encarnacion's household as Encarnacion (51), Margarita (44) [wife], and children: Virgilio (19), Enrique (18), Encarnacion Jr. (17), Heriberto (16), Jesus (13), Consuelo (12), Margarita Elva (9), Ruby Luz (8), Leslie (7). All of the boys, except for Enrique worked at the Loteria, Enrique worked as a bookkeeper. Also, living with the Mendoza's were: Margarita's mother, Mariana Garza (Ybarbo); Guadalupe Mendoza was listed as the Mendoza's servant and adopted daughter of Encarnacion, and Jose A. ("Pepe") as Guadalupe's son.

Carmen's best friend, Leonor, was on the same census record and lived at 814 15th Street. This was just one or two doors down from Enrique's house and directly across the alley from Carmen's house.

According to the 1930 United States Census, the population of McAllen was 9,075.[4]

The 1930 census also recorded Nueces County, near Robstown, where Estefana's brother, Guillermo Longoria, lived.[5] The 1930 census included Guillermo (45), Juana, wife (34), and children: Alberto (17), Teresa (14), Leandro (9). His daughter, Virginia, was not in this census. She was 15 years old at that time. The census taker had overlooked her (or she may have been away from home).

Alejandro Jr. (26) was working in Mexico, helping Anselmo with his businesses there. Cristobal Longoria (29) was living a few blocks away from Anselmo in 1930.

Enrique was love struck. He seemed to obsess over his new love. Perhaps his mother was moving things along when Enrique accompanied his mother to Estefana's home in the hopes that he might see Carmen. To Enrique, Carmen was a beautiful, fair-skinned redhead who seemed unattainable to him. She was not as lovestruck with him as he was with her. Carmen was more comfortable spending her free time with her friend, Leonor, than with Enrique. Carmen was a trophy to him, she thought.

The 4th letter was on Monday, May 1930.[6]

McAllen, Texas
May 19, 1930

Carmen Garcia

Adored and unforgettable Carmen,
    When you receive this, please have the certainty that I will be thinking of you. What could be more sublime in the world than to be loved with genuine affection? Have you found someone more interesting, more attractive [than me]? Lastly, did you know that I love you more than anyone? How

can you doubt, even for a moment, that I love you with all the strength of my heart; I have promised you and sworn to adore you forever?

If your affection for me is as you say, then what in the world could prevent our happiness? What could separate us, which was not by the will of God?

On Friday night, Mama and I went to your house. When we returned, we came by way of the yard of your uncle's house. You can't imagine the feeling, so pleasant that I experienced when I saw you, perhaps asleep, looking like nothing less than an angel. I was speechless, and as Mama was walking ahead of me, she said, "How wonderful she is!" Mama smiled as a sign of affirmation.

Without more, who loves you with all my soul.
Yours, Enrique
P. S. If you want, answer me.

Margarita's house was on the same lot about a half-block south of Anselmo's house on 15th Avenue. Estefana's house was directly behind Anselmo's house on 15th Avenue. For Margarita to visit with Estefana, she would walk up Houston Street for about 200 feet and then turn left at the alley (which was right before Anselmo's house). Then she would walk down the alley another 100 or so feet to Estefana's house.

Carmen worked hard and earned money by babysitting Anselmo's and Ofelia's kids, helping her mother or her sister pick cotton in the fields, or by working in a grocery store with her sister, Maria Luisa. She helped contribute towards the family expenses and saved a little for herself to go to the movies or buy beautiful clothes. Carmen dressed in comfortable, yet fashionable clothes. She had enough leisure time to go to the movies every so often with her friend, Leonor. For the first time in her life, Carmen didn't have to worry about her family losing their home or worry about going hungry. She enjoyed life. When her family lived in San Benito, Carmen didn't mind working on the farm. She loved to milk their cow. But now she had enough leisure time to go to the movies with her friend Leonor. Carmen loved her mother, her sisters, and her adorable toddler brother.

In June of 1930, Encarnacion (50) and his son Enrique (19) traveled to Monterrey, Mexico, and visited with Encarnacion's uncle, Jesus Maria Garcia (his mother's brother). He returned to McAllen on June 8, 1930. The border crossing record stated that Encarnacion had lived in Texas since March 2, 1927.[7] However, earlier border crossings seem to hint that he and his family may have moved to Texas a few months before that.

On Wednesday, June 18, 1930, in his 5th letter to Carmen, Enrique was very concerned about Carmen.[8]

McAllen, Texas
June 18, 1930

Ms. Carmen Garcia

Unforgettable Carmen,

I have to tell you a few words. I have no objection to telling you this so that you can take note of it and answer all the questions that I ask you in this letter.

In the first place, I want you to tell me why you have not answered my letters. I think that someone has advised you not to visit me.

I can't believe that you also have been advised not to write to me. Or perhaps you just don't want to write to me. I was told that you don't have the time, this I don't believe. Because if you don't have ten minutes to write a letter, the less time you'll have two or three hours to go out with Leonor or go to this house or [go to] your neighbor's house.

Now I think [and feel] that you have no desire to write. Since I never believed that you had such little appreciation for me.

You know perfectly well that my fondness for you is well-intentioned, and to demonstrate that to you, I have never walked with people of poor character.

Also, I wanted to make another particular recommendation that you've never wanted to carry out and that many times I have told you. On several occasions, you have gone out for a walk with Leonor. Sometimes, I've found out where you went, but not from you. That is to say, that you have not told it to me. [I heard it] from other people, who by chance saw you out, for example, in the Anahuac. I think this is very bad that you do not tell me where you are going, each time that you go out. In many cases, the reason is that you don't want me to accompany you. But you have no reason not to tell me where you are going to go.

I know perfectly well that you were given a lot of advice about our relationship. Many people have good advice, but more abundant are those that give bad advice. You've received - advice and you've followed it, i.e., you've done what you have been told. For example, a particular person advised that you not see too much of me. They say that the less you see me, the more affection I will feel for you. This cannot be regarded as good advice. Well, anyone could take this kind of recommendation from an ignorant person. How is it possible that the less you see a person, the more affection will come from it. I don't want to say that I have any less love for you; I know perfectly [well] that you get too carried away by what other people tell you.

To me, it seems that you think little of me. You have time to go to your neighbor's house, sometimes for the whole afternoon. You have the time to go to Leonor's house. You have time to go to the theater every once in a while. You have time for everyone else, except to go to my house. And when you do go, it's just for five minutes (I didn't know the reason before), and then you go. Some Sundays, you stayed all afternoon and sometimes two or three hours into the night. If your Aunt and Uncle do not want you to go, then why don't you tell me directly. This is not a bad thing if I know it, there should be no secrets between us, and especially those of this nature.

I hope you understand the reason for not hiding anything. It costs you little to let me know when you go out somewhere. Don't believe what other people tell you. Look for the best way to live by making your own decisions. It would be impossible to follow the advice from all the people that offer it to you. Some people tell you the reality wrapped in sacrifice. Others cover the lie [they tell you] with beauty. I don't want you to go out with whom I've told you. Take a walk with friends that are as honest as you; for example, Delia. Also, I would like that you do not go out on Sundays (no). Therefore, I tell you I want you to look for friends that are in your same class, i.e., good friends.

If in any of the parts of this letter I have been reckless, I beg your forgiveness; but my sole purpose is to bring to fruition a good outcome for our relationship and from this point on to become accustomed to knowing how to live, for one another, not to go to encounter difficulties for which there are no remedies.

Love, Yours, Enrique

On July 8, 1930, Enrique turned twenty. He was happy that he had a girlfriend, and life was good for him.

In early August 1930, Maria Luisa and her mother, Estefana, traveled to Brownsville, Texas. Estefana had lived in Brownsville and most certainly had relatives there. Likely, they went there to earn some money. Carmen had said that her mother worked on farms to make money. Although there is no border crossing found to support this, she may have been visiting relatives in Matamoros, Mexico. Her sister-in-law, Cecilia, and her husband frequented the border town of Matamoros, Mexico, Estefana's birth town. Without a doubt, Carmen stayed behind to care for Matilde, Marcolfa, and Alejandro. It is also possible that Estefana and Maria Luisa were working in the cotton fields near Brownsville to earn some money.

Estefana and Maria Luisa had stayed in Brownsville for a few weeks, likely working on a farm, harvesting some sort of crops. Estefana told Carmen in a postcard dated August 5, 1930, "I'll send you a gift of pearls soon."[9]

Maria Luisa also sent a postcard dated August 2, 1930, to her "amiga" Margarita (Enrique's mother) telling her that they had visited Harlingen High School.[10]

Life was good for them.

14 - Mamacita Danced - 9/1930 to 11/1930

Carmen was a well-mannered young lady. Her mother had instilled in Carmen a strong sense of morality. She was only fifteen years old, and her mother would have warned her to be cautious when it came to boys. Estefana had good reason to protect her daughter from those who sought to "own" her and then to leave her—perhaps referring to Carmen's biological father. In contrast, Estefana's husband, Crisanto, whom she loved dearly, had left her because of death. She had loved him and had been devoted to him until the day he died.

It appeared that Carmen was upset with Enrique. Is it possible that Enrique had knocked on Carmen's door while her mother and older sister were in Brownsville? If that happened, Carmen would have been unhappy with this and considered it highly improper, especially if her Uncle Anselmo or Aunt Ofelia had seen Enrique visit while Estefana was gone. Carmen's mother had trusted Carmen. Perhaps too, Carmen had not liked the tone of Enrique's last letter. On Friday, September 19, 1930, Carmen celebrated her sixteenth birthday. Maybe Enrique forgot to wish her a happy birthday.

On Tuesday, September 27, 1930, Enrique sent his 6th letter to Carmen. "Why are you angry with me since last Saturday?"[1]

* * *

McAllen, Texas,
September 27, 1930

Miss. Carmen Garcia
McAllen, Texas

My adored Carmen,

I received your letter. It is with my greatest pleasure to write back to you. I carefully read your letter. You say that you love me, and I hope that you do not forget the promise you made to me in your letter: "Yours until death." This makes me believe that you love me, and your kind words of affection support this.

My greatest desire is that you are mine forever. My heart does not have limits in loving you for the rest of my life.

Why have you been angry with me since Thursday? Do you think that I don't love you?

It is my greatest desire not to have issues with our relationship, and as soon as possible and that our love lasts forever.
I love you forever,
Enrique
Respond soon.

Enrique left with his family to Corpus Christi, Texas, to run the Loteria there and in the surrounding towns. She sent him back a letter and likely explained to him what he had done. Carmen was the understanding type with a big heart and she likely forgave him. There was something about him that she liked more and more. On Friday, October 3, 1930, Enrique wrote the 7th letter to Carmen:[2]

* * *

Migrants: Exploring the Colors of my Family History

Enrique Mendoza G.
1218 Leopard St.
Corpus Christi, Texas
October 3, 1930

Miss. Carmen Garcia
Mc Allen, Texas

Unforgettable Carmen,

With pleasure, I am writing this to tell you that we arrived well and without issue. Carmen, you can't imagine the good feeling that I get every time I receive a letter from you. Corpus, in my opinion, is no great attraction for me. But if you were here with me, I think it would be so delightful, mainly due to you, my lovely girlfriend, that I will never leave. I hope that (as you told me) you think the same way as I do concerning our friendship. I assure you that we will never have any obstacle that is opposed to our happiness that we almost have, but we have to sacrifice to achieve it fully.

Behave well, wait for me, and soon we will be happy.
I love you,
Enrique
Answer me as soon as you promised. I send greetings to your mother, Luisa, and your little girlfriend.

Enrique was happy that his girlfriend was "his." He couldn't help making a dig at Leonor, Carmen's best and trusted friend.

The business was going well for Anselmo. He was working hard to get a foothold in Mexico with his modern construction company. After one year in business in Mexico, he was hopeful that it would become as profitable as his construction business had once been in McAllen. Anselmo often advertised in the McAllen Daily Press to ensure that his lumberyard sales would remain strong while he traveled to Mexico to develop his construction business there.

Three other lumber companies regularly advertised alongside Anselmo's business, *Phoenix Lumber Company*. His competitors were *Independent Lumber Company* (M.R. Nelson, Owner), *Thomas W. Blake Lumber Company* (P.L. Haley, Mgr.), and *Valley Lumber Company* (L.M. Holland, Mgr.).

Incidentally, Anselmo used to work for M. R. Nelson. On October 5, 1930, all four companies advertised in a full-page ad in the McAllen Daily Press that was intended to promote building in McAllen.[3] Four lumber companies competing for customers in a small city was not easy. Perhaps most of Anselmo's customers came from the Mexican District. His business and his home were right in the middle of that district.

Despite the difficulties of a Mexican running his business in the United States amid the Great Depression, he had achieved a modicum of success. He was a brilliant architect and highly sought after. His family enjoyed the life that resembled the upper middle class of the time.

Enrique and his family were still in Corpus Christi running the Loteria. They went from town to town with the Loteria. After each city, they would dismantle the tent (and stands) and carefully pack it in the truck along with the prizes, the game tiles, and the rest of their belongings. When they went to the next town, they unloaded the truck and set everything up for the next game. They knew this process well and did it efficiently.

On the 8th letter on Thursday, October 9, 1930, Enrique wrote to Carmen:[4]

* * *

Enrique Mendoza G.
1218 Leopard St.
Corpus Christi, Texas
October 9, 1930

Miss. Carmen Garcia
Mc Allen, Texas

Loving and unforgettable Carmen,

I was glad to receive your letter. I am pleased with your demonstrations of affection that you show me in your letter. I understood from your letter that you love me. Hopefully, you never stop loving me. I promise you that we will be so happy when we are married, and we will not have any issues as long as we both think things through.

I wanted it with all my heart to put this letter in the mail today (Thursday). It was not possible because I was busy all day helping the boys to unpack the earthenware and set up the Loteria, and right now, it is 11:30 at night. Still, I decided to write to you so that you could reply as soon as you can, although it is not possible to receive your letter on Saturday like I wanted to; but I hope to receive your letter on Sunday or Monday.

In your letters, please tell me everything when you get into trouble, or when someone shows you some contempt. Because if you consider me trustworthy as your boyfriend, you will find me trustworthy when we are married. Don't think that curiosity is why I want to know everything that you want to tell me about yourself. It is because I want to start taking note of the people that we can consider as good friends when we go in real life and start knowing which are the people who are not friends and that their hypocrisy makes them smile to show us a false "good pleasure."

Say hello to your mother and Luisa. And receive my heart, and I love you with all my soul.
Yours,
Enrique

On Sunday, October 19, 1930, the families of Estefana, Anselmo, and the Mendoza's had a friendly get-together. It must have been a lovely party. Even though Estefana had been ill, she got up and danced. The Mendoza family had just returned from a very profitable tour of the Loteria from Corpus Christi and the surrounding towns. It was probably Margarita's idea for the festive event. She would have made sure that the local musicians provided lively music. All of the families were happy to share their blessings that they'd worked so hard to receive. The Mendoza's enjoyed the fast-paced and profitable Loteria, Anselmo enjoyed his very profitable construction business. Estefana's occasional hard work picking cotton or working at the local store provided her family with a little extra money. They were all blessed.

On the 9th letter, on Wednesday, October 22, 1930, Enrique talked a little about Carmen's mother.[5]

McAllen, Tex
October 22, 1930

Miss. Carmen Garcia

Loving Carmen, whom I hold in high regard,

With happiness, I answer your letter dated the 11th, which my Papa gave me. It came last

Tuesday, the day I was here.

I love you more each day more and more so that you see that my love for you is well-intentioned. And I hope you know how well Mama and Papa think of you and want nothing more than God grant that we do not stray from our aspirations.

Carmen, you can't imagine the wonderful time that I had on Sunday night when your Mamacita got better and danced – even though we were not allowed to go to the cinema; I say we were not allowed to go since they didn't let you go. Then I lost interest in going to the cinema. But it did not hurt my feelings; because I could see that she was a bit ill and had good reason not to permit you to go.

I'll send you a card, so you don't forget me, and you will remember me from time to time, as I remember you all of the time.

Receive the sincere affection of one who loves you and will always love you. I want you.
Yours,
Enrique

On Wednesday, November 12, 1930, Enrique wrote his 10th letter to Carmen.[6] Enrique had gotten into trouble when he had tried to visit Carmen while her mother was out of town a few weeks before. Enrique was bothered because of this. It still bothered Carmen that Enrique would show up at her house whenever he wanted. It bothered her mother too. Nothing would discourage Enrique from expressing his love for Carmen. He was quite persistent. Perhaps that was a quality that Carmen liked about him.

* * *

McAllen, Texas
November 12, 1930

Miss. Carmen Garcia

My loving and unforgettable Carmen:

With much happiness, I answer your letter, which left me thinking about what you said about permission to go to your house. Don't believe that I did this with bad intentions, but I talked to your Mamacita and asked permission to visit [your home] as your official boyfriend. She told me that she didn't know your opinion about this and didn't know Mr. Anselmo's either. I believe that your uncle [Anselmo] would have no problem with this. But it would have been preferable if it was closer to the marriage date to ask for permission, i.e., about two or three months before.

Have patience, which I hope God grant that our destiny will soon join for always, and to affirm tangibly, the great love that I have for you.

Don't doubt for a moment my love for you if you see me as pensive or sad; I do not doubt that there are times that I am because I don't see you often, and it has been a long time since we talked. I would like to be always by your side and that you love me as much as I love you, with all my soul.

It is 12 at night, and I am thinking of you and our future. Respond soon and write to me a lot and love me as much as you tell me you do in your letters. I love you,
Enrique

* * *

Enrique wanted to see Carmen more often, even if she was alone. He talked with her on occasion when she was out with her friend, Leonor, or when he went with his mother to Estefana's house. Additionally, he wanted everyone to know that she was his girlfriend. Carmen would not have liked for Enrique to go to her mother to ask to be Carmen's boyfriend. Carmen would likely have been annoyed with this. Carmen herself would decide if Enrique was her boyfriend or not.

15 - Mendoza Shakeup - 11/1930 to 12/1930

On November 3, 1930, Mariana Ybarbo, Mother of Margarita de la Garza Mendoza, wife of Juan Garza Espinosa, became ill with the influenza virus.

Sixteen days later, on November 19, 1930, tragedy hit the Mendoza family. Margarita's beloved mother, Mariana Ybarbo, passed from a terrible bout of influenza. As is often the case, it started with a mild weakness that crept up on her and progressed rapidly into a debilitating fever. Unfortunately, her influenza progressed out of control into pneumonia. She died of influenza, with a secondary cause of pneumonia. According to the death certificate,[1] she had been living in McAllen for three years (with Encarnacion and Margarita).

Mariana Ybarbo was born in Nacogdoches, Texas. Her father was Juan Ybarbo, born in Nacogdoches District, Texas; Her mother was Alafonsa "Ildefonsa" Flores, born in Natchitoches, Louisiana.

The census, taken just a few months before, had mistakenly indicated that she was 90 years. Perhaps Mariana Ybarbo had appeared older to the census taker. Probably, she'd already been ill at the time the census was taken (about five months before). In any case, she was a few years younger than that.

Was she born in 1840 (i.e., 90 years old in 1930) as the 1930 census had suggested?

The death certificate mistakenly stated that Mariana Ybarbo was born in 1876 and was 54 years old when she died. If that were true, she would have had her first daughter, Margarita, at nine years old – that's not possible.

According to the 1850 census in Nacogdoches, Texas, Mariana Ybarbo was two years old. Therefore, her birth year was more than likely in 1848. She gave birth to Margarita at age 37 in 1885.

Therefore, Mariana Ybarbo likely died at the ripe old age of 82 years (not 90 as the April 10, 1930, U.S. Census indicated and not 54 as the November 19, 1930 death certificate indicated).

Before she died, she believed that she owned land in East Texas. But if her husband, Juan de la Garza, were still alive, he may have told her that was no longer true. Juan de la Garza would have known most of the story about that land and how her father, Juan Jose Ybarbo, had once owned thousands of acres in East Texas.

On March 20, 1848, Juan Jose Ybarbo, father of Mariana Ybarbo, had an original patent for land in Rusk County.[2] It was situated about four miles Northeast of Henderson, Texas, on the "Left" side of State Highway 43.

Juan Jose Ybarbo had discovered that some sort of shenanigans had occurred regarding the ownership of his land. In 1877, he had enlisted the help of W. M. Cole and his brother in an attempt to reclaim his property. Juan Jose Ybarbo gave the Cole brothers power of attorney and agreed to provide them with half interest in any land that the brothers reclaimed.

In 1882, the Cole brothers filed suit. Two of the defendants, Jessie Walling and Elisha Roberts, could have been squatters if the land had been left vacant for an extended period. They contended that Juan Jose Ybarbo had conveyed the land to them in 1878. They couldn't prove it because they said that a courthouse fire had destroyed the record of the transaction. Juan Jose Ybarbo disputed their statement that he had conveyed the land to them.

The Cole brother's lawsuit failed, and Juan Jose Ybarbo lost his claim to his land in Rusk County. His loss was devastating - it was thousands of acres that he had lost. This land was part of Spanish and Mexican land grants that gave the Ybarbo family upwards of 20,000 acres.[3]

Juan Jose Ybarbo had been robbed of his land. What would he have thought about the rule of law? It appeared that the judge had favored the opportunists that had stolen his land. The judge had sent a clear message, "You have no rights here. You are not wanted here." During this era, the law would have favored Anglo Americans versus Mexicans in land disputes.

Juan Jose Ybarbo also had a land patent on thousands of acres in neighboring Anderson County (Deed Records W-51).[4] Not surprisingly, both Walling and Roberts had a partition deed for 200-1/2 acres of Ybarbo's land. However, many others laid claim to the several thousand acres that had belonged to Juan Jose Ybarbo.

In 1884, Juan Jose Ybarbo filed suit against the E. P. Jarvis and others to recover the title and possession of his land. By that time, many people had already claimed ownership of that land. Juan Jose Ybarbo settled for 2,302-1/2 acres. It was a small fraction of the property that he had once owned through a Spanish land grant.

Afterward, Juan de la Garza (born in General Terán, Nuevo Leon, Mexico) met Mariana Ybarbo near her home in Nacogdoches, Texas. Juan de la Garza, most probably a widower, had children from a previous marriage. Juan de la Garza had moved from General Terán, where his children still lived, to East Texas near to where Mariana Ybarbo was living.

Mariana Ybarbo and Juan de la Garza married about 1884 and later had a daughter, Margarita, in Floresville, Texas.

By 1901, Juan Jose Ybarbo, Mariana Ybarbo's father, had died.

Soon after, Vital Ybarbo, Juan Jose Ybarbo's son (Mariana's brother), filed suit to have the interests of all parties clearly defined.

It appeared that there was a dispute regarding property ownership of Juan Jose Ybarbo and P. L. Bradford. Vital Ybarbo, a civil war veteran, was a skilled attorney. As a result, the judge ruled that Juan Jose Ybarbo owned the 2,302-1/2 acres. As part of the ruling the sheriff, involved in the dispute, received 120 acres, perhaps as a bribe.

It appeared that P. L. Bradford benefited by Juan Jose Ybarbo's original lawsuit and by Vital Ybarbo's later lawsuit. Part of Mr. Bradford's land outside of the 2,302-1/2 acres had once belonged to Ybarbo. Presumably, Mr. Bradford paid Juan Jose's descendants (as well as the others) a small sum of money to make this problem go away. All of the "owners" of the 2,302-1/2 acres of land in question, including Juan Jose Ybarbo's descendants, quit-claimed that land to P. L. Bradford.

In 1902, Mariana Ybarbo had given her brother, Vital Ybarbo, power of attorney, and was not present when they made the deal. Her husband Juan de la Garza was there. It's unclear if Mariana Ybarbo knew about the quit-claim deed and might have assumed that her deceased father had left her at least part of the property in Nacogdoches. Certainly, Juan de la Garza, Mariana Ybarbo's husband, knew the truth.

Juan de la Garza, his wife, Mariana Ybarbo, and their surviving child, Margarita, right after receiving payment, they moved to General Terán. A young Margarita believed that her mother still owned thousands of acres in Nacogdoches. Years later (in 1945), Mariana Ybarbo's grandson, Jesus Mendoza, would rediscover the hidden truth about the Nacogdoches property.

Mariana Ybarbo had enjoyed an elegant and well-to-do lifestyle for her long life. She had experienced many challenges in her life; none of them detracted from her determination to live life to its fullest. Her daughter, Margarita, certainly had inherited her focused nature, her strong religious beliefs, and her appreciation for life.

According to Enrique, Mariana Ybarbo's grandson, she had

some property in General Terán. Presumably, this was her home, before she had moved with Encarnacion's family to Texas.

Soon after, life came back to normal, and Enrique continued with his letters.

On Thursday, November 27, 1930, Enrique sent the 11th letter to Carmen; "Tell me everything".[5]

McAllen, Texas
November 27, 1930

Miss. Carmen Garcia

My lovely Carmen,

With my greatest pleasure, I am writing this to answer your letter in which you speak to me of your love, which I appreciate more than my life.

I wish with all my soul to be always by your side; but I'm happy that we talk every once in a while, since it is not possible right now to be united as I desire; but God will grant this to us later, because of this we must not lose hope.

Carmen, I ask you please that you answer this letter early Sunday so that I can enjoy that day; you know how happy I am every time I receive your letter.

In your letters, tell me everything that you wish to. I am quite careful to save them in a safe place, and no one can see them.

With my greatest desires that you write back on the day that I say and the next letter that I send you will be very long. Who loves you and will not forget you. Yours,

Enrique
Receive this letter and receive my high regard for you and my love

On Saturday, December 20, 1930, Enrique sent the 12th letter to Carmen while he was in Mexico.[6] "I'll be back on Wednesday."

Mark: Monterrey, N. L. December 20, 1930.
Letter: Monterrey December 20, 1930

Ms. Carmen Garcia
Box 1141
McAllen, Texas

Ms. Carmen Garcia
McAllen

Unforgettable Carmen,

With pleasure, I write to you and tell you of my sadness because I am not by your side, but I implore you to know that I have always been thinking about it. Later, I'll explain why I had not written before today.

I will be back on Wednesday that if God wants. I have a lot to tell you.

Regards to your Mamacita and Luisa - and, receive the heart of your inseparable,

Enrique

Even though Enrique thought that his family would be returning the next Wednesday (December 24, 1930), his family's border crossing indicated that they returned on Tuesday, December 30,

1930.

About December 26, 1930, Encarnacion and Margarita traveled to Monterrey and visited with his uncle, Jesus Maria Garcia (his mother's brother). Enrique had accompanied them there. Once in Monterrey, Encarnacion's uncle, Jesus, took them to General Terán, where they assessed Mariana Ybarbo's property. Enrique later said that after his grandmother died, they sold Mariana Ybarbo's property and gave the proceeds to his sister, Ruby Mendoza. Although, a few years later, Encarnacion would receive an overdue property tax bill from General Terán, Nuevo Leon, Mexico for Ruby Mendoza. This suggests that maybe, they just put the property in Ruby Mendoza's name and continued to rent it.

While Encarnacion was in Monterrey, he bought a Mosler safe for $50[7] [about $1,000 in today's money]. Was Encarnacion making further preparations to move to Monterrey, Mexico? Did he buy the safe to leave in Mexico to begin to put money in there to prepare for his trip back? It doesn't make sense that he would buy an expensive and heavy safe in Monterrey to bring it back to Texas. There's every indication that he was planning to move his family into his mother's house who had died in 1920.

16 - Making Moves - 1/1931 to 3/1931

Anselmo was spending more time in Mexico trying to make his business there profitable. He was determined to become a wealthy contractor and builder in Mexico. The United States economy was suffering and making it almost impossible to compete with the other builders in the United States. Being of Mexican descent was also problematic for a businessman in the United States. Mexico, on the other hand, was continuing to rebuild itself (after having been embroiled in a revolution and internal conflict for 20 years). Anselmo knew he had a good chance at becoming Mexico's premier building contractor. He decided to spend more time developing his business in Mexico. His wife and children would stay behind in McAllen, Texas. It was a steep price for him and his family to pay for success. Perhaps, he had hoped to move his family there once his business in Mexico was profitable. Ofelia, most certainly, did not like this arrangement. About this time, Anselmo borrowed at least $2,000 and used his home and rental properties on Houston Avenue as collateral.

Ofelia told Carmen, "Viene como si no me coneciera." ["When he visits me, it's as if he doesn't know me."]

Ofelia lived with her children in the main house. It was a duplex that had a large "sala" [living room], "comedor" [dining room], "cocína" [kitchen], bedroom, bathroom, and another bedroom. On the other side, there was an office, bedroom, and the kitchen that she used for ironing the clothes. She occasionally took her children to visit her family. She continued to socialize with Margarita - sewing and talking about each other's personal affairs. No doubt, Margarita had told Ofelia about her and Encarnacion's plans to move back to Mexico. Ofelia wouldn't have liked this either. She and Margarita had become very close friends. It seemed to Ofelia that everyone was leaving her.

Encarnacion would travel to many Texas cities with his Loteria. He carefully planned which cities he would visit in advance in order to obtain the necessary paperwork to operate it legally. Occasionally he received mail at the local post office in the city where the Loteria was. If someone needed to reach him by mail, he would simply tell them to address the correspondence to the city where he planned to be. In those days, the recipient went to the post office to pick up his mail. One such letter arrived at the Kingsville, Texas, post office. It was addressed to Encarnacion Mendoza and had a postmark of January 4, 1931.[1] The letter was from R. Martinez in Monterrey, Mexico. Encarnacion had just returned from his Monterrey trip, so it probably had something to do with the business that he had conducted there. The envelope undoubtedly contained important paperwork concerning his planned return of his family to Mexico.

On Friday, January 9, 1931, Oscar Vale, superintendent of City Schools, Rio Grande City Independent School District, wrote a letter for Margarita Mendoza stating that she and her family were of good standing in the community.[2] Margarita seemed to collect these sorts of letters when her family was planning a major move (or other important events where she would need proof of her loyalty to the United States). Mr. Vale stated, "[Margarita] . . . is of good moral character and of unimpeachable reputation and law-abiding qualities. . ."

Years later, Enrique said that Oscar Vale had recently become a lawyer and had helped him when he ran the clothing/shoe store for the old man (Mr. Garza) in McAllen (July/August 1929).

On Saturday, January 10, 1931, Enrique wrote his 13th letter to Carmen.[3] He asked her to let him know when she and her best friend, Leonor, were going to the cinema so that he could join them.

McAllen, Texas
January 10, 1931.

Ms. Carmen Garcia

Loving and unforgettable Carmen,

With pleasure, I write this to answer your kind letter, which brought me much joy in what you wrote to me. Your Aunt and Uncle and other members of your family will eventually come to realize that the objective of the relationship that you and I have is good. That is to say, don't doubt that our love will stay alive as we wait for our union. That is our destiny; because it is my firm belief that God will destine for us to have happiness which, I do not want to miss.

Only one thought makes me sad. It's that Mama and the whole family are thinking of living in Monterrey but understand that it would be better if I stayed here; they know very well that I love you very much. And I think that each day that Papa is more certain of our union.

If you are going to the cinema on Sunday with Leonor, let me know if you are going in the afternoon or evening and to which theater so that I can join you.

With all my heart, [it would be good] to talk a while with you even if it's in the cinema.

Write back soon, as I always do.

Accept my most sincere appreciation for the attention that you give me, and to present to you with my faithful love from someone who loves and adores you. Yours,

Enrique

Carmen had told him that day that she and her friend, Leonor, planned to go to the cinema. Perhaps, she'd told him just to appease him. He was very demanding of such things. She probably wouldn't have expected him to go to see a movie with her and Leonor. First of all, he didn't care for Leonor, and secondly, they would need to be accompanied by an adult chaperone. The large group would indeed have spoiled the movie for her. Imagine trying to have fun watching a movie with her, Leonor, Enrique, and a chaperone (instead of just her and Leonor). She might have thought it would have been a bit awkward and uncomfortable. Going to the neighborhood cinema was a pleasant escape from her hardworking days. It was so fortunate for her that there was a cinema nearby.

Her good friend, Leonor and Carmen and her good friend, Leonor, walked the six blocks to the Azteca. This was a beautiful theater nestled in the middle of the Mexican District of McAllen. They saw each other nearly every day. The backyards of their houses faced each other, with only the alley separating the two properties. When they arrived at the theater, they sat down next to each other and waited for the movie to start. The lights had dimmed as the piano player began to play. Carmen and Leonor looked anxiously towards the screen as the pictures flashed brilliantly across the screen.

Migrants: Exploring the Colors of my Family History

The feature had barely started when Enrique walked into the semi-dark theater. It was bright enough for him to see Carmen and Leonor sitting side by side. He grimaced a little as he walked up. Leonor noticed him walking towards them. Enrique moved quickly and sat right between Carmen and Leonor. It was uncomfortable for Carmen with Enrique sitting tightly between her and Leonor. He started to say something to her when she stood up quickly and walked past him. Leonor quickly followed Carmen out of the theater. Enrique sat dumbfounded.

Years later, Enrique had said that Carmen and Leonor had made room for him to sit between them. Then Carmen said that she didn't remember making room for him. She recalled that she was incensed that Enrique would have the audacity to plant himself tightly between her and Leonor. Carmen said it was improper for a boy to make such an advance like that. She said that her aunt and uncle would disapprove, and that is why she left. It was improper to be on a date with Enrique without an adult chaperone. She said that Enrique knew full well that her aunt, Ofelia, did not want her to be alone with Enrique. [Note: The theater had bench-style seats instead of individual seats.] Perhaps it was Leonor who moved over to make room for Enrique.

After this incident, Ofelia and Anselmo became leery of Enrique. Carmen must have admitted to her mother or her aunt as to what Enrique had done. She wouldn't have kept it a secret. Her mother, uncle, and aunt would not have liked this at all.

Margarita, along with Encarnacion, would by now be planning a move to Mexico. She had a habit of obtaining references from prominent local officials when she and her family were planning to move. No doubt she started this practice years before when her family had fled from General Terán.

She believed it very important that her family comports themselves as good citizens wherever they were. She was not a strict person in her customs, but rather a person who demanded the very best of her family, and her authority was never challenged. She had long felt unwanted in her home country of the United States. She felt that now that the Cristero Rebellion was over in Mexico (as well as seeing the waning power of President Plutarco Elias Calles), it would be much safer for her family to live there. In Monterrey, they could all live happily without the prejudice she had so often felt or witnessed in the United States.

Her husband had no doubt conveyed his feelings and experiences to her. He was strong-willed and not likely to have appreciated how some of those with whom he did business treated him. Strangers often denigrated him because he had a dark skin color (due to his Mexican heritage). He learned early on when he started the bakery in Weslaco or traveling along the South Texas region with the Loteria to pay a little extra to the sheriff or the carnival owners who might cause him trouble. He knew that money talked. He knew that greed often trumped prejudice. In Mexico, he would be around people that spoke his language and looked more like him. He most certainly recognized that Mexico would ultimately yield a much better, safer life for his family. The United States was wrought with violence against Mexicans like him.

On Sunday, February 8, 1931, Enrique sent his 14th letter to Carmen[4] "Anselmo said to stop bothering you."

McAllen, Texas
February 8, 1931

Miss. Carmen Garcia
McAllen,

Unforgettable Carmen,
I am writing to say hello to you and your Mamacita and all at your house.
Carmen, perhaps you're not surprised that I

haven't gone to your house. You must understand that I have not gone to see you because your uncle Anselmo asked me to stop bothering them. I know now what has bothered them, and I have my greatest desire to marry you, to ask him about you and me - both Don Anselmo and Ofelia, the good intention that we both have in marriage.

Hopefully, you don't get to regret getting attached to me; I assure you that in a short time, our sacrifices and hopes will be rewarded with the happiness that unites our souls.

When we, you and I, have the opportunity to talk, we will discuss this matter, and I will take good care to speak with your Mamacita, to see what the three of us agree on.

Without more, you receive the appreciation and affection of one who loves you and don't forget. Yours,

Enrique
P.S. write back soon

On March 1, 1931, Carmen worked at a clothing store across the street from Enrique's store. Enrique wasn't allowed to visit her there, but he was happy that she was near to him. In an interview with Margarita Elva (daughter of Encarnacion and Margarita), she said that Estefana worked at the store too. Perhaps it was Estefana who got the job and brought her daughter, Carmen, there to work with her. According to Estefana's daughter, Matilde Escobedo, Maria Luisa Garcia also worked at that store.

On Sunday, March 1, 1931, Enrique sent his 15th letter to Carmen.[5] You acted properly, I have no ill-feeling; I have no objection that you have gone to work.

Roger Mendoza

* * *

McAllen, Texas
March 1, 1931

Miss. Carmen Garcia

My unforgettable Carmen,

With pleasure, I reply to your letter, of which I am duly aware, although it is not so warm as I would expect. But I think that you acted appropriately, and I do not have any ill-feeling by this triviality; since I desire, with all my heart, to be in alignment with you. For this reason, I try to avoid, as much as possible, any little displeasure among us; For what is easily fixable is not as important.

I have no objection that you've gone to work, and I hope you keep your promise, which I sincerely appreciate. Allow me to make comments, which I think are essential to telling you, to treat you, so that you understand what you should do.

Carmen, I will not write more because the time you'd use reading a longer letter, you could instead spend writing a reply, In this way, you'll have to mail me sooner and know that each of your letters is a flame that lights up our future and the happiness of us both.

Without more, receive the appreciation and affection of one who loves you with all the force of his soul and doesn't ever forget. Yours,

Enrique
What is the main object that makes us love each

other, you and I? I desire to be happy when God permits it.

Meanwhile, Aunt Ofelia told Carmen that she should go out with her brother Laurio Montalvo. Carmen said to her that she didn't want to because she already had a boyfriend.

Ofelia was likely disappointed and would not be happy about it.

Years later, Carmen said about Enrique meeting her mother, "Enrique rarely visited me at the house. But, when he did, he would sit at the table with Mary, Mama, and me. I would just be sitting there quietly while Enrique would speak to my mother. On more than one occasion, he had pulled out his handkerchief and wiped his nose. He told my mother that he couldn't stay long because he was catching a cold."

On Friday, March 13, 1931, Enrique sent his 16th letter to Carmen.[6] I answer your affectionate letter:

McAllen, Texas
March 13, 1931

Miss. Carmen Garcia

My unforgettable Carmen,

With enjoyment, I answer your very affectionate letter, in which I see the goodwill that you have for me. This makes me very happy since there is no girl in the world that I love so much. The only hope in my life is founded on your affection. I think that I will love you forever. I do not want to stop thinking about you, my idol, Carmencita - for all time.

From the first day that God had willed that I meet you, I have loved you so much, or rather a lot, but I hesitate to tell you about my love because I see how beautiful you are, very beautiful (really wonderful). I have feared that you would have many admirers, which I do not doubt that you do, that perhaps of the many you have, I would stand out; and what bothers me the most is that yesterday I thought that you might stop loving me and love someone else. But because of your strength of will, you would be inclined to keep the promise you made to me that you would love me for all of my life. I believe that your force of will is unwavering. I will show you tomorrow (or the day after) that you will be my beloved wife (when you want it to be). This is the right way to live happily; when we are over there, far from these places, where the air in our country gives us the necessary encouragement so that our union is not a failure. Because I have to tell you that, if you think the same way as I do regarding marriage – it should be forever. Therefore, we must take necessary measures to not give reason to either one of us to bother the other with nonsense or whims. In telling you this, I do not wish to offend you even in the least because this is what we both will want to avoid.

Continue being a wonderful girlfriend, and soon you will be a wonderful wife. Keep nothing from me that we should both know, as I do with you.

Without more, receive my appreciation and appreciation of the love that I dedicate to you. Yours,

Enrique

Migrants: Exploring the Colors of my Family History

* * *

Perhaps Enrique was feeling a bit more insecure than usual. His father was probably excited at the prospect of moving back to Mexico. He would soon be traveling to Mexico again. Enrique might have felt that his relationship with Carmen and their future together might be at risk if they were to move back to Mexico.

According to Enrique, his father didn't drive. Therefore, either Enrique, Canacho, or a hired hand would drive Encarnacion. On March 12, 1931, Encarnacion (50) traveled with his son, Canacho (19), to Mexico. They went to Monterrey and visited with relatives as Encarnacion continued with his preparations for his family's move back to Monterrey. He and his son, Canacho, returned to McAllen on March 18, 1931. The move back to Monterrey was proceeding well.

There was a boy that sent Carmen a card. She told Enrique about the letter. He told her, "Give me that letter, and I'll take care of it." Years later, during an interview, Carmen turned to Enrique and said, "He's already dead. What did you tell him?" Enrique answered her softly and said that he told the boy, "no," and then said something that only Carmen heard. After he said that, both Carmen and Enrique laughed. It was their little secret. What had happened to that boy?

The Great Depression that began in 1929 in the U.S. was getting worse. The residents of McAllen had hoped that they would not suffer much from its ill effects. However, McAllen, Texas, was not spared from the financial disaster. Rumors were rampant as banks began to encourage borrowers, in the firmest possible way, to repay their loans.[7]

Encarnacion's family had minimal debt but saw that fewer customers were willing to part with their money to play the Loteria. To them, it was a game of chance. The players hoped that they would enjoy a little bit of fun and excitement in contrast to experiencing the dismal effects of the depressed local economy.

Anselmo, on the other hand, had borrowed money using all of his properties as collateral. The stakes were much higher for him. He also had a business in Monterrey that he'd tried desperately to make successful. It was not. He immediately set about to sell the Monterrey business. Unfortunately, he sold it at a loss. His company, *Phoenix Lumber Company*, was also experiencing a decline. He had been traveling back and forth between his apartment in Monterrey and his home in McAllen and devoted his attention to *Phoenix Lumber Company*.

Estefana certainly felt the ill effects of the Great Depression. She was finding it harder to afford food and other necessities. Perhaps by this time, they had been let go at the clothing store. She discovered that she could still earn enough money to support her family if she and Carmen picked cotton in Mission, Texas. Both of them had done that back-breaking and strenuous work before. They desperately needed money. Maria Luisa could stay home and care for Matilde, Marcolfa, and Alex.

17 - We Need Money - 5/1931 to 10/1931

On Tuesday, May 12, 1931, Enrique sent his 17th letter to Carmen.[1] Searching for work. Sad about your upcoming trip to Mission.

McAllen, Texas
May 12, 1931

Miss. Carmen Garcia,

My esteemed and unforgettable Carmen. With pleasure, I answer your letter that has made me very sad and pensive about what you wrote concerning your trip to Mission. I assure you that if I had a way to prevent you from going, I would for two main reasons. The first is because you're going to be doing a lot of work; the second, because it bothers me that you're going to be away from home. You know how much I love you, and you can imagine my concern. For this reason, I have decided not to search for work outside of here, so that I can be close to you. With this, I wish to say that if I commit to working in any large population as Corpus, Brownsville, or Monterrey, I would have to live there. And that is not what I want, as I told you before. I want to be near you. I don't want to say that I have the chance to get a job in any of these three cities, mainly in Monterrey, because it would be unnecessary to tell you. The only thing that I want to say to you is that I don't want to be far from you. And God will grant that our happy day will soon come, that you have waited for a long time and I hope with all my heart I hope that it happens soon; to build our small home, but with much luck and happiness. Many times, I think that your mother and Luisa believe that we have been dating for too long, and I have still not asked you to marry me. It is by God. Don't be discouraged or doubt that I will find a way to ask you soon [to marry me] and to bring us happiness with the help of God.

I was delighted to read your kind letters, in which I see your expressive phrases of affection.

Without more, receive the appreciation and affection of the one who loves you with all his soul and will love you forever. Your faithful,

Enrique

On May 12, 1931, Estefana and her daughter, Carmen, picked cotton in Mission, Texas. Even though automated picking machines promised to make picking cheaper, they broke down often and didn't work very well. The cotton farmers in Mission, Texas, had to hire locals to pick the cotton. There was no shortage of workers. It was grueling, back-breaking work. Prickly, hard husks held the cotton tightly. The razor-sharp shells would easily tear at the hands of even the most skilled picker. Long-time cotton pickers had scarred hands from past harvests. Callouses covered their hands that made it a little easier to pick the cotton. The cotton pickers would eventually fall into a rhythm as they crouched along the rows, picking at the plants as they slowly moved from plant to plant.

Now that the Great Depression was hitting the region hard, the farmers weren't able to get a good return on their crop. They had to hurriedly hire workers to harvest the crop and get it sold before the price fell too low. Even though the farmers couldn't pay pickers as much as they used to, the workers were plentiful and often turned away from work. Fortunately, Estefana and her daughter Carmen were selected to pick the cotton. Although Estefana would have felt tremendous pressure and stress, she worried about providing for her family while performing labor-intensive work. It certainly would not have been healthy for her or her daughter.

While they were there, Carmen dutifully sent a letter to Enrique, who was in McAllen, Texas.

On May 12, 1931, Enrique was probably still working at Mr. Garza's store. It was not the same kind of exhausting work that Carmen was doing.

On Sunday, May 24, 1931, Enrique sent the 18th letter to Carmen.[2] "Hope your finger is healed. You seem to like Mission more than McAllen."

McAllen, Texas
May 24, 1931

Miss. Carmen Garcia
Mission, Texas

My unforgettable Carmen,
 With pleasure, I answer your letter. I hope that when you receive this, your finger is healed. It is

my greatest desire.

Carmen, I have not written to you because of things beyond my control. You know well that there are times when I have a lot of work, but I am happy to write now.

Here is a verse that I wrote, especially for you:
It is you
Which I will never forget;
So, wherever I go in life,
A picture of your dear image,
I always have with me recorded.

These five lines occupy a very small space of paper, but they mean a world of love that I feel for you.

In your reply tell me what is new, write to me as much as in your previous letter, since the longer your letters are the more joy it gives me to read them.

Tell me when you're coming home; you seem to like Mission more than McAllen.

Without more, as always, Your most faithful,

Enrique

In this letter, Enrique seems to acknowledge Carmen's pricked hand but immediately switches back to his display of love. She must have said something about working hard in the fields in her letter, and he responds with, "I have a lot of work. . . ."

Carmen and her mother, Estefana, were still hard at work picking cotton in Mission, Texas. Mission is about eight miles west of McAllen, Texas. It appeared that Carmen was "busy" picking the cotton and didn't having much time for anything else. It's not surprising that Carmen might have delayed writing back to Enrique because she had little time or energy after working in the fields.

On Tuesday, June 2, 1931, Enrique sent his 19th letter to Carmen.[3] "Why do you take long to write back; We had many customers in the shop. We were unable to help all of them."

McAllen, Texas
June 2, 1931

Miss. Carmen Garcia
Mission, Texas.

My unforgettable Carmen,

With pleasure, I reply to your letter, which did not fail to amaze me by your way of thinking about me. I am not surprised that you think that way. There are several times that you say the same thing or something similar. You know very well that I have promised to see only you, you know that you're the only girl that I love and I am surprised that you have such opinions about my conduct.

Carmen, I can't imagine why you take so long to reply [to my letters], being that you promised me to respond [to my letters] quickly. At present, you often break your promises, but I do not believe that you treat your [promises] like a child's play.

On Sunday, I received your letter and today (Tuesday) I'm writing this to show you that it doesn't matter how much work I have, I want you to receive my replies in the shortest time possible.

On Sunday you told me you were going to go for a walk. Tell me, how was your stroll? Also, tell me if you're prepared to get married to me, with the same desire that you had before you went to Mission, When I come to see you, I will ask you a question. Do not answer [my letter] the same way [as your last letter], that is to say, there is doubt in your letters. For this reason, I believe that you've changed something in the time that you've been there [in Mission].

On Saturday, we had many customers in the shop. Many were angry and didn't buy anything. We could not help them all because we were overwhelmed.

I hope you answer soon to make it valid for your promise.

Without more, I received the mementos that your mother gave you and that you gave CHITA [Margarita Elva].

Your Enrique, who adores you.

By Tuesday, June 2, 1931, Estefana and Carmen continued the back-breaking and tedious work of picking the cotton crop in Mission, Texas. Enrique continued to work in the store. It had become a family store as he and his sisters helped with the sales while Enrique did the bookkeeping. Carmen most certainly did not enjoy the harsh effects of picking cotton. She was most likely happy that her mother was with her. Carmen knew that her mother understood how unpleasant and painful the work was. She was beginning to realize that Enrique did not fully appreciate her hard and painful work. Perhaps she'd even been disappointed that he didn't seem to understand how hard picking cotton was. Instead, he'd complained about how hard he was working. She would most likely have been annoyed, but too tired and worn out to be utterly angry.

On Tuesday, June 9, 1931, Enrique sent his 20th letter to

Carmen.⁴ "I lost your address [in Mission] then found it."

McAllen, Texas,
June 9, 1931

Miss. Carmen Garcia
Mission, Texas

Unforgettable Carmen,

With my greatest pleasure, I write this and beg forgiveness for my delayed response. There is no way that it would be okay that you do the same with me. As I told you on Sunday, I had lost your address, and thank God that I found it.

I send you the letter that I wrote to you last Tuesday, the one that I had not sent to you as I said above.

Never forget me and respond soon. I will never stop loving you,

Your Enrique

Margarita continued to obtain good references for her family. Soon, she and her family would move safely to Monterrey, Mexico. That was where Encarnacion had grown up with his parents, Jesus and Guadalupe Mendoza. It's interesting to note that both Margarita and her husband, Encarnacion were making meticulous preparations to move to Monterrey.

On July 2, 1931, Margarita received a letter from McAllen public school that stated that the Mendoza children attended Roosevelt School.⁵ In that letter, Miss Zara Thigpen, Principal, stated, "This is to certify that I have known Mrs. Margarita Garza de Mendoza and family for four years and as far as I am able to say, they are honest, honorable people."

Roosevelt was a grade school in their neighborhood. Anselmo's company had built a four-story building for the school a few years back.

Sometime in July 1931, Estefana and Carmen returned home to McAllen with a little extra money. Perhaps things would be getting a bit better for Estefana's family in the coming months.

Anselmo was concerned about his finances. He was not making much money in McAllen and had invested heavily in new business ventures in Mexico. Although Anselmo had sold his business in Monterrey at a loss, a financial crisis was still on the horizon ahead. Perhaps he thought that he could sell enough of his inventory in *Phoenix Lumber Company* to pay off his creditors, especially the bank.

On September 15, 1931, Anselmo advertised in the McAllen Daily Press. He took out a large ad that was titled "Closeout sale."[6]

WE DON'T MEAN MAYBE....!
OUR CLOSING OUT SALE IS GOING FINE

We are putting out sensational values

Our materials are getting to move rapidly, but we have plenty yet. Remember we must pay our bills. And how? By sacrificing our stock, of course. What do you care? The profit is yours.

LOOK! Some of our other bargains.

Mortise Door Set 40c
3x3 and 3 1/2

On Wednesday, September 16, 1931, Enrique sent his 21st letter to Carmen.[7] ("Sorry didn't write sooner, been busy"):

* * *

McAllen, Texas
September 16, 1931

Miss. Carmen Garcia

My unforgettable Carmen,

    You can't imagine my greatest pleasure that this letter brought me because I suppose you will receive it with my affection as always. I hope that you aren't upset because I didn't answer you sooner. As you know perfectly well, that myriad circumstances have prevented me from responding more promptly, perhaps by God. But we both, that is to say, you and I, try when possible to avoid the minor annoyances so that tomorrow or the day after God grant us that we marry and get our home even though we are more or less poor. But we shall reign in the happiness and love if we both propose to cement this great happiness. To be happy tomorrow, we must begin today. I hope that, with your cooperation, we both arrive at our aspirations and show all the people that know us, that our love has been and always will be genuine and real. Hopefully, the principles of great happiness will last a lifetime with the help of God and our valuable cooperation.

    Respond soon, to keep writing to each other often.

    Without more, receive my sincere appreciation, the highest consideration, and my most faithful affection from someone who loves you with all the strength of his soul, and I hope that you respond in the same way. Your most faithful, Enrique

***

Margarita, Encarnacion, Anselmo, and Estefana were well aware of each other's troubles. Margarita and Encarnacion were planning a move to Monterrey. Anselmo was selling off his inventory to build up his business in Mexico. Estefana undoubtedly had grave concerns about the financial future of her family, especially if Anselmo moved away and also because she was feeling ill. Perhaps, the long grueling hours picking cotton in Mission, Texas, had been significantly detrimental to her health.

Mr. Garza, the old man that had once gone to the Mendoza's to ask them to re-open his store, was most certainly experiencing the ill-effects of the Great Depression. The meager $15 rent that Enrique was paying him for the building rental was not enough. Perhaps, it was time for Mr. Garza to find a way to get some more money. He decided to sell the business to Enrique.

Enrique was surprised when Mr. Garza told him that he wanted to sell the business to him. Enrique told Mr. Garza that he didn't have the money to buy the store. Enrique said to him that he wasn't even sure that he would be able to (or even wanted to) be responsible for the outstanding debt. At this point, the store had about $3,500 in debt, and the business checking account had a balance of $1,000 and change. The business was going very well for the store.

Mr. Garza said that he wanted to sell the business for $1,500 and then rent the building for $20 per month.

Mr. Garza said, "Write me a check for $1,000 from the business checking account."

He told Enrique to pay him the rest (about $500 more) in payments. Mr. Garza assured him that if he did this, then he would pass the business to him. Enrique may not have realized that in addition to the $1,500 that the man would receive for the store, Enrique would assume the store's $3,500 debt.

Enrique thought that this was a good deal. Mr. Garza insisted that Enrique write the check right away, and then when Enrique returned, they could complete the transaction.

Enrique told Mr. Garza that he would have to talk it over with his father. And, his father was away at the Loteria. Mr. Garza seemed impatient with Enrique. Enrique relented and wrote Mr. Garza the check for $1,000 from the store's bank account. Enrique told Mr. Garza that he would return on Sunday with his father.

On Friday, October 2, 1931, Enrique sent his 22nd letter to Carmen.[8] Enrique has a lot to tell Carmen.

McAllen, Texas,
October 2, 1931

Miss. Carmen Garcia

My unforgettable Carmen,

With my greatest pleasure, I answer your letter, of which I will speak to you personally.

You can't imagine the pleasure that I experienced now that I understand that the relationship between your family and mine has become much stronger. I have the firm belief, without any doubt, that you and I are very important for the relations [between both families]. As it is, I desire that we not falter in our purpose, and hopefully with patience and calm for the blessed day, that God will grant us his valuable help, and we must discount the most insignificant incident that may disturb our love.

I have a lot to talk about with you, but I'll save it for another letter when you answer this one.

Have faith in my love that is as big as "the greatest."

Without more, farewell affectionately your most faithful,

Enrique

P. S. Do not forget the one who loves and adores you with all of my soul
Yours = FOREVER=

It appears that the news that Enrique wanted to share with Carmen had to do with the store that he was running for Mr. Garza. Perhaps, he wanted to tell her that he was going to buy a store.

18 - One Door Closes - 10/1931 to 12/1931

That weekend, Enrique's father was at the Loteria in Alice, Texas. Enrique went there and asked his father about Mr. Garza's store. His father thought it was a good idea and told him that he could loan Enrique the $500 from the Loteria.

The following Sunday evening, when Encarnacion and Enrique returned to McAllen, they went to visit Mr. Garza at his home. Mrs. Garza answered the door and told them that her husband was no longer interested in any business deal. She told them to go away.

When Enrique and his father went to the store, they found that most of the newer inventory was missing from the store. He later found out that the old man had moved the stock into his house and was selling it from there. Enrique found that the cash register that his father had loaned him was also missing from the store.

A relative of Enrique (on his mother's side), Oscar Vale, had recently become a lawyer and had told Enrique not to worry.

Enrique worried anyway because the business was in his name (at least with the bank and the creditors). The lawyer told Enrique to draft a letter to the bank, telling them to stop payment on the $1,000 check. The bank was closed on Sunday, so Enrique felt that he had time to take care of this the next day. He thought that there was no way that the man could have cashed the check yet.

Early Monday morning, Enrique delivered the letter to the bank, and they assured him that the bank would not cash Mr. Garza's check. Enrique didn't know that the man had friends at the bank that bypassed the payment hold and cashed the check anyway.

By the end of the day on Monday, Mr. Garza had the cash; the business bank balance was at zero, and Enrique had $3,500 in business debt with his name on the credit accounts.

The lawyer told Enrique to take legal action against Mr. Garza. The judge scheduled a court date.

Enrique and his father arrived promptly for the court date. Mr. Garza didn't show up. The judge was lenient and scheduled another court date. Mr. Garza didn't show up for that court date either. The judge ruled in favor of Enrique. Mr. Garza was ordered to pay Enrique $1,718.76 and was liable for the debt to the creditors.

Mr. Garza had several houses and other properties, and Enrique's lawyer suggested that they put a lien on Mr. Garza's property.

Mr. Garza was crafty. His lawyers claimed that Mr. Garza was not right in the head (he was crazy) and should not have to pay the debt. The judge agreed with the lawyer and ruled that Mr. Garza didn't have to pay Enrique anything.

Later, Enrique explained to the creditors what had happened, and they admonished Enrique for writing the check to Mr. Garza. The creditors each told him that he was not liable for the debt since the judge had previously ruled that Mr. Garza was legally responsible for the store's debts.

The creditors went to the store to repossess the merchandise. To their surprise, they found that all of the new merchandise was gone.

Enrique never received a penny from Mr. Garza, and Enrique wasn't liable for any of the business's debts that totaled $3,500. Enrique was relieved that he had dodged this very serious bullet. However, Enrique had lost his income that he had earned while running the store. He would need to go back to working full-time at the Loteria.

Migrants: Exploring the Colors of my Family History

The lawyer, Oscar Vale, wanted to introduce Enrique to his relative (perhaps his niece). Enrique immediately told him that he had a girlfriend. In an interview, Enrique recalled that her name was Elia but wasn't sure. Carmen immediately disagreed with him and said that her name was Elsa.

There is a picture of Oscar T. Vale in the La Familia Mendoza Photobook.[1] He was superintendent of schools on January 9, 1931, and may have been the same person as Enrique's lawyer.

On October 17, 1931, Encarnacion and his son, Canacho traveled to Monterrey. They stayed with Encarnacion's uncle, Juan Maria Garcia, in Monterrey. Encarnacion visited Ramon Elizondo, a Monterrey bank manager. Ramon Elizondo "Gerente" of *Banco Comercial de Monterrey* in Monterrey, Mexico, was a friend of his.

While there, Encarnacion had made some arrangements to facilitate his family's move to Monterrey. He spoke with the Bank Manager, Ramon Elizondo, and obtained two letters from him. The first letter was addressed to Encarnacion and stated that Ramon would help his family move back to Monterrey. The second letter was for Encarnacion to give to Don Candelario Guajardo. In that letter, he asked Mr. Guajardo to assist Encarnacion and his family for a problem-free/safe travel across Mexico on their move back to Monterrey. Encarnacion had carefully folded both of the letters and put them away for safekeeping. Encarnacion had previously purchased a $50 safe in Monterrey, presumably to safeguard his money.

On October 31, 1931, Encarnacion returned to McAllen from Monterrey with the two letters that the bank manager had given him. Encarnacion thought that it was imperative to have those letters to travel safely with his large family to Monterrey. It was still dangerous to go in certain parts of Mexico, and it was still risky traveling with all of his belongings to Mexico's interior.

On Thursday, November 5, 1931, Enrique sent his 23rd letter to Carmen.[2] ("Appreciate your sacrifice in waiting.")

***

McAllen, Texas
November 5, 1931

Miss. Carmen Garcia

My unforgettable Carmen,

    I also support you in hope [for our relationship]. I am writing this to show you that my love remains and will continue to be faithful until the last day of my life. But the circumstances have been contrary to our own desires. But it is not surprising that sooner or later, our desires will come to be. I appreciate your sacrifice in waiting, but I "hope" that you realize that I too impatiently wait for the blessed day of our marriage. And I hope that with God's will and our cooperation, we will be happy all the days of our lives.

    Trust me and all the demonstrations of love that I show you are from the bottom of my heart. It is not selfishness, which makes me love you. I look for happiness for us both. Your most faithful,

Enrique Mendoza G.

    Carmen received his letter and read it with hopefulness and optimism. She was excited that Enrique was talking about marriage. And it seemed like he was trying to find work here in McAllen, instead of going to Monterrey with his family. Carmen didn't seem to have much interest in moving there.

    Carmen couldn't think too much about the letter anymore since her mother seemed to have had a lengthy illness. She was worried about her mother.

No doubt, her mother told her not to worry as Estefana forged ahead with her household chores with her chronic cough.

Carmen and Maria Luisa both noticed that the color had faded from their mother's face. Estefana's body resisted her illness as she worried about money and the family. Estefana was weak and moved slower than usual. She had worked hard to save enough money to keep her family fed. But it was getting more challenging to make enough money. She was getting sicker and taking remedies that were sure to help her to recover. But now something was really wrong.

Carmen and Maria Luisa got scared when they discovered that their mother's fever had soared out of control. Estefana finally collapsed into bed, and her two oldest daughters, Maria Luisa and Carmen, would have to take care of the family and the household chores. Both of them took care of their mother while they kept the younger siblings away to let Estefana rest and recover. Christmas was fast approaching, and Estefana wanted this Christmas to be special for her family. She got worse. Her illness had progressed into pneumonia.

Carmen and Maria Luisa prayed from the depths of their souls to save their mother. Maria Luisa carried the burden for her siblings of wondering how their family would survive if anything were to happen to their mother.

After suffering from pneumonia for ten days, Estefana Longoria died on Thursday, December 24, 1931, at 5:35 a.m. (she was born in March of 1892). Maria Luisa or Carmen had found her lifeless body when they woke up the next morning. Or perhaps they had sat next to Estefana as her life left her (while the younger ones slept).

Years later, Matilde remembered that day clearly and said, "I saw Maria Luisa crying by my mother's bed."

Maria Luisa had looked over at nine-year-old Matilde and said to her, "Don't get near her. She's asleep."

"I was never told by anyone that my mother was dead," Matilde said.

On that day, Ofelia and her kids were visiting family, and Anselmo was in Mexico. Margarita was the only one at home and brought Estefana's children to her house.

Estefana's brother Cristobal was living in McAllen at the time and notified the authorities of Estefana's death. He also was the informant on her death certificate.

"We had the "velorio" [wake] in the "sala" [living room] of our house," said Matilde. "My mother was buried in a pauper's grave in McAllen."

So now Maria Luisa (19), Carmen (17), Matilde (9) Marcolfa (7), and Alejandro (5) were orphaned. The future must have looked very frightening for them. Who would take care of them, where would they live, how would they manage without their mother?

In a 1983 interview, Enrique and Carmen were asked, "What was Estefana like?"

Carmen looked up and hesitated before starting to speak. Enrique cleared his throat loudly and quickly spoke up. He knew that Carmen, after 52 years, still missed her mother.

Enrique said that Estefana was kind, serious, sincere ("buena, seria, sincera.").

Carmen smiled and then said, "She was very shy. She was a reserved person."

There's no doubt that she was a powerful woman too.

Estefana had four surviving brothers, Guillermo, Anselmo, Alejandro, and Cristobal. In death, Estefana had joined her two sisters, Luisa and Matilde, her mother, and her brother, Benjamin.

"Maria Luisa, Carmen, Marcolfa, Alex and I ... walked to my mother's gravesite every Sunday," Matilde said. "We had to cross a small bridge over a canal to get to the graveyard."

All of Estefana's five children continued to live in the house that their uncle, Anselmo, had provided for their family. Ofelia,

Anselmo's wife, worried about how Estefana's children would be able to pay the rent that was due to her each month.

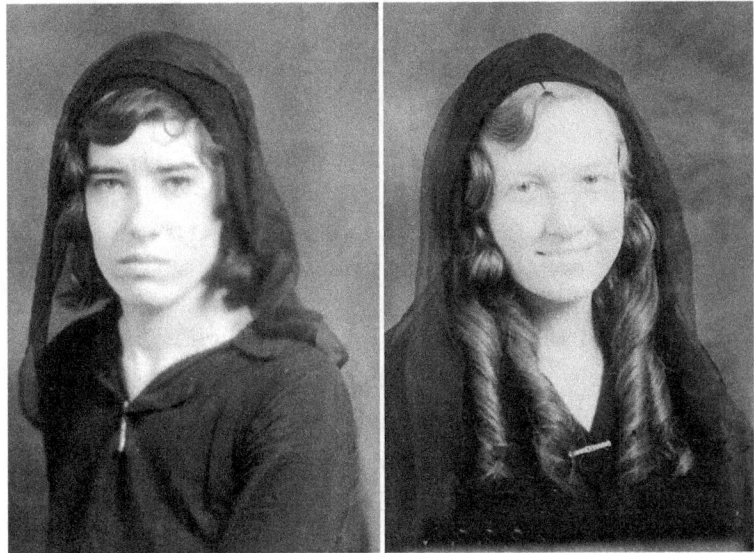

Maria Luisa and Carmen Garcia

19 - A New Loteria Tent - 1932

The name of the game played inside of the Loteria tent was also called *loteria*. It was a game of chance and was very similar to bingo. In the game, the moderator called out symbols like El Sol (The Sun), El Diablo (The Devil), La Dama (The Woman), etc. Each player paid five cents for a card that had sixteen symbols in total - four across by four down. Some versions of the game had a different number of symbols on them. After the moderator called out a symbol, the players placed a bean (used as a token) on the same symbol on their card (if the symbol was on their card). A winner screamed, "Loteria!" or something similar when he won. The winner's card would have had beans that covered all of the symbols on his card or had four beans in a row. Of course, Encarnacion chose what rules to follow. Sometimes the symbols had numbers on them, which made it easier for those that didn't speak Spanish.

Encarnacion's Loteria was often part of a carnival with many vendors and carnival rides that lasted the entire weekend, from Friday until Monday.

Encarnacion's crew, which consisted of his sons and the hired help, would arrive early on a Friday morning to the city where the carnival was. They would set up the tent and then spend a few hours setting up the interior tables where the prizes would be displayed. Next, they would set up the benches where thirty to forty players would sit while they played. There were two thirty-foot-long benches, one placed on the right and the other on the left side of the long side of the tent. At the rear of the tent was a twenty-foot long bench. Players would sit facing the center (where the prizes stood) with their backs towards the outside. Then Encarnacion's crew would unpack the prizes and carefully place them so that they were displayed conspicuously on a two-tiered table. At the front of the tent stood a stand where the moderator would call out the numbers.

Players would start to gather anxiously around the tent, starting at about 4:00 p.m. or 5:00 p.m. They would wait impatiently until the stand opened at 7:00 p.m.

The Loteria would operate continuously for 72 hours. The crew would grab a quick sandwich and drink sodas to keep them going.

Encarnacion would usually have four or five "cabritos" [goats] that he would use as premium prizes for the Loteria. He would buy them for $2 each. To win a goat, the players would have to buy two cards. The first one they would play for a regular prize; the second play would be for a goat. The Loteria had plenty of business.

At the beginning of 1932, Enrique was working with his father, Encarnacion, with the Loteria. Enrique helped with the setup of the tent for the Loteria, along with his brothers and the hired help. Enrique would not have enjoyed the process of assembling the tent. It was labor-intensive and very different than balancing dollars and cents in an accounting journal while sitting at a desk. He wasn't lazy; he just wasn't used to "construction" work.

The original size of the Loteria tent was sixteen feet by twenty-eight feet. They used to spend all day assembling the tent since they would use hammer and nails to construct it. The wood would have to be replaced every so often because of all the nailing. The repeated nailing on the edges of the canvas would eventually result in irreparable damage to the fabric too.

Dozens of two-by-four boards formed the frame for the Loteria tent. It also had two-by-six boards lengthwise along the top of the tent – three on each side. A canvas then covered the structure on the top and sides. However, the sides hung like curtains that rolled up neatly when the Loteria was in operation. Stakes anchored the tent to ensure that it was stable. When the Mendoza family was at home, they would set the tent up in the vacant lot next to their house to sell merchandise.

Encarnacion's Loteria (Virgilio and Heriberto in center) after a rain storm

Phoenix Lumber Company was located directly across the street from Encarnacion's house. The lumber company was located in McAllen, Texas, on 10th Avenue (later renamed Houston Street) and belonged to Anselmo Longoria (Estefana Longoria's brother). Encarnacion bought white pine lumber from the lumberyard, indeed with a family discount from Anselmo's lumberyard. This arrangement was quite convenient for Encarnacion because he would set up his tent in the lot right next to his house when they were not traveling with it.

On Friday, January 15, 1932, at about 2:00 a.m., a fire started in the *Phoenix Lumber Company* yard and crept throughout the facility. Although Anselmo had begun to sell off the inventory in September of 1931, there were several thousand dollars of building materials still in the yard at the time of the fire. The fire destroyed most of it (about $6,000 worth). The office building, which had his architecture business and the hardware store was next to the yard.

The volunteer fire department quickly arrived; however, the plug [hydrant] next to the lumberyard had failed. The fire quickly spread through the dry lumber and progressed towards the *Phoenix Lumber Company* office while the firemen unsuccessfully jigged the plug in an attempt to get it to give up its water. The firemen went to the nearby hydrants. The water flowed conservatively from those adjacent water spigots while the flames engulfed the lumberyard. There was insufficient pressure to squelch the lumberyard flames. The raging fire had started to threaten the neighboring homes. The Central Power and Light company increased the water pressure to the neighboring plugs.

Across the street at Encarnacion's home, the smoke must have been thick as it blew over their house. The burning embers would have rained down on their house and onto their Loteria tent (if it was there). The Loteria tent fabric, coated with flammable paraffin, would have been at risk if it was standing next to Encarnacion's house. Although, Encarnacion and his family were likely running the Loteria in the neighboring cities that weekend. Enrique never mentioned much about the fire in his letters to Carmen, nor in his interviews of 1983 or 1984.

Four hours later, the firemen had the fire under control. They had focused on preventing the fire from crossing to the neighboring houses instead of quenching the lumberyard flames. The firemen contained the fire to the lumberyard. Piles of ashes lay where the neatly stacked lumber had been. The building where Anselmo Longoria had met with customers to finalize architecture designs was left with charred walls nimbly holding up black remnants of a wet, smelly ceiling. In the nooks and crannies, where the flames weren't as intense, were hidden some of the hardware like hinges, nails, and other construction material. The losses were enormous ($6,000 in the lumberyard and $1,000 for the building) and it was only partially covered by insurance. The early morning fire was one of the biggest that McAllen had ever faced. The failed plug was partly responsible for the complete devastation to Phoenix Lumber Company.

To Anselmo Longoria, having just lost his loving sister three weeks before, he might have been devasted by despair. Instead, Anselmo went through the charred remains later that day and salvaged some of the inventory. He put the salvage for sale and decided to focus exclusively on his business in Monterrey, Mexico.

Certainly, Enrique would have seen the lumberyard fire directly across from his house had he been home. Or, if he'd been out of town with the Loteria, he would have seen the remains when he got back home.

Enrique found boxes of metal hinges for sale at Anselmo's lumberyard and bought them. It occurred to Enrique that instead of nails, he could join the two-by-four boards of the Loteria tent frame to each other with hinges.

Enrique numbered each of the two-by-four boards so that it was easy to assemble the frame quickly. For example, two-by-four board "1" was connected via a hinge to two-by-four board "2", etc. When he was designing the structure, he decided to make the tent larger. The new tent was now twenty feet by thirty feet.

Anselmo sold the hinges to Enrique. Enrique had paid 10 cents for each hinge set and paid $50 for the whole box of them. There were more than enough hinges for the newly designed tent that used hinges instead of nails to assemble the tent frame.

The tent originally had used "Manta" (a tightly woven blanket) on the roof and the second layer of Manta above that. The top "Manta" kept some of the rain out, and the second one at the ceiling kept the rest of the rain out.

Later, a newer, even tighter weave canvas replaced the old "Manta." But it may not have required a coating of paraffin to waterproof it (like the old one did).

When the Loteria came to San Antonio one time, Encarnacion bought "lona" (canvas) from a friend. They put "agujeros de ojales" (eyelet holes) along the edges. The new canvas lasted much longer because nails went through the eyelets instead of through the canvas fabric. It didn't require the use of paraffin to waterproof it.

Enrique integrated the new canvas tent into the new hinged two-by-four lumber design.

The newly designed tent took two or three men less than 1-1/2 hours to set up. This efficiency was a far cry from the all-day affair with four or five men and the old tent setup that required hammers and nails to assemble.

20 - Two Become One - 1/1932 to 7/1932

On Wednesday, January 20, 1932, Enrique sent his 24th letter to Carmen.[1] He's not written to you for a long time.

McAllen, Texas
January 20, 1932

Miss. Carmen Garcia

My idolized Carmen,
With the immense love I always have for you, I write these few lines, that I hope you like.
Even though I have not written to you for a [long] time, I have not stopped thinking of you and our love; because I cannot find enough ways to describe the nobility of your heart, the purity of your soul, and how big it is. This is why I do not doubt that you're a wonderful girl; the proof of your good manners and your generosity, both by your simplicity as by the good way that you live. You're a model of truth, and I hope, with all my heart, that your qualities continue to be so sublime, as I have told you before. I have never stopped

loving you, and I believe that I have found you on my journey, lighting the path that will illuminate my future, or rather, our future.

Hopefully, we are both thinking in the same manner, so that we do not have any stumbling blocks in our future; so much pride I have for my girlfriend to have a girl that meets all these virtues. God wants, as always, for our affection to stay strong and not to have difficulties with our great love. Without more, I conclude, your most faithful,

Enrique

With Anselmo's *Phoenix Lumber Company* in McAllen reduced to ashes and his looming debt with the bank, Anselmo poured his heart and soul into the company he was cultivating in Monterrey.

Ofelia, Anselmo's wife, did not like this at all. As it was, Anselmo had been traveling back and forth between his businesses in Mexico and McAllen (*Phoenix Lumber Company*). She had hoped when he sold the Polygonal Business in Mexico, that Anselmo would stay in McAllen with his family. Now that *Phoenix Lumber Company* was gone, Ofelia knew that he'd spend less time at home. Even though Anselmo handled the finances, Ofelia could see that they were falling into abysmal debt. She was worried. She didn't like that Anselmo had an outstanding loan and that he had used their properties as collateral.

It was probably Anselmo's idea to pay Carmen to do housework for Ofelia. Estefana's family needed the money too. Ofelia might have had mixed feelings about this arrangement.

Ofelia began to take control of the finances at the house because Anselmo was spending more time away [in Mexico]. She was well aware that they would lose everything if the bank demanded payment of Anselmo's loans. Most of their money was invested in the business in Monterrey, and their savings were dangerously low. The worsening Great Depression hung over them like a dark cloud that could soon erupt into a terrible storm.

Anselmo would have reassured Ofelia that all would be okay. He was determined to reclaim his wealth and to save them from his precarious financial position.

In February of 1932, Anselmo went alone to Mexico to his other business, "Mansional Mexico."[2]

The following excerpt is from Chemo's biography of his father, Anselmo Sr., from March 27, 1990:[3]

"In 1932 he [Anselmo Sr.] invented and patented, in Mexico, a building board very similar to our sheetrock. This board was made with fiber scraps from a rope factory and a special formula of ingredients, and these ingredients were made by boiling and using the soup, as they used to call it, and mixed the gypsum with it. The mix was poured in a 4x8 mold, and the finished product was ready to use after a period of about 10 hours. He named this board "MANSIONAL." There again, he had trouble in introducing this product to the Mexican builders as they built all of their interior walls out of brick or concrete and covered them with plaster. It was very hard to educate the Mexicans to use faster methods in building inside partitions and ceilings with a lighter material."

Estefana's sister-in-law, Cecilia Escobedo Contreras (Crisanto's sister), was undoubtedly concerned about Estefana's children. Cecilia and her mother, Anastasia Escobedo (Crisanto's mother), traveled the twenty miles from San Benito to McAllen to visit with Estefana's children. Carmen's two friends from San Benito came with Cecilia. Presumably, Carmen's friends were Josefina and Antonia. Carmen was thrilled to see her close friends from San Benito.

On Friday, February 19, 1932, Enrique sent his 25th letter to Carmen.[4] He hopes for a job in McAllen, not Monterrey.

McAllen, Texas
February 19, 1932

Migrants: Exploring the Colors of my Family History

Miss. Carmen Garcia

My very lovely Carmen,

You can't imagine the pleasure that you gave me to read your flattering letter in which you never cease to amaze me how favorably you wrote about your affection. I do not doubt that you have exaggerated a bit in what you wrote. But the main thing is to have love and truth, like what you tell me and I have always shown you. And hopefully, our aspirations will be cemented for our happiness to be complete, as we hope. I know perfectly well that some people criticize our relationship because they believe that it is not as positive as you and I know that it is. But someday we will be vindicated in their eyes, that in our love there is nothing false and that everything will become a reality with the favor of God. Don't doubt that there is happiness for all and that we have a right to it. Even if we have to face difficulties, we will overcome them little by little. Because I must tell you that the troubles are for us to overcome, not to dominate us.

Many times, I have doubted your love for me a little bit. Because you are very frank and kind to your friends and, occasionally, you are less so with me. But now that I read your letter and that in it you say that you only have love for me, and you would love me forever. I wish with all my heart that this is the case.

Concerning what I told you about going to Monterrey to work, I am telling you only because I have no desire to go. I hope for a job opportunity here so that I can stay until we get married. In front of God, I tell you.

Don't let the lack of ink keep you from writing to me, you can write with a pencil. It is crucial to understand what you and I tell each other, which we will not forget, and we will keep in our hearts the essence of our oaths, which dwells in our love.

Without more, who loves you with all my soul,
Yours, Enrique

On Monday, February 22, 1932, Carmen wrote to Enrique.[5] This letter was the ONLY letter that Carmen had saved. Years later, Carmen said that in a fit of anger, she had destroyed all of the letters that she wrote him, except for one that she had missed. She kept the ones that Enrique had sent to her, though. Even in her anger, those letters were special to her. When asked why she had destroyed the letters she'd written to Enrique.

She chuckled and said, "I wrote those letters, so they belonged to me. Besides, I was angry with Enrique about who knows what at the time, and that's why I destroyed them."

McAllen, Texas
February 22, 1932

Mr. Enrique Mendoza G.

Unforgettable Enrique,

It is on my wall, a very high [inspiring] letter, which gave me great comfort and hope.

Enrique, you say that you will do everything possible to stay here, of that I am delighted.

You also say in your letter that I say that my

affection for you is not as you expect.

I don't want you to doubt my love for you, my love for you is faithful; never doubt what I tell you in my letters, everything that I wrote to you is true.

Nothing much more to tell than Cecilia was here and her mom and my two friends. Cecilia says that they will come next Sunday, and she thinks she will stay with us.

Well, I will end my humble writing. Your faithful,
Carmen Garcia, that is funny.
Forgive the letter, but this is what the time allows.

Carmen was working for her aunt Ofelia [Anselmo Longoria's wife]. Ofelia was paying her $4 per week to do most (if not all) of the housework.

Ofelia could not have been happy to be left at home with all of their five children. Her husband lived mostly in Mexico at the time. She resented his infrequent trips to their home. He focused on building his new business in Monterrey and restoring his wealth and financial security. *Phoenix Lumber Company* was gone, and he likely had poured some of the money he'd gotten from the insurance company into his business into the Monterrey business, *Mansional Mexico*.

He was very motivated to rebuild his wealth with his new factory in Monterrey. He was hopeful for the future, especially since the political climate had improved towards the rebuilding of Mexico's infrastructure. To Anselmo, this meant building/construction opportunities galore. He knew he could be successful again.

Almost every day, Carmen would report to her Aunt Ofelia's home to clean her house, wash the clothes, and iron the clothes. Ofelia did the cooking. Years later, as she described working for her aunt, she said, "None of Ofelia's children would ever lift a finger to help with the cleaning. She paid me $4 each week."

In the kitchen of the second apartment of the duplex, there was a large tub where Carmen handwashed all the clothes for Ofelia's family. She ironed clothes in that room too. It was next to Anselmo's office. After she finished the washing, she cleaned the house. In an interview from 2007, Margarita Elva, Enrique's sister, said that Ofelia was a tyrant and had made Carmen work much too hard - the classic Cinderella story. Carmen was quite efficient and completed her chores, no matter what Ofelia demanded from her.

By the end of the day, her hands were raw from washing the clothes, and her body exhausted. Years later, she would say that she enjoyed doing the housework. Perhaps, it had distracted her from the grief of losing her mother. In any case, it would have prepared her for what was to begin in the next few months.

By 1932, the Great Depression was at its worst, whose crushing weight caused widespread suffering.

On February 27, 1932, Cecilia Escobedo Contreras again visited with Estefana's children. It was only for a few days. After this, Cecilia decided that it would be best for Matilde (9) and Marcolfa (6) to go back with her to San Benito - at least for a little while until they could sort things out. Carmen (17) and Maria Luisa (19) kept Alejandro (4) with them. It could be that taking Alejandro would have been a burden to Cecilia; he was too young to do any chores and would have to be looked after.

Matilde and Marcolfa would soon learn that living with their Aunt Cecilia wasn't as comfortable as they had expected. Aunt Cecilia was very strict with them. They would have lots of chores to do and not much time for play, but they were safe and well-fed. Many years later, Matilde shared the experience of living with her Aunt Cecilia, saying that her aunt often told her, "no estes dioquis" (don't stand around doing nothing).

Enrique was feeling insecure as he saw Carmen's family falling apart. He would undoubtedly be concerned that she might move to

San Benito to join her siblings. He was used to being the privileged child as Margarita's and Encarnacion's firstborn. It's not unusual for the firstborn to expect a higher level of privilege from his family and those in his circle.

On Friday, March 18, 1932, Enrique sent his 26th letter to Carmen.[6] It was a love letter.

> McAllen, Texas
> March 18, 1832
>
> Miss. Carmen Garcia
>
> My adored Carmen,
>   I received your very kind letter, of that I have been aware of it and very happy for what you say in it, and I am confident that your love is so loyal and true as you tell me; because mine has no limits, each day. I love you more and more, so I hope that you appreciate my love for you and how I adore you. Many girls are very fond of their boyfriends, and I'm speaking of the good qualities that they have. And what they do is to increase their wellbeing to such a degree that having the boyfriend is nothing special to them, and they despise and resent their [boyfriend's] presence. Her vanity obscures her good qualities that the boy so appreciated (and immeasurably loved).
>   But of this, I do not care; because I have the firm belief that between you and me, this has never existed (and could never begin to exist). Because the reality is that I will always tell you that I am proud of you; because you have a myriad of excellent qualities that will bless both of us.

And even though no cloud has obscured our good aspirations, we must always have faith and hope in what we want to realize, for the benefit of our love.

Don't think, even for a moment, that I will waver in what I have promised you. I only hope to overcome any difficulties which happen to us (now and in the future).

To achieve this, I need your valuable help; because only the both of us (you and I) can be depended upon to realize our dream, with the favor of God, of course. That is how it has been for the last two years; why doubt one or the other? Why don't we work together to prove that we love each other? I tell you "that we both love each other" because we promised this to each other. Why give us reason to doubt this? You are quite convinced that my affection is genuine. Why do you question this sometimes? OR why do you show that on certain occasions that you do not love me? OR at least, why do you make me doubt your affection? Being that I have always shown that I adore you (even though you want to deny this), everything I say in this letter is true.

So, I hope, in the future, you will stop talking about the advantages or disadvantages that refute what we have already proposed. My desire and yours should be in harmony, that we always strive to improve our good way of thinking, and therefore, as time progresses, our great love will become more apparent.

I want to write much more, but I figured that if I write too much, some detail that I write might make you believe the opposite. I have good intentions for you in my letters to not make you lose faith and hope in what we both want. But, at the same time, I understand perfectly well that your kind heart does not make you think badly of me in the slightest detail.

I think I have written too much already, and I leave you with the most fervent hope that our relationship will improve day by day, as can happen between two people who both love each other, as I adore you. Yours,
Enrique
P. S., A small bit of your love, is huge in my life. I imagine that it will always be that way!

The world was both emotionally and financially crashing around the families, and Enrique seemed emotionally insulated from it all. He did not like that she created a "pros and cons" list about the two of them being together. He undoubtedly interpreted this as her hesitation about their relationship.

The fire at the lumberyard across from Encarnacion's house alone was enough to put his family in a state of insecurity. The newspaper never reported the cause of the fire. It merely stated, "of unknown origin." Anselmo might have been suspicious about how the fire had started. Perhaps Margarita or Encarnacion assumed that it was an ominous warning to hasten their return to Mexico. The anti-Mexican sentiment was quite possibly somehow involved in the fire. However, there is no evidence to determine the actual cause of the fire. In any event, it was a terrifying event to have a fire raging out of control across the street from Encarnacion and Margarita's home.

Encarnacion and Margarita had postponed their return to Mexico because of the death of Estefana. Also, their son, Enrique, had a serious relationship ("comprometidos") with Estefana's daughter, Carmen. They, especially Margarita, certainly would not have wanted to leave their eldest son behind in the United States while they moved back to Mexico. They'd done that before when they had moved to Texas. Margarita would most likely have assured Enrique that everything would work out.

Enrique was an insecure young man, and the only thing that would help him to have a semblance of normalcy was to be reassured by the woman with whom he'd fallen in love. Reassurances from his mother were no longer enough for him. He'd become blinded by his passion for Carmen. Unfortunately, this intensity might have been a bit overwhelming for Carmen. Although, it might have served as a useful distraction from the grief of losing her mother. Carmen must have written another letter to Enrique to, once again, reassure him.

On Thursday, April 28, 1932, Enrique (21) sent his 27th letter to Carmen (17).[7] "I only adore you—"

McAllen, Texas
April 28, 1932

Ms. Carmen Garcia

My adored Carmen,

With pleasure, I write this, in reply to your letter, from which it appears that you have some love for me, which leaves me very satisfied and pensive at the same time, for the reason that I wish, with all of my heart that henceforth there is no lack of love, the realization of our hopes. Also, because I understand that you will do everything you can to cement our aspirations in favor of our happiness.

In each letter that I write to you, I tell you that

"I only adore you," so I hope you'll always know to conduct yourself in a manner that you understand that all your love is for me.

Wait with patience and keep in mind this letter; if we go forward in agreement, our dreams will be possible. I give you all of my affection. Yours, Enrique

In a picture from May 23, 1932, Carmen Garcia (17), Alejandro (4) and Leslie Mendoza (8) posed for a picture in McAllen, Texas. Maria Luisa, Carmen, and Alejandro were still living in Estefana's rented house.

On Thursday, June 2, 1932, Enrique sent his 28th letter to Carmen.[8] "Erase from your heart any doubt."

McAllen, Texas
June 2, 1932

Miss. Carmen Garcia

My dearest Carmen,

With all the pleasure that exists in my soul, I am writing this. I hope that when you receive it, you experience in your heart my firm conviction of all of my love that I give you. And also [I give you all] the confidence that a man can give to a woman he loves (when it is deserved). To whose affection corresponds in the same way, with a healthy desire to carry our sweet and robust objectives to a happy conclusion.

I would like, with all my love, that you could erase from your heart the slightest trace of resentment that you have of me.

So, I wait for you to do your part in favor of us both, since our goal that we so eagerly desire, is delayed [temporarily unreachable]. Respond soon.
Your most faithful, Enrique

Sometime between February and June 1932, Enrique and Carmen went out riding in his car. Years later, when Carmen was recounting this story, she smiled and said, "and I drove it. Just that one time. It was at nighttime, and the only time we were alone."

Anselmo had used the property on Houston Street in McAllen, Texas, as collateral to pay for his Mexico construction businesses. When the banks crashed, the McAllen bank asked Anselmo to repay the loan balance. Anselmo had thirty days to pay off the loan.

On June 21, 1932, Encarnacion sent a registered letter (or package) to Ingeniero Plutarco Elias Calles, Jr. ("Aco"), son of the former president of Mexico, Plutarco Elias Calles. Aco owned a citrus orchard in General Terán and was living there when Encarnacion and his family lived there (about 1926).

At one time, Encarnacion and Aco were friends. But their friendship had soured due to political reasons. Encarnacion knew Aco's father too. Why is Encarnacion sending a registered letter? The citrus orchards that Aco owned were in Soledad de la Mota in General Terán (a gift from his father). His father lived in Mexico City. Aco's father would often vacation at his son's estate.[9] Aco's wife was Elisa Saenz. Was she related to Enrique's cousin, Méme Garza's wife, Juana Saenz? These questions remain unanswered today.

On Wednesday, June 26, 1932, Enrique sent his 29th (and last) letter to Carmen.[10] "talked at midday; going to Weslaco."

McAllen, Texas
June 26, 1932

Migrants: Exploring the Colors of my Family History

Ms. Carmen Garcia

My very dear Carmen,

After very affectionately greeting you, I tell you the following: as I do not doubt that in the time that we were talking today at mid-day, I overstepped the rules that we must observe with our love.

But as any person should express their feelings to our loved ones, always you've noticed that I have been frank with you, and I have demonstrated that to you.

So, if your conscience and your heart tell you that you should forgive, that is your choice, if your answer is favorable to our desires, I beg you, with all my heart, to do what is possible to cooperate in favor of us (both you and I). I will do the same in the future. In a few moments we are going to Weslaco, write back to me as soon as I return.

Your most faithful, Enrique

Ofelia was upset that the bank had called the loan and decided to take action. She thought that if she could rent out the house where Estefana lived, they could begin to pay off the loan. Of course, the rent from that little house would barely be enough even to begin to repay the loans. The loans totaled $2,000. Anselmo was in Mexico at the time.

Margarita had always been very involved with charities, giving money to the Red Cross and giving food to the church. She would make beans and rice for the church. Carmen said that Margarita's rice and beans were always delicious. She noted that Margarita would cook the beans, and just before they were ready, she would put in a "pierna" (ham hock/leg). Carmen would help Margarita with the food donations to the church.

One day, Ofelia was having a bad day and was venting out her frustrations to Carmen. She yelled at Carmen and told her, "I'm not paying you so you can help Doña Margarita. I pay you so you can work for me."

Years later, as Carmen remembered the event, she said, "But I did everything for her. After I ironed for her, then it was my time to do as I please."

On June 26, 1932, Enrique went to Weslaco - probably with the family for the Loteria.

Ofelia went to Estefana's house and argued with Maria Luisa. Maria Luisa had recently sprained her ankle and was not the type to be so easily pushed around.

"She was barely able to walk," Carmen said years later about her sister Maria Luisa.

Ofelia told Maria Luisa, "Get out of this house. I don't care if you have to drag your foot behind you as you leave." Carmen was shocked that her Aunt Ofelia had come into their home and evicted Maria Luisa.

In an interview years later, Carmen said, "Hopefully, God has forgiven Ofelia. Ofelia despreciaba [disrespected] a Mama and threw Mary out."

Carmen then said, "Cuando uno aga un daño, yo creo que uno paga un ["When someone does something bad, I believe you pay a price in your life]. That's why I have my [illness] . . . Toda paga una en esta vida [All pay in this life]. Por eso a mi . . . y a ella por [For me . . . and for her] - For . . . kicking Mary out, Despreciar a mi mama [Disrespect my mother]. "That's why I say: Toda paga una en esta vida [all pay for their actions in this life]." Note: In the 1984 interview, Carmen was quite upset while talking about this. She jumped back and forth from speaking Spanish to English while she spoke about her aunt Ofelia, her mother, Estefana, and her sister, Mary (Maria Luisa). She'd been very upset with Ofelia about this.

Carmen went on to say that maybe God had punished Ofelia because Anselmo took all of the banco de madera [lumber business] to Mexico and moved to Mexico without her. He left Ofelia alone to raise the kids. At the time Chemo was in boarding school in Monterrey. Anselmo would come home to McAllen for an occasional visit.

"Viene como si no me coneciera [When he visits me, it's as if he doesn't know me.]," Ofelia had told Carmen.

By June of 1932, Maria Luisa and her little brother, Alejandro, had left for San Benito, Texas, to join their siblings, Matilde and Marcolfa, to live with their father's sister, Cecilia.

A few days later, Cecilia went to Estefana's house to bring Carmen back. There was no way that Cecilia would allow Carmen to stay there by herself.

When Cecilia got to McAllen, she talked with Margarita.

Margarita told her [as recounted by Carmen], "She's not going back with you. She's going to marry my son."

Years later, as Carmen said, "Cecilia left empty-handed, and Margarita took me in. And that's how I got married to Enrique." Carmen winked and smiled after she said that.

Matilde remembered, "Mary took a job at a second-hand furniture store. She earned $2 a week. Marcolfa and I went to school during the week while Alex [her brother, Alejandro] stayed at home "solito" [alone]. He was about four and a half years old. Each day when we left for school, we would leave Alex sitting on the stoop to our house, and that is exactly where we found him . . . [when we] returned. Alex was a quiet, well-behaved child who spent hours out in the yard, entertaining himself with large red ants. He would hold a "palito" [stick] on the ant pile. When the ant reached the top of the [stick] close to his hand, he would turn it around [and] make them crawl up the [stick] again and again. They never stung him even though my sister Maria Luisa kept warning him."

". . . te van a picar esas ormigas [those ants are going to sting you], Maria Luisa had said.

Years later, Matilde recounted another story about her brother, Alejandro Escobedo, when they lived in San Benito, "One weekend, Marcolfa, Alex, and I went to the "cine" [theater]. We were crossing an intersection and told Alex to hurry. As we rushed across the street, we left Alex behind, and he got hit by a car. Luckily the car was moving slowly. We ran back to Alex, dusted him off, examined him, and he looked okay except for the "bola" [bump] on his head."

"Don't tell Maria Luisa!" Marcolfa and Matilde had told him.

Matilde continued with her story.

"We continued to walk toward the "teatro" [theater] while Alex complained that his head hurt."

"Do you want to go back home or to the movies?" Marcolfa and Matilde had asked Alejandro.

Matilde finished her story, "Needless to say, he quickly forgot the pain, and we all had a great time at the movies."

The three young siblings kept the incident a secret from their sister, Maria Luisa. Although, years later, as an adult, Alejandro's bump turned into a large cyst that had to be removed. Matilde's daughter Olga later remarked, "Oddly enough, he died of brain cancer."

Estefana's family was now irretrievably fractured.

Soon after that, Ofelia had expressed that Encarnacion and Margarita's boys were a troublesome bunch. She had contradicted her earlier statement when she first met them and said that the boys were such good children.

On July 8, 1932, Enrique Mendoza celebrated his 22nd birthday. He'd received his best birthday present ever. After a two-and-a-half-year courtship, he was going to marry the love of his life, just as his mother had told Cecilia.

On July 18, 1932, Enrique Mendoza (22) and Carmen Garcia (17) got their wedding license.

On July 24, 1932, Enrique Mendoza married Carmen Garcia. The priest, Reverend P. Montero, who married them, was the Pastor at Sacred Heart Church. Carmen and Enrique were married there, just blocks from their home. The church was special to Carmen because her uncle, Anselmo Longoria, had built it.

Carmen wore a beautiful flowing wedding gown with a pearl lace crown with a flowing veil. Margarita had spared no expense for the church wedding and the reception at Anselmo's house. The wedding gown had cost $25. Anselmo was there, although, Carmen's siblings weren't in attendance.

On their wedding day, Carmen and Enrique received a postcard from Eutermio Longoria (a relative of Carmen's on her mother's side) and a Western Union telegram from Jesus Valdez (Méme's uncle) and his wife, Maria Garza, from San Antonio, Texas. More letters came from family and friends from Monterrey congratulating Enrique and Carmen. All of these letters were addressed to Box 1141, McAllen, Texas.

In the January 5, 1984 interview, Carmen said, "When one is young, one is "feliz" [happy]. When one gets married, then one has obligations. "Hacerle de comer" [Fix dinner]. It's never the same." She also said, "Thank goodness that I just have a cough and some phlegm, but I feel good. Thank God. I could even go outside."

Enrique looked crooked at her and told her that it was far too cold for her to go outside.

Carmen ignored him and said, "Hay que recibir las malas y las buenas. No nomas las buenas [You must receive the bad with the good. Not just the good]."

As the world around them seemed to be crumbling, the Longoria family and the Mendoza family had united as one. Encarnacion and Margarita's son, Enrique, and Estefana Longoria's daughter, Carmen, became Mr. and Mrs. Enrique Mendoza.

* * *

Enrique and Carmen Garcia Mendoza Wedding Party

21 - Goodbye, McAllen - 8/1932 to 9/1932

Anselmo was unable to come up with the $2,000 that he owed to the bank in the 30 days they'd given him to repay the loan. He lost all of his properties on Houston street, including the houses where his family, Estefana's family, and Encarnacion's family lived. The new owner purchased the properties at ten cents on the dollar. Anselmo made arrangements with the new owner to rent one side of the duplex house. The Longoria's moved all of their belonging into one side of the duplex. He told Encarnacion and Margarita the sad news.

Anselmo and Ofelia Longoria's home

Encarnacion and Margarita had planned to take the Loteria on a multi-city tour. They decided that they would tell their family to pack up for a long trip in addition to the Loteria.

On August 26, 1932, Encarnacion received a letter from Teodoro Elizondo.[1] Teodoro Elizondo owned the property that was adjacent to Encarnacion's building in General Terán and had allowed Encarnacion to set up his tent on a corner of his property. Teodoro Elizondo was extremely concerned that Gaspar Cantú Garza had sold some of Teodoro's land.

TEODORO ELIZONDO

Gral Terán, N.L.
August 26, 1932

Mr. Encarnación Mendoza
McAllen, Texas, USA

Dear friend,

Most attentively, about the sliver of land that is adjacent to the back of your property that is part of my property that I let you use, in the presence of Arturo García, who was then-Mayor 1 / a. and Tomas Botello who was Sindico 1 / o. Well, now Solomon Moya sold the house to Dr. Joaquín R. Toba, and Gaspar alleges that this sliver of land belongs to him, because you had bought it from me. I argue that I let you use it so that you could [put your outdoor market on that sliver of land], having with it the right to mediation.

So to clear up this matter as soon as possible, because the doctor [Dr. Joaquin R. Toba] is moving in there this coming September, please answer me by return mail, and tell me the truth of the deal, so that I can show your letter to Gaspar and the doctor to resolve this matter.

Without further business, and waiting for your letter on the subject, I remain, as always, your friend. Your attentive friend and S.S.,

Teodoro Elizondo

Of course, Teodoro Elizondo was right. On April 5, 1924, Encarnacion had enlisted the help of Arturo Garcia, then Municipal President of General Terán to politely ask Teodoro Elizondo to permit Encarnacion to put his Loteria tent on Teodoro Elizondo's property. Being the good neighbor, Teodoro Elizondo agreed to let Encarnacion use his property. Encarnacion was busy making preparations for the next Loteria and decided that he would travel to General Terán to resolve the property dispute matter after the Loteria had completed its tour. With only a few days left before leaving, he'd purchased all sorts of prizes for the Loteria. He told his family that everyone would need to bring enough clothes for a several-day tour.

Encarnacion and Margarita's family had packed the truck with the tent, the prizes, and all that they needed for a successful Loteria. They had plans for several carnivals in towns that traveled from southern Texas up through central Texas. They would often run two Loterias simultaneously on the weekends. They were quite prosperous. Enrique and some of the brothers, along with hired help, would work one of them while Encarnacion and Enrique's brothers would work the other.

After an exhausting multi-city tour with the Loteria, the brothers and the hired help disassembled the tent. The hinges at the end of each two-by-four made the tear-down relatively simple. Each two-by-four was numbered and stowed in numbered order in the back of the truck.

Even after they paid the law enforcement and others who required their cut, Encarnacion was quite happy with the remaining profits. By 1932, just three years after the Great Depression had started, they had saved enough money to live comfortably for a while.

Near the end of the tour, Encarnacion's family gathered for dinner. They expressed their thanks for their profitable Loteria and enjoyed the food. Perhaps, Margarita had made her delicious rice and beans. After dinner, Encarnacion made an announcement.

"Hijos," he might have said as he got their attention. For several weeks, Encarnacion and Margarita had made no secret of the plans they were preparing to move the family from their home in McAllen. However, it appeared that Encarnacion and Margarita had decided to move immediately. They told the children that they would not be returning to McAllen. The children were likely surprised. They'd thought that they were going on a regular Loteria trip and would eventually end up back at home in McAllen. But something more than Anselmo losing his properties must have changed Encarnacion and Margarita's minds to move immediately. There's no way to know exactly what the reason had been, except perhaps they'd had their fill of all the turmoil that they had recently experienced in McAllen. In addition to the loss of Anselmo's property, they may have considered: the death of Estefana, the issues they'd had with Ofelia, the lumberyard fire across from their home, and countless other mishaps. Encarnacion would have told them that they would return to McAllen sometime later to get the rest of their belongings, but for now, he and Margarita wanted the family to decide where they wanted to move. Of course, they wanted to live in those places where the locals would tolerate Mexicans.

There were two choices: Monterrey, Mexico, or San Antonio, Texas. In both of those places, Encarnacion was confident that he would be able to continue with the Loteria to support the family. When he lived in Monterrey, he had run the Loteria there. He had family there. He had numerous business contacts, including at the

Bank of Monterrey. Encarnacion had already made most of the arrangements for his family's return to Mexico. He had wanted to be sure that if the family chose to move to Monterrey, it would be possible. Also, the Cristero Rebellion had ended years earlier in 1929, and the political climate in Mexico had started to calm, especially in Monterrey. It's interesting to note that San Antonio and Monterrey appeared to be their only two choices. Most likely, Encarnacion and Margarita had narrowed the choices before presenting the options to their family.

Margarita was a United States citizen and had been born in Floresville, Texas. She had relatives in Mexico, in San Antonio, and other places in Texas. Her late mother, Mariana Ybarbo, was also born in East Texas. San Antonio was a relatively safe place to live for many Mexican families who had fled the religious persecution during the Cristero Rebellion that had started in 1926 in Mexico. San Antonio had a significant population of Mexicans. Of course, Encarnacion and Margarita's family would never escape the prejudice against them as long as they lived in the United States. The anti-Mexican sentiment of the 1930s was something that the family could endure if they were careful.

Encarnacion had made careful plans to return to Monterrey. Why would he be moving to Monterrey instead of General Terán where Margarita still had relatives - her half-brother, Salomon de la Garza, and others? In Monterrey, he would be returning to his birth town. Perhaps it's entirely plausible that his mother, Guadalupe Mendoza, had owned substantial property there.

Perhaps Encarnacion had inherited the property from his mother, Guadalupe Mendoza, after her death on August 26, 1920, at the age of 59 from tuberculosis. Encarnacion frequently traveled to Monterrey and kept close ties to his relatives there.

Encarnacion was a very skilled entrepreneur. He most certainly had the necessary connections (i.e., a business network) to restart his businesses there. Also, General Terán was only sixty miles from

Monterrey.

Encarnacion always kept aware of the political problems in Mexico. The local newspaper, *The Brownsville Herald*, reported about Mexico every so often. The presidency for Plutarco Elias Calles had ended in 1928. That news would have thrilled Encarnacion. Calles had been responsible for the higher taxes he had to pay when he had his businesses in General Terán. Encarnacion must have believed that Calles was responsible for the corruption that came with the collection of those taxes. Calles had also implemented stringent health regulations on Encarnacion's businesses. Perhaps Encarnacion would have felt that it would have been safer to return to Monterrey, where he had relatives, but not to General Terán. In General Terán, Aco (son of former President Plutarco Elias Calles) had a considerable influence on the town. Aco would most certainly not have been welcoming to Encarnacion's family to General Terán (even though they had once been friends).

Margarita might have been leery of returning to Mexico. She had relatives in General Terán, but she had quite a few more in the United States where she had been born. Margarita had family throughout Texas, such as Donna, Seguin, San Antonio, and McAllen from her father's side of the family (De La Garza). On her mother's side (Ybarbo), she also had family in Nacogdoches, Texas and Natchitoches, Louisiana.

Margarita and her family had grown accustomed to the modern niceties and conveniences in the United States, such as indoor plumbing, toilets, clean, orderly streets, and much more. In the United States, she no longer feared the possibility that political rivals might have her or her family jailed, or worse, murdered for having stood up for her political beliefs or religious views. It had only been five years since she and her family had fled for their prosperity and their lives from General Terán. The politics of Mexico had threatened the safety of their family and the ability to operate a business free from government corruption. In the United

Migrants: Exploring the Colors of my Family History

States, she suffered the malady of prejudice because of her Mexican heritage. Her father, Juan de la Garza, was Mexican, and her mother, Mariana Ybarbo, was from the United States with French and Spanish ancestry.

But her face portrayed more of her father's Mexican heritage rather than her mother's European ancestry. She most certainly would have felt a bit safer with an occasional bigoted, cowardly neighbor in Texas rather than a gun-toting group of rebels at her front door in Mexico - as had been the case so often at their business in General Terán. Like her husband, Encarnacion, Margarita would also have made plans to find a place to live in San Antonio. She had relatives in San Antonio, Texas. Her half-brother's son, Méme Garza, lived there.

Perhaps the choice for Encarnacion and Margarita had been: "Do we want to live near Encarnacion's relatives in Monterrey or Margarita's relatives in San Antonio.

Enrique would later say in an interview that the family decided to move to San Antonio. But in another interview, the next year, when asked about the move, he hesitated before he answered and said that most of his family, but not all, voted to move to San Antonio. Encarnacion would have wanted to move back to Monterrey, where they respected him. He would not be denigrated as he was in the United States. Margarita might have felt comfortable there with people who would not condescend to her because she looked Mexican. In Mexico, the Cristero Rebellion was over, and she would no longer feel threatened to practice her Catholic religion.

Encarnacion and Margarita must have been disappointed at some level that their children voted to go to San Antonio instead of to Monterrey. Even so, it was imperative for Margarita and Encarnacion to keep the family together and safe.

Soon Encarnacion and Margarita's family would learn that a move to a big city like San Antonio had many benefits as well as a few culturally challenging issues.

Years later, Enrique said that he and his siblings found that life in the United States was much more comfortable and faster-paced than it had been in Mexico. The modern day conveniences, like bathrooms and indoor plumbing, were much better.

Encarnacion and Margarita, after much thought, must have agreed that the lifestyle in the United States was much more comfortable for their family. They couldn't deny that they enjoyed the creature comforts while living in the United States.

Encarnacion and Margarita, along with their children, had found the United States incredibly alluring. Encarnacion agreed to forgo his plan to move to his birth town of Monterrey, Mexico and move to San Antonio. He had previously moved from his beloved home of Monterrey to General Terán in 1908, just after he had married Margarita. Encarnacion and Margarita had concurred that their family would be happier and safer in San Antonio, Texas.

In September 1932, Encarnacion traveled to General Terán to resolve the property dispute matter that Teodoro Elizondo had written about. As was usually the case, Encarnacion traveled to Monterrey to stay with his uncle, Jesus Maria Garcia (his mother's brother). Once there, they went to General Terán to resolve the matter.

While Encarnacion (50) was taking care of his property dispute in Mexico, Margarita (47), Virgilio (26), Enrique (22), Canacho (21), Heriberto (19), Jesus (16), Margarita (13), Ruby (11), Leslie (9), and Enrique's wife Carmen (18) headed to San Antonio. In their own way, each had said their final goodbyes to McAllen. Even with the support of her new family, Carmen must have had some sorrow.

22 - San Antonio - 9/1932 to 12/1934

Margarita and her children had arrived in San Antonio in September 1932. Why did they choose to move to San Antonio and not to another city in Texas? It was a big city, the third-largest in Texas, according to the last United States Census (population in 1930 was 231,542). She and Encarnacion had been there before visiting family (such as Margarita's nephew, Manuel "Méme" Garza, and his family and other relatives of hers). Enrique had later said that Margarita was extremely close to Meme's mother Juana. Margarita seemed to have relatives everywhere, sprinkled throughout Texas. Additionally, the beauty and charm of San Antonio would have been enough for anyone to want to live there.

Just like Encarnacion, Margarita was a planner, leaving nothing to chance. It's unclear where they stayed on the day that they arrived in San Antonio, but it was likely that they stayed at a relative's house. Perhaps a hint came when, on September 20, 1932, Margarita bought a Baker's console gas range from Walker Furniture for $50.[1] She'd put her address at the corner of N. Frio and Leal Streets. This was just a few blocks from the house on Hill Street where they would soon move to.

Certainly, Margarita would have seen the Hill Street house when they arrived in San Antonio. Or maybe Margarita's nephew, Méme, would have told her about it in a letter or a phone call. The house was at 219 Hill Street and was large enough to fit multiple families.

As you entered the front door, there was a long hallway. As you walked down the hall, there were four large bedrooms on each side. At the end of the hallway was a bathroom. It was a luxury to have an indoor toilet that Encarnacion and Margarita did not have in Mexico.

To the left was a large kitchen. Just beyond the kitchen was a large storeroom. As you walk out of the kitchen, into the hallway, just past the bathroom, was a large room that held a massive table at which the family could enjoy a meal together. They could also hold essential family meetings there when they wanted. The houses in that area were worth anywhere from $3,000 to $5,000. But the house at 219 Hill Street in 1933 was not for sale. It was for rent and a perfect place for the Mendoza family to live.

Méme's family would have been quite familiar with San Antonio, which had a public library on Main Street, the San Antonio Zoo at Brackenridge Park, and the beautiful River Park in downtown. San Antonio was home to Kelly, Brooks, and Randolph Air Force Bases. Radio broadcasts from several English-speaking stations like KONO, WOAI, and more.

Méme would undoubtedly have told Margarita that there was freedom to worship her Catholic faith without worry. San Fernando Cathedral would have been a beautiful church and historical site for worship.

Of course, Margarita would expect that a city as large as San Antonio might have some less than desirable elements like prejudice, bigotry, and crime. Margarita would have known how to keep her family safe from that. Her husband, Encarnacion, would have known that too, but as a business owner, he had to interact with people from all different walks of life. Margarita would most certainly have witnessed those times while visiting the United States when Encarnacion was humiliated because of the color of his skin or his notable Mexican Indian features.

Undoubtedly, both Margarita and Encarnacion were used to dealing with all sorts of people. They ran businesses that catered primarily to Mexicans but welcomed all customers. Encarnacion focused on operating his businesses and making a profit rather than worrying about the prejudices that he'd experienced. That's why he was such a successful entrepreneur. Anita, Margarita, and Encarnacion would have all agreed that the potential for happiness and well-being was in store for their families in San Antonio.

After having resolved the property dispute between Teodoro Elizondo and Gaspar Cantú Garza in General Terán, Encarnacion returned to the United States on September 21, 1932.

Encarnacion and Margarita were undoubtedly delighted with the house, and so were their children: Virgilio (27), Enrique (22) and his wife Carmen (18), Canacho (21), Heriberto (18), Jesus (16), Maria Consuelo (15), Margarita Elva (14), Ruby de la Luz (11), Leslie (10), Encarnacion's "adopted" daughter, Guadalupe (21), and her son, Jose Armando ("Pepe") (2). [Guadalupe was the trusted housekeeper].

A few years after moving to San Antonio, Margarita obtained a letter of recommendation from the Police Chief of San Antonio (in 1936). In that letter, he stated unequivocally that the Mendoza family had lived in San Antonio since September of 1932.

Even though Encarnacion and Margarita's family moved into the house on Hill Street, they rented the house in McAllen for a few weeks longer. All of their furniture and other belongings were still there. They would have returned shortly to McAllen to collect all of their belongings and bring them back to San Antonio. That trip would have taken them about five hours each way. However, because of the Loteria, they were used to traveling throughout South Texas, so it would not have been difficult to make the journey to and from McAllen.

Also, the McAllen Post office would hold any correspondence sent to Encarnacion and Margarita's family there in Box 1141. As before, Encarnacion or someone in his family would pick up their mail when they were near there. Also, the Loteria still traveled throughout South Texas, including McAllen. That would give them the opportunity to stop by the post office and pick up any mail.

In 1933, the Reynosa-McAllen international bridge replaced the crossing between Tamaulipas, Mexico, and McAllen, Texas (i.e., the Port of Hidalgo). A severe hurricane had severely damaged the previous one.[2] This new bridge made it easier and safer to cross between the United States and Mexico.

On January 18, 1933, the United States issued a quarantine identification card to Enrique Mendoza.[3] According to his application, he had black hair, 5'7", 22 years old, a United States Citizen, and occupation of a bookkeeper.

On March 25, 1933, Maria Luisa sent a postcard to her sister, Carmen.[4] The front of the postcard had a picture of Harlingen High School. Maria Luisa had addressed the postcard to Mr. and Mrs. Enrique and Carmen Mendoza at Box 1141 in McAllen, Texas.

At the time, Maria Luisa, Matilde, Marcolfa, and Alejandro were living with relatives in San Benito. Perhaps Maria Luisa had not known that Carmen and Enrique had already moved to 219 Hill Street in San Antonio, Texas. Ofelia Longoria, who was still living in McAllen, would have picked up the postcard from the Post Office and forwarded it on to Carmen in San Antonio. It's a little unusual that Maria Luisa hadn't been informed of Carmen's new address in San Antonio.

Harlingen, Texas – With Love
March 25, 1933

Dear Sister,
    I send you this postcard to say hello to you and everyone in general.

Migrants: Exploring the Colors of my Family History

Maybe when you receive this card, you are running on horseback.
Hello from all
Well. G A Jesus
Today, we passed by this place.

Your sister,
M. L. Garcia

Around this time, Carmen's uncle, Anselmo Longoria, had a fully operational lumberyard or factory in Monterrey, and he was no longer living with his wife and children in McAllen, Texas. Ofelia and the children were living on one side of the duplex and renting it from the new owners. Anselmo was living alone in an apartment in Monterrey and working obsessively to make his business successful. He would work all day to expand his business and then come home and unwind. In the evenings, he would make business plans for the next day, write poetry, or play the violin. Somewhere around this time, Anselmo's two brothers, Alejandro and Cristobal, went to work with him at his business.

On April 28, 1933, Encarnacion and Margarita celebrated their 25th Wedding Anniversary.[5] One of their sons, presumably, Enrique Mendoza on his typewriter, wrote a toast for their momentous event. It was a welcomed respite from their grueling past few months.

Ladies and gentlemen.

Today April 28, 1933.
I'm happy to address you. A few sentences or words in honor of the those that gave me life, and I hope that all who are present here will know how to forgive me for the simple but frank way of

expressing myself. I want to pay tribute to those who today have been married 25 years, and at this time, , It is very proud of a son to witness such a solemn event, how happy he feels, how many thousands of young people would like to have this joy.

Dear Brothers and Sisters; here is an example, how the life of a marriage is preserved: by fighting with destiny and overcoming obstacles as they arise. (And all because) Because they walk united with a common purpose, when they undertake a project, they both do it in full accordance with each other. And if they succeed, they are proud, and if they fail, they still feel happy because they were in accordance with each other.

Let's imitate this great example, and now, let us give the most expressive thank you to GOD, our Lord, for having allowed them to live their lives and preserve their health. For them [Encarnacion and Margarita] for having guided us on the strict path of righteousness and honesty, and also to the people present, we give them the most deserved thanks for having attended this humble event where we celebrate the silver wedding anniversary of Mr. Encarnación Mendoza and Mrs. Margarita Garza, to whom we wish them one hundred more years of life and congratulations,

I have spoken.

Life for Encarnacion and Margarita's family was settling into a beautiful, pleasant rhythm. They kept up with the news from Mexico.

On July 8, 1933, The Mexican states of Nuevo Leon and Tamaulipas were hard hit by severe hurricane damage.[6]

1933 July 8 Saturday - *Abilene Reporter News*

TWO STATES IN MEXICO ARE HARD HIT BY GALE
by the Associated Press

MEXICO, D. F., July 7. - Reports from northeastern Mexico tonight indicated heavy hurricane and flood damage in the states of Tamaulipas and Nuevo Leon. No loss of life was reported, although it was feared.

These two Mexican states were lashed yesterday and most of today by high winds and a torrential downpour which brought rivers up at an alarming rate, especially at Monterrey, industrial city of northern Mexico.

As all rivers in that vicinity drain into the Rio Grande between Laredo and Brownsville, floods may be expected along the lower Rio Grande. A dispatch from Monterrey reported wind and flood damage at Linares, Montemorelos, General Terán, Sabinas Hidalgo, Salinas, and Cuidad Victoria, widely separated towns.

Roads were impassable throughout the section. Highway traffic between Monterrey and Saltillo was stopped by raging river floods, and the suburb of Colonia de la Independencia was cut off from Monterrey this afternoon, and rescue crews began taking out the residents.

Bridges were washed away, and homes were

flooded. The rains stopped in Monterrey in mid-afternoon, but skies continued overcast. Several busloads of passengers were isolated in a canyon west of the city.

Airplane pilots reported all villages within a 28-mile radius of Soto la Marina, on the coast north of Tampico [Tamaulipas], were leveled by the storm. It was impossible to determine if there were any casualties as the section is isolated from communication lines.

On July 23, 1933, the Mendoza's received a wedding announcement/invitation for the wedding of Maria de la Luz Sanchez and Méme Garza. Méme was Enrique's cousin by way of his mother.[7] The wedding was to take place at San Fernando Cathedral in San Antonio, Texas. The bride, Maria de la Luz Sanchez, lived at 312 Perez Street in San Antonio, Texas. This address was about four blocks from the Mendoza's residence at 219 Hill Street.

On July 26, 1933, Margarita obtained an affidavit that stated that Martina Garcia had known her since birth (years later, Carmen remembered having an aunt named Martina).[8] The affidavit also said that she lived in McAllen, Texas. As she'd done many times before, Margarita continued to obtain references that she could use to collect evidence that her family was of good standing in the community. They'd been living happily in San Antonio for about ten months. Margarita was meticulous about obtaining and using these types of references for establishing a bank account, getting a job, filing citizenship papers, and a myriad of other reasons. Margarita kept busy. She became more active with the church, just as she'd done at Sacred Heart Church in McAllen, Texas. She always made it a point to give them donations of her time and money.

Migrants: Exploring the Colors of my Family History

Although Encarnacion's Loteria business was doing well, the rest of the family would soon need money to support their own growing families. Enrique worked the Loteria, and Carmen went to work making clothes as a sewing machine operator.

Canacho started a neighborhood grocery store soon after arriving in San Antonio at a building at 401 Arbor Place on the corner of Arbor Place and San Marcos Street. The store was named "La Tienda de No Aye" and was not far from downtown San Antonio.

Heriberto and a business partner opened a small store a few blocks away from Canacho's store. They offered basic items, such as bread, milk, eggs, etc.

There was a story that the Mendoza family ran a store by the name: "M&M Grocery (i.e., Mendoza and Mendoza Grocery). There is a strong possibility that one of these two stores had this name.

By October of 1933, Maria Luisa, Matilde, Marcolfa, and Alejandro left San Benito and moved into a room in 219 Hill Street, next door to Enrique and Carmen's place. There must have been correspondence between Carmen and Maria Luisa to plan this move. They must have been very excited to be near to each other after a year's separation.

Matilde recounted her family's history while they lived at 219 Hill Street, San Antonio, Texas.[9]

"Alex was barely five years old when we got to San Antonio, and he had to stay home alone while we attended school. I attended Stephen F. Austin Elementary School in the 5th grade and Marcolfa in the 2nd grade. I went on to the 6th and 7th grade at Hawthorne Junior High School. That is as far as [I] got, was to junior high school, and Marcolfa also left school. Once I left school, I took care of Alex and Marcolfa full-time. I cooked, washed, and cared for Marcolfa and Alex full time. I was about 13 or 14 years old. I had to help because Maria Luisa's job was labor-intensive. She worked as a seamstress, putting overcoats together. It [was] a government-owned factory. As far as I can remember, my sister always walked to work to save money on bus fare. In [the] winter, she left and returned home -- when it was dark. When not doing housework for Maria Luisa, I would spend my time playing with my childhood friends, Leslie and Ruby Mendoza."

Maria Luisa had a boyfriend named Pedro "Pete" Herrera. He would, at times, call on Maria Luisa at her residence at Hill Street. On one of his visits, Margarita Elva Mendoza (Enrique's younger sister) answered the door.

"He was ugly. He had a big belly, and often the button that held his shirt closed over his belly button would come loose." She said she was disgusted with his belly protruding unnaturally through his unbuttoned shirt.

After living at the Hill Street room for a short time, Carmen's sister, Maria Luisa Garcia (21), moved into an apartment at 214 South Laredo Street. Maria Luisa brought her siblings, Matilde (11), Marcolfa (8), and presumably Alejandro (6).

As Matilde had remembered (above), Maria Luisa worked as a seamstress. She was quite skilled at it. She was tall, slim, and often dressed fashionably. Perhaps, her job had allowed her to wear the latest fashions. According to Mary Lou Gomez-Rettie, she recalled her mother, Matilde had shared that Maria Luisa had beautiful blue eyes. It seemed that Maria Luisa was well dressed, had good looks, and was very independent.

In 2007, Margarita Elva, daughter of Encarnacion and Margarita, remembered that she had told Maria Luisa to make some sort of cosmetic alteration to her nose. Margarita Elva was not cruel, but it suggests that Maria Luisa might have been self-conscience about her nose for some reason. For everyone who saw her, they would have only noticed her striking beauty.

In the later part of 1934, Chemo visited his father's (Anselmo Longoria Sr.) Mansional factory in Mexico. His uncles, Alejandro

Longoria and Cristobal Longoria, were working for his father when Chemo visited. Chemo was amazed at the busy factory that sat next to the railroad tracks.

In Mexico, Lazaro Cardenas was inaugurated to the presidency of Mexico on December 1, 1934.[10] Mexico's turbulent past was about to make a sharp turn into a balanced and prosperous direction. Up to this point, former President Plutarco Elias Calles had quite a bit of influence in Mexican politics. He lost that power very quickly after Cardenas became president.

Encarnacion and his family would most certainly have been pleased with this shift in power that was happening in his home country. Was Encarnacion's heart still missing his country of birth? He certainly would have pondered how different their lives would be if they had decided to return to Mexico.

23 - Family Life - 1/1935 to 10/1936

Encarnacion and Margarita, their children were living at 219 Hill Street in 1935. Margarita controlled the finances in the household. On January 19, 1935, Margarita opened a bank account in her name at Frost National Bank in San Antonio, Texas. In those days, a woman needed her husband's permission to open a bank account. Perhaps Encarnacion or another male relative had accompanied her to the bank when she opened the account. Perhaps, the bank had not allowed Encarnacion to open the account because he was not a United States citizen. In any case, her bank account held the sizeable income from the Loteria. At last, balance and prosperity had returned to Encarnacion and Margarita's family as they continued to set up roots in San Antonio, Texas.

In March of 1935, Carmen quit her job (she was seven months pregnant). Her employer had told her that his company's insurance policy didn't cover her pregnancy. She was disappointed and agreed to leave the following month. She loved to sew, and it was satisfying to earn money for her family. It gave her a sense of independence. It was there that she'd sewn hems and seams on all types of fabrics. She was a highly skilled sewing machine operator, and this job was a creative outlet for her. On one of her days working there, she was battling a particularly tricky piece of cloth. She corralled the piece through the sewing machine as the sturdy, threaded needle pierced effortlessly through the multiple layers of fabric. Perhaps she'd been upset as she flung the material into its proper place under the presser foot. She put the sewing machine foot down hard and started the machine at full speed as she pushed the fabric forcefully under the pounding needle. The machine took the fabric aggressively along with her finger. The needle pierced her finger, leaving the needle and its bloody thread painfully bonded to her finger. She picked up the foot and quickly withdrew the needle from her finger. The pain was horrendous, but she took care of her finger and finished her work. After a long day, she went home to her extended family at Hill Street.

When Margarita's daughter, Margarita Elva, was interviewed in 2007, she said that her mother had a broken arm, but she wasn't clear exactly when it happened. She hinted that it had occurred at Hill Street. On May 13, 1935, The Physicians Health and Accident Insurance Company sent a letter to Encarnacion at 219 Hill Street, San Antonio, Texas, responding to a claim that he had filed.[1] Perhaps that was for Margarita's broken arm.

Enrique and Carmen lived in the first room at the Hill Street house. Carmen gave birth to their first child, Enrique Jr., there. Although Enrique and Carmen proudly called him Junior. Perhaps they did this to avoid confusion between father and son. However, it's probably because they were proud of their first son. In Mexican culture and many others, the birth of a son, especially a first-born son, was a big deal. Years later, Enrique and Carmen continued to call him Junior, and his siblings called him Henry. Enrique's parents, Encarnacion and Margarita, were delighted with their first grandson, Enrique Jr.

Carmen had wanted to go back to work, but Enrique had objected. He wanted her to stay home and take care of their first-born child. In those days, Carmen complied without much of an objection. Perhaps it was because she loved spending time with her beautiful new baby boy.

On June 12, 1935, Enrique Mendoza Sr. sent a postcard from San Angelo, Texas, to his wife, Carmen.[2] Carmen read the postcard:

My unforgettable wife,

Receive this postcard in proof of my love that I have for you.
Your husband that loves you. Say hello to all, kisses for you,

Enrique

On the postcard, Carmen later wrote in pencil "Bebe al mes 9 lbs. 4 onzas" [Baby at one month old, 9 pounds, 4 ounces]. Carmen used any available paper to write information that was important to her. Presumably, Enrique and his father were traveling with the Loteria. Enrique and Carmen now relied soley on Enrique's income now that Carmen wasn't working anymore. Enrique would soon learn that supporting a family of three would cost more.

Carmen was frugal and found ways to save money. She made clothes for herself and Henry. Most of Enrique's clothes were suits, shirts, and ties that he bought. Carmen saved any spare nickels, dimes, or pennies away. They always had enough money to cover their expenses. Enrique's income from the Loteria was very good, and his family lived comfortably with the rest of Encarnacion and Margarita's large family.

Encarnacion was doing very well with the Loteria. The economy in the United States was recovering from the devastating effects of the Great Depression, and the Loteria's customers were more willing to spend their money on Encarnacion's exciting game of chance. Encarnacion was optimistic that his Loteria business was earning his family a steady income. Good fortune and hard work were rewarding his family.

Migrants: Exploring the Colors of my Family History

Encarnacion was in need of a new truck for the Loteria. He relied heavily on a reliable truck to move his Loteria from town to town. Perhaps his old truck was giving him trouble. He still didn't drive the truck. One of his son's (or the hired help) drove it for him. He went to Ormsby Chevrolet on September 25, 1935, and found a reasonably priced truck.[3] He put $20 cash down payment and promised to return the next day to make arrangements to buy the truck. The following day, Encarnacion returned to the dealership and paid $130 as a down payment and obtained a loan for the balance. The terms of the loan were $72.19 as the first payment followed by fifteen monthly payments of $36. The total cost for the truck was $762.19. With this new truck, he could carry more merchandise along with everything he needed for the Loteria. Life was good for his family.

About this time (mid to late 1935), Canacho ran a small general store on the corner of San Marcos and Arbor Place. Carmen later said that Canacho had passed his store to Enrique. The store sold a wide variety of items from toilet paper, soaps, and other household items to canned food, beans, flour, and coffee to refrigerated items like milk, cheese, and meat. It was like a small grocery and department store. They even sold costume jewelry and other such items. The store was neat and orderly, and no doubt, Enrique prepared the bookkeeping records for the store. About this same time, Heriberto had another store that he ran with a partner a few blocks away. Years later, Carmen said that they (Enrique, Carmen, and Henry) moved to the building where the store was. The two-story building still stands in 2020. It has a basement where meat was processed.

Back in Mexico, Mexican President Cardenas, who was elected in 1933, deported former President Plutarco Elias Calles to the United States on April 9, 1936. Calles, with his wealth acquired during his years in power, lived comfortably in Southern California.[4]

Sometime in 1936, Enrique had to close the store that Canacho had passed to him. Years later, Carmen said that the store was not doing well, mostly because Enrique spent more time at Heriberto's store playing pinball instead of working at his store. Enrique said that he did the bookkeeping for Heriberto's store. He didn't deny playing pinball, though.

On May 6, 1936, there was a promissory note from Frost National Bank for Canacho (Encarnacion Mendoza Jr.) to pay $50 with interest at 10 percent per annum[5] due in 90 days. His mother, Margarita, had also signed for that loan. Margarita had an account in good standing with Frost National Bank and was trusted by the bank to secure this loan. In 2020, when adjusted for inflation, $50 was worth about $931.07.[6] A portion of the note ($15) was paid on July 11, 1936, after the loan was called by the bank. It appeared that Margarita had paid the balance on August 19, 1936. It's unclear why Canacho (24) was borrowing $50 at the time, but this transaction demonstrated that his mother, Margarita, was ready to help her children when they needed financial assistance. Perhaps, this promissory note had something to do with the store that Canacho had passed to Enrique.

On September 16, 1936, Encarnacion made the last payment of $120.40 on the Chevrolet Truck that he'd purchased from Ormsby Chevrolet[7] in September of the previous year. He had previously made each payment promptly until December 27, 1935, and for some reason, skipped the January 1936 payment. Starting in February 1936, he made only partial payments. Perhaps this was an indication of some minor financial difficulties for his family starting in January of 1936. Encarnacion's Loteria was extremely profitable, but only when it operated. If they could not run the Loteria for one or more weekends, they would have no revenue coming in. Although, he would set up the tent next to his house to sell some of his Loteria prizes or vegetables that he'd buy for resale. It was also the dead of winter, so it would not be unreasonable to suspect illness or inclement weather to interfere with the operation of the business.

For a while now, Encarnacion and Margarita had been concerned about their family being deported back to Mexico. Encarnacion and most of his children were Mexican citizens and could be deported at any time. They had no proof that they were in the United States legally. Margarita wanted to ensure that the paperwork for her family was in order. For some reason, Margarita was unable to obtain a birth certificate stating that she was born in Floresville, Texas and that she was a United States Citizen. This was alarming to her, so she and Encarnacion went to the United States Department of Labor, Immigration Service on September 23, 1936, to begin the process of documenting their legal status in the United States.

In order for Margarita and her Mexican born children to file naturalization papers, Encarnacion had to prove that he was in the United States legally. He filled out the form "Declaration Regarding Last Entry into the United States"[8] as follows:

> "To the U.S. Immigration Office in charge, at the port of Laredo, Texas, my wife, whose name and address appears below, has applied or will apply for immigration visas under the Immigration Act of 1924, as amended. Name of prospective immigrants: Margarita Garza de Mendoza. Exact foreign address: Montemorelos, N.L., Mexico. In connection with such application, I desire that the American consul at Monterrey, Nuevo Leon, Mexico, be informed as to my last entry into the United States, as shown by the records. The following statements relate to such last entry and, to the best of my knowledge and belief, are accurate. I am not a citizen of the United States."

* * *

The rest of the form stated that Encarnacion Mendoza was born in Mexico and was 54 and married when he entered the United States. His entry dates were September 21, 1932, February 25, 1934, and April 18, 1936. However, he was first admitted at Hidalgo, Texas, on March 2, 1927, with a non-quota immigration visa obtained in Monterrey, Mexico. He entered his address as 219 Hill Street, San Antonio, Texas, and signed it Encarnacion Mendoza.

Now with this step completed, Margarita likely felt that Encarnacion's paperwork, proving his United States status was secure. Margarita next went to Frost National Bank and requested a letter of reference for her. On September 24, 1936, the Vice President of Frost National Bank issued a "Favorable Consideration" letter to Margarita Mendoza.[9] Margarita appeared to be in the process of obtaining letters from officials to show that she and her family were, in their opinion, good citizens. As mentioned earlier, she usually did this when she was preparing for a family move or filing some sort of official paperwork. In this instance, it was for her to obtain citizenship papers for herself and later for her family.

Margarita went to the San Antonio Police Department to obtain proof that each of her family members was a good upstanding citizen in the eyes of the law. On October 8, 1936, the Chief of Police of San Antonio, Owen W. Kilday, issued a letter ("To Whom It May Concern") that the Mendoza family had no criminal record. He further stated that "that the family had lived in San Antonio since 1932 and would shortly leave the state to Nuevo Laredo, Mexico, to properly return to this City, State, and Country per our Immigration Laws."[10]

Margarita went back to the United States Department of Labor, Immigration and Naturalization Service with all of the supporting documentation on October 27, 1936. Margarita filled out the application: "United States of America Petition for Naturalization."

Margarita provided the following information:

A list of her children (all resided in San Antonio):
- **Enrique Mendoza**, born Seguin, Texas, on September 8, 1910 [Actual date was July 8, 1910];
- **Encarnacion Mendoza, Jr.** born General Terán, Mex., November 9, 1912;
- **Heriberto Mendoza**, born General Terán, Mex., February 10, 1913;
- **Jesus Mendoza**, born General Terán, Mex., April 15, 1916;
- **Consuelo Mendoza**, born General Terán, Mex., August 2, 1918;
- **Margarita Elva E. Mendoza**, born General Terán, Mex., September 23, 1919;
- **Ruby de la Luz Mendoza**, born General Terán, Mex., July 21 1921;
- **Leslie del Roble Mendoza**, born General Terán, Mex, September 25, 1922.

Margarita signed the form "Margarita Garza Mendoza." Two witnesses also signed the document who swore that they knew Margarita: George Downs, a health officer at 410 Topeka, and her physician Dr. C. B. Alexander, at 2003 W. Magnolia [Dr. Charles B. Alexander was the family physician for her children and their families.]

Now that Margarita had filed all the appropriate paperwork to secure the safety of her family. She certainly must have breathed a sigh of relief and felt safe that her family would not be deported.

Despite some minor obstacles, Encarnacion and Margarita's family life was relatively stable and now secure in San Antonio.

24 - Sacrifices - 11/1936

Anselmo Longoria was born on April 21, 1895, in Los Cuates, Matamoros, Tamaulipas, Mexico. Not far from the United States border near Brownsville, Texas. His parents were Alejandro Longoria Sr. and Estefana Martinez.

By 1900, Anselmo (5) and his family immigrated to the United States and settled in Brownsville, Texas. According to the United States Census of 1900, his parent's family included: Alejandro Longoria Sr. (41), Estefana Martinez (33) wife, Guillermo (15), Louisa (13), Matilde (12), Estefana (10), Anselmo (6), Alejandro Jr. (2). Estefana Martinez had had two other children who had died before the date of this census.

By November of 1936, Anselmo Longoria (42) had been living alone in Mexico for the previous three years working hard to make his construction business successful. He was well-educated in the construction business and wired for success. He wanted to achieve the same level of success that he had once known in his prosperous engineering company in the United States. That business had ultimately extinguished itself after the harmful effects of the Great Depression and the suspicious fire that had destroyed his lumberyard and construction headquarters.

He brushed away the memories of his McAllen construction business as if they were ashes and focused his attention exclusively on his new business in Mexico. He devoted his full effort to apply his golden touch to his Mexican business. He paid an enormous price for this, as did his family. He had left his wife and his seven children behind. His wife, Ofelia, raised their children only with rare visits from Anselmo. On occasion, his son, Chemo, had visited his father at his factory. Anselmo hired his two brothers, Cristobal and Alejandro Longoria, to work at his business. By June of 1935, Cristobal was managing the Mansional factory in Culiacán, Sinaloa, Mexico. Likewise, his brother, Alejandro, was also working at the business. The Mansional product was very similar and a predecessor to modern-day sheetrock.

Anselmo Longoria, Sr.

Anselmo, on March 16, 1936, wrote a letter to his daughter, Delia (14), in McAllen.[1] He wrote from the city of Gómez Palacio, Durango, Mexico. In the letter, Anselmo hid his feelings behind his typed words of despair. He told his daughter that he had fought hard to obtain a future that he may never find. And as the days passed, he felt annoyed because of it. The letter sounded as if he was saying, "no matter how hard he tried, he could not see a future where he would be successful." He told his daughter that he had found a distraction when he was tired, and that was to write poetry.

Delia,

My beautiful daughter,
In the years that I have been alone here in Mexico,
Beautiful, but to this date unruly,
I've been fighting for a future that I haven't achieved.
And every day I've been annoyed.
I've searched for a distraction, and I've found it,
Writing in verse when I'm tired.

So, taking advantage today of my free time,
I write to you to request that you
receive my original composition that I dedicate to you,
that captures your essence, and being that I am a poet,
also explains my great advice to you
that you will always remember with love.

Your papacito,
Anselmo

* * *

Anselmo's poem to his daughter, Delia (preserved in Spanish):

- LA VOZ DE TU PADRE -

Tu juventud vale un millón entero,
consérvala pura como la Aurora,
tesoro de este mundo placentero....
Ama lo bello y al paisaje divino adora.

-

Alegre serás; desafía la voráz pena,
de admiradores la sana conducta.....
A tus padres dá la Felicidad eterna
y a tus hermano Evita la disputa.

-

En el baile, un hombre será tu camarada,
rodeará con su brazo fuerte tu frágil sintura,
y te hablara de amores....Mi hija adorada.....

-

¡Dile! No entiendo....Quiero por fortuna,
gozar mi juventud sin estar enamorada
y ser admirada hasa mi edad madura.

Anselmo's poem to his daughter, Delia (translated into English):

THE VOICE OF YOUR FATHER

Your youth is worth a whole million,
keep it pure as the Aurora,
treasure of this pleasant world....
Love the beautiful and the divine landscape.

-

Cheerful you will be; defies the laziness of sorrow,
of admirers of good behavior.....

To your parents, give eternal happiness
and your brother Avoid the dispute.

-

At the dance, a man will be your companion,
he will hold you with his strong arm around your fragile waist,
and he'll tell you of love....my beloved daughter.....
Tell him! I don't understand....I want, with good fortune,
to enjoy my youth without being in love
and be admired for my mature age.

Anselmo was not giving up, as his letter might have suggested. He was incredibly thoughtful and remarkably driven. Anselmo certainly was introspective. His right slanting signature, with its slightly upwards rise, demonstrated that he maintained a semblance of optimism while at the same time, he was tethered tightly to his past.

He was successful, but not in the way that he wanted. He had provided for his family back in Texas and perhaps felt the guilt for not being with them. Anselmo thought about the future of his family. He was determined to succeed, no matter what. In addition to his poetry, he played the violin and loved the beauty of quiet solitude.

In November of 1936, Anselmo drove to Mexico City in the hopes of starting a new factory there to build his patented Mansional product. This factory would be a considerable achievement towards arriving at his goal. A factory in the capital of Mexico would have certainly brought him the wealth that he desired - not just for him but for his family. At that time, new construction in Mexico was in full swing. If his pitch to build the factory was successful, he would have established three factories in Mexico. After a long and grueling day, he was hopeful as he left the proposal meeting in Mexico City and headed home.

His son, Chemo, provided the following account from his tribute to his father on March 27, 1990:[2]

> In November of 1936, he went to Mexico City to establish a new factory to manufacture MANSIONAL, but to this day, we don't know what the outcome was on this venture. He was returning to Monterrey and left Mexico City late in the afternoon, he drove all night and was passing through one of the highest points on the highway that is built on the Sierra Madre, close to a small town called TAMASUCHALE, in the state of San Luis Potosi, he fell asleep at the wheel and instead of making the curve his car went straight down to the bottom of the cliff, about 200 feet deep. He was thrown out of the car almost to the bottom and died of multiple head injuries. His car landed a few feet away from an Indian hut at the bottom of the cliff. These Indians were the ones that took the body up to the highway; otherwise, not a soul would have found out what had happened or found the body. The town authorities were notified.

Anselmo died on November 27, 1936 (b. April 24, 1884), at the age of 42, and was buried in Monterrey. Anselmo was survived by his wife, Ofelia Montalvo (36), Chemo (17), Delia (15), Elida (13), Ofelia (11), Heron (8), Jose Eduardo (7), and Alicia (5).

Anselmo's brothers, Alejandro and Cristobal, stayed in Mexico, to run Anselmo's businesses.

Years later, Carmen recounted a story that one of Anselmo's in-laws (that lived in Pharr, Texas) had told her about her uncle Anselmo's death.

"He said that Anselmo wasn't alone in the car [when he crashed].

He said that Anselmo was with a beautiful woman."

She grimaced and then continued, "Despicable! I don't believe that."

Of course, it wasn't true. Chemo, Anselmo's son, had many pictures and firsthand evidence that Anselmo had been alone in the car.

Anselmo's in-laws were not particularly fond of Anselmo. To them, Anselmo had left his wife, Ofelia, in Texas while he was off in Mexico following his passion for business.

When Anselmo died, his family was still renting the house on Houston Avenue in McAllen. Perhaps, Ofelia must have worried how she would raise her children as she grieved the loss of her husband. No longer would she be receiving any money that Anselmo would send her. Life was about to get very difficult for Anselmo's wife and his seven young children.

Carmen and Maria Luisa would have quietly mourned the death of their maternal uncle, who had saved their mother, and her children from destitution in 1929.

July 19, 1936 - Anselmo's seven children: Alicia "Licha," Jose Eduardo "Pepe," Delia, Chemo, Heron. Back: Ofelia, Elida (301177)

25 - More Family - 4/1937 to 12/1939

On April 25, 1937, Jesus Mendoza and Delia Garza were married at the Inglesia de Nuestra Señora de Guadalupe in San Antonio, Texas.[1] After they married, Jesus and Delia were both living in one of the rooms at Hill Street.

In May of 1937, Carmen was pregnant, and her baby would be due soon. Enrique was concerned because he had to leave town to work the Loteria with the rest of his family. That was Enrique's only source of income for his family.

Enrique said to Carmen, "Don't have the baby until I get back. Wait for me."

Carmen laughed. Of course, she thought to herself that the baby would come when the baby was ready, whether or not Enrique was there.

A few days later, their second child, Minerva ("Minnie"), was born at home in the second room from the left at 219 Hill Street. Minnie had black hair and was about eight pounds when Dr. Evan delivered her - the same doctor had delivered Henry. Enrique was there to witness the momentous event. Minnie cried early-on because she wanted to sleep near her parents. Carmen put Minnie's bed closer to her, and there was no more crying.

One day, when Henry was about two or three, his aunt Leslie (Encarnacion and Margarita's daughter) was holding him while

Carmen tended to some household chores. Leslie was chatting with Carmen and Guadalupe ("Lupe"). Carmen was busy with housework, and no doubt, Lupe was helping her.

Lupe had been with Encarnacion and Margarita ever since they lived in McAllen, Texas. She was devoted to Encarnacion and Margarita and did most of the cooking. And she kept the house clean and orderly. Carmen, Leslie, and Lupe had a great time chatting away. Carmen soaked up every word that Leslie and Lupe spoke. They weren't gossipy women, but they did enjoy sharing exciting tidbits about the families.

Perhaps the conversation got a bit too lively when Leslie sat little Henry down on the ledge of the open window.

It was likely hot that day, and the window didn't have a screen on it. Leslie loosened her grip on Henry. And to her horror, Henry squirmed and fell backward. Leslie reached out to grab at Henry, but she missed him. Henry fell a couple of feet to the ground. Lupe and Carmen gasped in horror at the site.

Years later, as Henry recounted the story that Carmen had told him, he said, "I must have fallen on my head. That's why I. . . ."

Henry thankfully survived that fall with just a few minor scratches and bruises. After recounting this story, years later, he added that he loved the Mexican chocolate that Lupe would make for him. Perhaps, Lupe had prepared a nice cup of sweet Mexican chocolate to calm him down from his harrowing fall out that window.

By 1937, Maria Luisa (22), Matilde (16), Marcolfa (12), and Alejandro (10) had moved to an apartment rented from an Italian landlord (possibly at 214 S. Laredo Street).

Maria Luisa's boyfriend, Pete Herrera, would come by the Laredo Street apartment on occasion to take her out for dinner or perhaps a nice walk in the park. Maria Luisa met Pete Herrera shortly after moving to San Antonio. Maria Luisa was quite attractive, so it would not be surprising that she could have her pick of men if she were that kind of person. Maria Luisa likely cared more for the type of man that was kind and caring. Perhaps she thought that the character of a person was more important than their looks. Matilde remembered, "My first memory of Maria Luisa having a "novio" [boyfriend] was when we lived at the apartments. She told me [that] he planned to marry her [Maria Luisa], but he never did. He used to call me "La India."

On June 4, 1937, Enrique's sister, Maria Consuelo Mendoza ("Consuelo"), at 19 years old died from "bronco-pneumonia" with a contributory cause of epilepsy. Dr. Charles B. Alexander had treated her from June 1 to June 3, 1937. She was buried at San Fernando Cemetery No. 2 in San Antonio, Texas.[2]

The death certificate reported that Consuelo was born on August 2, 1922 (at 10 a.m.). But according to her birth certificate from General Terán, Maria Consuelo was born on August 2, 1918. Her sister, Ruby, was born on June 17, 1922 (according to Ruby's birth certificate from General Terán). It's possible that in her grief, Margarita reported the wrong birth year. It's understandable because her precious daughter had just died, and Margarita was undoubtedly full of pain from the loss.

Margarita asked Carmen for the veil and corona that Carmen had worn for her wedding. Margarita wanted her daughter, Maria Consuelo, laid to rest with them. Of course, Carmen said yes because Margarita had paid for them. Carmen later admitted that she wanted to keep the veil and corona, perhaps to pass it on to one of her daughters.

On August 6, 1937, Encarnacion bought a new 1937 Chevrolet truck for $1,137.50.[3] The details were: Model No. 157 Dual Stake; Serial No: 3SD04-11172; Horsepower: 29; 1-1/2-ton capacity; 384 cubic ft. capacity; 18-gallon gas tank; 6 tires, two axles, two-wheel drive.[4]

He paid $500 cash and traded in his old Chevy truck that he'd bought in 1935. The balance of $190.50 was due in 90 days. The

$500 was paid by check according to a Frost National Bank statement from October 13, 1937. The check cleared on August 7, 1937, from the account of Margarita G. de Mendoza.[5] Margarita managed the checking account.

Encarnacion and Margarita must have felt that their records were in order with the United States Immigration and Naturalization Service and planned a nice trip to Monterrey. Perhaps they went to Monterrey to visit Encarnacion's side of the family. Encarnacion's family made the trip in November of 1937. A border crossing into Laredo, Texas was recorded for each family member on November 16, 1937:

Margarita[6] (United States born), Heriberto,[7] Jesus[8] (wife Delia Garza), Margarita Elva,[9] Ruby Luz,[10] and Leslie.[11]

Enrique, Canacho, and Virgilio were not in the border crossing records. Even so, it's likely that one of them had driven the family there.

The following year, on April 5, 1938, Margarita got a new pair of glasses on special for $10.[12] On April 28, 1938, she received an invoice for $19 ($10 for the glasses and $9 carried forward. $6 payment was due each month). It appeared that the family was still carrying on with the same degree of prosperity.

Carmen's younger sister Matilde remembered when Maria Luisa's boyfriend, Pete Herrera, brought a friend over to Maria Luisa's apartment, "In June of 1938, he brought over a friend named Abel Gomez. Abel was wearing a suit when I first met him. He looked very handsome. He was thirty-three years old, and I was sixteen. I must have caught his attention too because three days later he asked me if I would go meet his parents. I agreed to go with him. I was extremely impressed by his family. His father, Santos Coy Gomez,[13] was a very warm and charming person. He was a tall, thin man with . . . fair complexion and blue eyes. Abel's mother, Maria de Jesus Cadena Gomez[14] was warm and charming as well. She was short in stature with hazel eyes. I was also impressed by

Abel's sisters, Eva Slightom,[15] a saleslady at Ben Franklin's Clothing Store, Lupe Villalogin[16], a film processor at Studer's Photo Shop, and Stella Ondarza, a bank teller at Citizen's Bank. I quickly took note that Abel's family was a very cultured, refined family. Three months later, Abel, a confirmed bachelor, proposed to me. I said, yes. When I told Mary [that] I wanted to get married, she gave me a sermon."

"Once you get married, you do not return home, it is forever," Maria Luisa had said to Matilde.

Matilde continued, "Another condition that Maria Luisa set on me was that I had to take Alex with me."

Abel Gomez (34) and Matilde Escobedo (16) were married on September 18, 1938, at 4:30 p.m.

Matilde described her wedding, "I got married in an exquisite gown purchased by Abel's family. We got married at St. Agnes Church, 803 Ruiz. It was an old wooden church at the corner of Ruiz and San Jacinto that has since been torn down and rebuilt across the street from the original site. Abel's twin brother Abelino was my best man, and Bella, his wife, was my matron of honor. After the photographer took our pictures, we had a reception in the back yard of my in-law's house at 534 Delgado. We had [a] musician [mariachis] for our guests, and we danced until 3:00 in the morning. I even got to dance a rock and roll number with Abel's nephew, Manuel."

Abel, Matilde, and her brother Alejandro Escobedo (11) moved into 219 Hill Street by September of 1938. At about the same time, Carmen's younger sister Marcolfa met Claude Ordonez. Marcolfa and Claude became quite close and perhaps intimate. It's unclear what exactly happened next, but Maria Luisa or Matilde discovered that Marcolfa and Claude had become a bit too serious about each other. Maria Luisa or Matilde acted swiftly. They sent Marcolfa to stay with Abel's sister [Eva Gomez Slightom]. Marcolfa was not happy about this. One night she snuck out her bedroom window [at

Eva's house] and went to seek Claude. Some believe that she and Claude eloped that night. That's probably true.

After a few months, Marcolfa had begun to show that she was pregnant. Although she was just thirteen years old, she was tall and had started to look older than her age. Her face seemed to fill out a bit, and she likely carried herself a bit more like a person who was a few years older. Maria Luisa, in particular, would have been infuriated that her thirteen-year-old sister had become pregnant and involved with Claude. Claude was short and looked like a young teenager, even though he was nineteen.

Carmen's older sister Maria Luisa would have wanted Marcolfa to be married when she gave birth to her child. Maria Luisa and Matilde acted to ensure the wedding happened. They obtained a wedding license on April 14, 1939, in San Antonio, Texas. Two days later, on April 16, 1939, Marcolfa Escobedo, at age thirteen, married Claude W. Ordonez (19). However, the marriage license showed that Marcolfa presented herself as seventeen years old. The two witnesses who signed the marriage license were: Maria Luisa Garcia (Marcolfa's sister) and Pedro Herrera (Maria Luisa's boyfriend).

Matilde remembered, "Marcolfa got married shortly after me. She borrowed my wedding gown and veil for her ceremony. She married at St. Henry's Church at 1619 South Flores. She was thirteen years old when she married Claudio 'Joe' Ordonez."

On April 12, 1939, Enrique bought a 1935 Chevrolet sedan from the owner of Rodriguez Wholesale Grocers, located at 502 S. San Jacinto Street in San Antonio.[17] Enrique worked for Rodriguez Wholesale Grocers at that time.

Soon after, Irma was born at 219 Hill Street. She was born in the first room (same room as Henry). "Irma cried a bit because she had earaches," Carmen later said.

On August 27, 1939, Ruby de la Luz Mendoza (18) (daughter of Encarnacion and Margarita Mendoza) married Ernesto Reygadas

(27) (son of Elena Fierro Vda. De Reygadas).[18] The ceremony was held at the Iglesia de Nuestra Sra. de Guadalupe Catholic Church in San Antonio, Texas. She left the Hill Street home (sometime before the 1940 census) to live with Ernesto close to his family, which was a few miles from the Hill Street home.

On December 28, 1939, Encarnacion received a past due state tax bill for 8.40 pesos from General Terán, Nuevo Leon, Mexico. The taxes were five years past due and sent by Luis Elizondo. The letter was addressed to Encarnacion Mendoza Sr. at 219 Hill Street, San Antonio, Texas. On the bill was written: "Causante: Ruvess(?) de la Luz Mendoza Garza."

Luis Elizondo, "El R. De Rentas del Estados" signed the document. Why was Encarnacion receiving a tax bill from 1934? Perhaps there had been a dispute on the tax bill when the property that had belonged to Mariana Ybarbo had been sold a few years before.

Enrique later said that his grandmother, Mariana, had given his sister, Ruby ("Rube") de La Luz, her property in General Terán. Sometime after Mariana had died (November 19, 1930), Encarnacion had gone to General Terán and sold the property. There had been another bill for back taxes on December 10, 1927.[19] The latter tax bill may have also been for Mariana's property.

These tax bills showed that Encarnacion Sr. still had ties to his home country of Mexico. By the end of 1939, Enrique's younger siblings Canacho, Jesus, Ruby, and Margarita Elva, were now married. Carmen now had three children, and her two younger sisters were now also married. The families were growing and going their own ways.

26 - Old Soul - 4/1940 to 12/1941

On April 1, 1940, the United States Census for San Antonio[1] at 219 Hill Street indicated that the Mendoza families and Matilde Escobedo's family were still living on Hill Street. According to the 1940 Census, they rented the house. Five families lived in that house. Each family paid $3 rent (total was $15 per month).

The five families consisted of the following:

Unit #1:
- Encarnacion Mendoza, head, 62; Completed the 3rd grade; Born in Mexico; Occupation: Proprietor, Carnival Show Staff
- Margarita Mendoza, wife, 53, Completed 8th grade, Born in Texas
- Heriberto Mendoza, son, 27, Completed 8th grade, Born in Mexico, Proprietor, Carnival Show Staff
- Leslie Mendoza, daughter, 17, Completed 6th grade, Born Mexico
- Guadalupe Galvin, daughter, 39, Completed 5th grade, Born in Mexico
- Jose Galvin, Grandson, 10, Completed 3rd grade, Born in Texas

Unit #2:

Migrants: Exploring the Colors of my Family History

- Enrique Mendoza, head, 30, Completed 8th grade, Born in Texas, Bookkeeper, Wholesale Grocery
- Carmen Garcia Mendoza, wife, 26, Completed 4th grade, Born in Texas
- Enrique Mendoza, Jr., son, 5, 0th grade, Born in Texas
- Minerva Mendoza, daughter, 3, 0th grade, Born in Texas
- Irma Mendoza, daughter, 1, 0th grade, Born in Texas

Unit #3:
- Encarnacion Mendoza, Jr. (Canacho), head, 25, Completed 6th grade, Born in Mexico. Deliveryman, Drugstore
- Enriqueta Chapa Mendoza, wife, 22, Completed 3rd grade, Born in Mexico
- Fernando Mendoza, son, 1, 0th grade, Born in Texas

Unit #4:
- Jesus Mendoza, head, 24, *H1 Grade, Born in Mexico, Packer, Wholesale Grocery
- Delia Mendoza, wife, 21, Completed 6th grade, Born in Texas
- Maria N. Mendoza, daughter, 2, 0th grade, Born in Texas
- Jesus Jr. Mendoza, son, 1 month, 0th grade, Born in Texas

Unit #5:
- Abel Gomez, head, 35, *H1 Grade, Born in Texas, Plasterer, Own business
- Matilde Escobedo Gomez, 18, Completed 6th Grade, Born in Texas
- Abel Gomez, Jr., son, 10 months, 0th Grade, Born in Texas
- Alexandro Escobedo, brother-in-law, 12, Completed 4th grade, Born in Texas

*H1 *means high school 1st year*

By now, all of Maria Luisa's sisters were married: Carmen Garcia to Enrique Mendoza; Matilde Escobedo to Abel Gomez; and

Marcolfa Escobedo to Claude Ordonez. Yet, Maria Luisa (28) was the oldest and still unmarried. Maria Luisa told Matilde, "Now it's my time to get married, so save your wedding dress for me because I'm going to be the next one to use the dress." Maria Luisa must have been hopeful that her boyfriend would someday become her husband.

On August 19, 1940, Enrique sent a letter to his son, Henry (5) (translated from Spanish).[2] Enrique was in Corpus Christi, working with his father and others at the Loteria.

Corpus Christi, Texas, August 19, 1940

Sr. Enrique Mendoza,

Loving son,
   I send to you, Carmen, and the children much happiness and a hello.
Your father who loves you,

E. Mendoza

About October of 1940, Carmen said that she moved from one side of the house (on Hill street) to the apartment across the hall. She said she moved the bed herself. She was probably able to move to the room because one of the other tenants had recently vacated the apartment. It's not known who might have moved out.

On October 16, 1940, Méme Garza (Enrique's cousin), Abel Gomez (Matilde's husband), Claude Ordonez (Marcolfa's husband), and the Mendoza boys registered for the draft (for World War II).

- **Virgilio Mendoza** (34), 603 No. Frio Street, b. April 25,1906, Carta Blanca Restaurant[3] Mole on the right cheek, Wife: Genoveva Sanders Mendoza

- **Enrique Mendoza** (30), 219 Hill Street, b. July 8, 1910, works at Rodriguez Wholesale Grocers,[4] Appendix operation
- **Encarnacion Mendoza Jr.** ("Canacho") (28), 219 Hill Street, b. Dec. 9, 1911, works at Summers Drug Store,[5] Left Arm
- **Heriberto Mendoza** (27), 1419 Saunders, b. Jan 26, 1913, works at Pedro Salas[6]
- **Jesus Garza Mendoza** (24), 219 Hill Street, b April 2, 1916, unemployed[7]
- **Manuel Saenz Garza** ("Méme") (32), 915 N. Comal, b Feb 13, 1908, works at J. Valdez Meat Market and Grocers,[8] (Small-pox scars on Face), Wife Mrs. Maria De La Luz Garza
- **Abel Gomez** (35), Jr. 219 Hill Street, b. June 27, 1905, unemployed[9]
- **Claude Ordonez Sr.** (21), 220-1/2 S. Laredo,[10] [Note: Maria Luisa, his sister-in-law, was living at 214 S. Laredo]

Later, Heriberto Mendoza and Jesus Mendoza served in World War II. They may have left in 1941.

By the end of 1940, Maria Luisa was feeling ill more often than usual. There was no indication that her boyfriend Pete had proposed marriage. Maria Luisa had developed tuberculosis and she was hospitalized in the Grace Lutheran Sanatorium for Tuberculosis at 701 S. Zarzamora Street in San Antonio.

On December 10, 1940, Carmen and Enrique's fourth child Ricardo ("Richard"), was born at 219 Hill Street in the room she had moved to three months before. Carmen regretted that she had moved to this room because it was way too cold in there for her newborn baby. She wished that she had stayed in the first room where Henry, Minnie, and Irma were born. In any case, Carmen was blissfully happy with her baby. He hardly ever cried.

Years later, in an interview, Carmen said that Dr. Evan had delivered the four older children. However, her daughter, Irma, remembered that her mother, Carmen, had told her that a midwife had delivered her. Although, Carmen was very specific in two interviews (1983 and 1984) when she said that Dr. Evan had delivered the four older children.

Why had Dr. Evan not delivered any of the children after her fourth child (Richard) in 1940?

Carmen was a practical woman. She had always dealt with life's challenges head-on. Carmen dealt with the loss of her mother by being strong for her siblings and working hard at her Aunt Ofelia's to earn money for the family. She had always approached life with a common-sense logical approach. In other words, when she got knocked down in life, Carmen stood right back up, endured the hardships, and moved on. She was by no means perfect, but she was kind and goodhearted. She said that her sister, Matilde, was so much kinder than she ever was. Matilde and the others appreciated Carmen's "old-soul" wisdom. Carmen, now married with four children, was pregnant just a handful of months after giving birth to Richard.

She had been careful, even to the point of getting birth control, to prevent another pregnancy. She was deeply religious, and the church forbade the use of artificial contraception. However, she considered very carefully why she would have to break the Catholic Church's rule to protect her family. She carefully measured the pros and cons of having more children and being able to support them. She loved children, especially babies, and would certainly sacrifice to have more.

As the doctor (presumably Dr. Evan) examined her, she remembered the night that Enrique had been excessively affectionate with her. She couldn't get to her birth control in time.

Migrants: Exploring the Colors of my Family History

Now, she was pregnant again.

At her next exam, the doctor told her that both she and the baby were at risk if she were to continue the pregnancy. She was horrified when the doctor suggested that she should immediately end her pregnancy. Enrique seemed to agree with the doctor. He didn't want to lose Carmen and wasn't sure that he could afford to support his growing family. Carmen resisted. The doctor claimed that if she were to continue, there could be dire consequences for her and her baby.

At the time, Carmen firmly believed that she should be obedient to her husband. Years later, during an interview, she regretted that she had not told Enrique no, when she didn't want to do something that he wanted of her.

Her mother-in-law, Margarita, whom she adored would also (most likely) have advised Carmen to end her pregnancy. One of Enrique's sisters had experienced something similar but had fled from the doctor's clinic before anything could happen.

Carmen's sister-in-law had said, "I saw blood-stained sheets in the clinic and then realized what the doctor was going to do. I ran..."

Carmen wasn't able to run away like Enrique's sister had done. She had four young children to consider.

In an interview in 1984, Carmen said, "Cuando un aga un daño, yo creo que uno paga un ["When someone does something bad. I believe you pay an enormous price]. That's why I have my [illness] . . . Toda paga una en esta vida [All pay in this life]. Por eso . . . a mi por tener el aborto . . . [Because of that . . . because of the abortion]. "That's why I say: Toda paga una en esta vida [All pay in this life]." Carmen had severe asthma for much of her adult life.

Carmen seemed to part ways with Dr. Evans after that. No records indicated that she ever saw him again.

Years later, after she'd had all of her ten children, she had read in the newspaper that Dr. Truitte [Note: spelling may be incorrect], a doctor she thought highly of, had been charged and convicted of performing an illegal abortion. Carmen was angered that the law had condemned such a good doctor. She said in the 1984 interview, "He is a good doctor!"

About March of 1941, Enrique, Carmen, and the four children moved to the Alazan Courts at 710 Colima Street They were newly built and had six apartments in each of the buildings. Richard was about three months old. Henry went to the elementary school that was near the corner of Guadalupe and Colorado streets.

The Alazan Courts, constructed in 1939, were the first low-income, public housing in San Antonio, Texas. Families of Mexican descent primarily occupied them. Tenants occupied the building starting in August 1940. Years later, Minnie described them as beautiful new homes. Each home had a private bathroom.[11]

Historical Note: Father Carmelo Tranchese, the pastor of Our Lady of Guadalupe Church (Nuestra Sra. De Guadalupe Catholic Church), supported the Alazan housing project. He was one of the five commissioners on the newly created San Antonio Housing Authority ("SAHA"). Coincidentally, Father Tranchese was the priest that performed the marriage ceremony for the parents of Eddie Alejandro[12] (future spouse of Minnie).

Enrique worked for Rodriguez Wholesale Grocers in San Antonio as their bookkeeper. After this job, he never worked again as a bookkeeper. Later, Rodriguez sold his inventory of dried shrimp and spices to Enrique. Enrique handled the bookkeeping, so he knew the suppliers if he needed more product to sell. Carmen packaged "camaron" (dried shrimp) and "pimento," "canella," "comino," and other spices that Enrique would sell to vendors. The shrimp and spices were very smelly. Years later, when she was recounting this story, she said that her children had not liked the smell. Her neighbors most certainly didn't like the smell either.

At the apartment at Colima (Alazan Courts), Carmen packed the "camaron" in the kid's bedroom. She was up late doing the packing. A lady would come by to help her iron and tidy up the house. It was similar to what Carmen had done for her Aunt Ofelia back in McAllen as a teenager. Carmen appreciated the lady's help caring for the children while she packaged the "camaron." She was careful to have it packed and ready to go before she went to bed.

Enrique was the first in San Antonio to sell the dried shrimp packages to the bars. At the time, no one else did it. Carmen said that the dried shrimp was salty and was delicious with beer.

It was reported in print news, former Mexican President Plutarco Elias Calles had returned to Mexico and was politically powerless. Encarnacion's family had been so negatively impacted by Plutarco Elias Calles and his family, which caused them to move to Texas permanently. This news may have caused some trepidation to Encarnacion and Margarita, while thinking of their future.

On May 14, 1941, the Brownsville Herald reported about Plutarco Elias Calles:[13]

CALLES Returns to Mexico City

Mexico City - Mexico's former strongman president. Plutarch Elias Calles has returned from five years of exile in the United States without rancor against Ex-President Cardenas, who expelled him and determined to remain aloof from Mexican politics.

The 63-year-old Calles made these statements to a representative of Mexico's leading newspaper, Excelsior, in an exclusive interview.

Calles was interviewed on his son's ranch near General Terán, a small town not far from Monterrey, Nuevo Leon state.

Asked directly whether he still was bitter against Cardenas for exiling him in 1936 after he had helped put Cardenas in the presidential chair, Calles answered immediately, "No."

He also asserted:

"Under no circumstances will I ever mix in Mexican politics, again."

On August 18, 1941, Margarita applied for a job through the Texas State Employment Service.[14] She got a job at Radio Cap Company that manufactured caps and hats, for which she sewed and embroidered the lettering. Margarita was a power machine operator. She worked there until January 12, 1942.[15] She renewed her application at Texas State Employment Commission on January 19, 1942.

By 1941, Maria Luisa left the tuberculosis sanatorium, presumably to marry her boyfriend. She must have felt a renewed hope after having seemingly recovered from her treatment. Perhaps she thought that her life was turning around.

Matilde said, "Her boyfriend, Pete, didn't stick around much after Maria Luisa got sick."

She went to a friend's house and became violently ill. She was readmitted to the hospital and five days later, succumbed to the ravages of tuberculosis. She died in the most horrible, vicious way because of that disease.

On October 8, 1941, Maria Luisa died. She had just turned 29 years old. Maria Luisa could finally breathe easily in heaven and stay peacefully with her mother, Estefana, at her side.

Her siblings, Carmen, Matilde, Marcolfa, and Alejandro, were devastated. Matilde's husband, Abel Gomez, informed the coroner of Maria Luisa's death. On the death certificate, Abel Gomez listed his address as 719 Camada Street, San Antonio, Texas. Abel had stated that Maria Luisa had lived at 214 S. Laredo and had been

Migrants: Exploring the Colors of my Family History

living there for eight years (since 1933).

Matilde's wedding dress was a beautiful lace wedding gown that would surely have made an angel cry from its beauty. Matilde remembered, "We buried her in my wedding dress and veil. I couldn't forget that she wanted to be a bride and be the next one to use my wedding dress. My husband bought her a beautiful pink granite headstone with the inscription: *Best is Thine and Sweet Remembrance is Mine.*"

Carmen, Matilde, Marcolfa, and Alejandro would often cry as they remembered their beloved sister, Maria Luisa, and their mother, Estefana. Maria Luisa was buried at San Fernando Cemetery No. 2 in San Antonio, Texas.

Some years later, after Maria Luisa's death, her boyfriend crashed his vehicle into a car and critically injured a young boy who was a passenger. The young boy's father rushed from his car and attacked Maria Luisa's boyfriend, Pete Herrera. They said he died of fright, but in all likelihood, he'd died of a heart attack or similar condition. Like Maria Luisa's sister Carmen said, "When someone does something bad, I believe that you pay a large price. Everyone pays in this lifetime." Maria Luisa's fiancé, some felt, had promised her something that he had no intention of delivering.

There is a death certificate from the State of Texas that listed: "Pedro (Pete) E. Herrera, born on March 25, 1904, had died of a cerebrovascular hemorrhage with an antecedent cause of hypertensive heart disease on June 18, 1951. The certificate revealed that he was married.[16]

Maria Luisa never gave up hope. She was the oldest daughter of Estefana Longoria. Carmen believed that her sister had a different father than hers. On the death certificate, Abel Gomez and Matilde had listed Maria Luisa's father as "Manuel" Garcia. Carmen's father was named Canuto Garcia. Several relatives in the Rio Grande Valley confirmed this.

Soon after Maria Luisa died, Carmen got tested for tuberculosis

(TB) along with all of her kids: Henry, Minnie, Irma, and Richard. They all tested negative.

On December 20, 1941, Estefana's brother and Carmen's uncle, Guillermo Longoria (50), a farmer, died in Robstown, Texas, of Dropsy [also referred to as edema, a condition which is characterized by swelling of the body tissue due to accumulation of fluids] . Carmen used to talk about picking cotton on a ranch near there and that she was born in Robstown, Texas.

By the end of 1941, Carmen (26) had lost her beloved older sister Maria Luisa and her Uncle Guillermo, and in the last ten years, she had lost her Mother Estefana, her Uncle Anselmo. Carmen knew she had to keep strong and carry on because she loved and cherished her husband and four children.

27 - New Home - 1/1942 to 5/1945

On January 12, 1942, Margarita Garza Mendoza lost her job as a seamstress at Radio Cap Company.[1] She got a friendly letter of recommendation from them. Margarita wasn't the type to give up with this bad news. On the following week (January 19), she reapplied for another job.[2]

Encarnacion and Margarita had felt financially secure. Margarita had saved some of her earnings from her past job, and the Loteria was going well.

On January 22, 1942, Encarnacion and Margarita purchased new furniture on credit from Bell Furniture Co. at W. Commerce at Main Avenue for about $154.45.[3] They paid off the loan in full on June 19, 1942. Both Margarita and Encarnacion were determined to remain in good standing with their creditors. Certainly, Margarita was always vigilant in maintaining a good reputation in her community, lest her family gain the attention of immigration authorities.

On January 27, 1942, Encarnacion reported his 1937 Chevrolet truck (model no. 157, dual stake) to the War Department.[4] World War II was raging, and all United States Citizens were required to supply this information if the government needed to "Hire or "Lease" the vehicle. The heading for this document read: "CONFIDENTIAL; Highway Traffic Advisor Committee to War

Department; The government needed urgently for planning for National Defense. Please fill out and return promptly using a separate card for each vehicle you own."

On May 27, 1942, Enrique received a letter from the United States Civil Service Commission, Board of Civil Service Examiners at Fort Sam Houston. It was a notice of rating that stated that he was eligible for employment as a "Storekeeper." The document indicated that the period of eligibility for potential employment with them was one year. The letter was addressed to Enrique Mendoza at 710 Colima Street.[5] Being the sole family provider, Enrique had taken this examination in the hopes of obtaining a civil service job. At that time, Enrique and his family were living at the Alazan Courts (710 Colima Street), and he probably worried that he needed extra money to support his family and to pay the rent. The source of his income was from small bookkeeping jobs, the Loteria, and delivering dried shrimp and spices, that Carmen packed, to the bars and stores.

Encarnacion kept up with the news from Mexico; it was his home country. On September 15, 1942, in honor of Mexican Independence Day [Dies y Sies de Septiembre], the Mexican ex-presidents (de la Huerta, Portes Gil, Ortiz Rubio, Rodriguez, Cardenas, and Plutarco Elias Calles) and the current president, Avila Camacho, stood on the city center stage of Mexico City together to show their support of National Unity.[6] This united display of Mexico's leadership also demonstrated support to Britain and America in the second world war.

Enrique received an invitation to the wedding for his sister, Leslie (postmarked Kingsville, Texas, December 22, 1942).[7] It's interesting to note that Kingsville was a regular destination of the Loteria. Encarnacion and Margarita likely had relatives that lived there. Margarita seemed to have relatives all over Texas. And on several occasions, Encarnacion had received mail from Mexico and the post office there.

Migrants: Exploring the Colors of my Family History

On January 3, 1943, Leslie del Roble Mendoza (19), daughter of Encarnacion and Margarita, married Carlos del Moral, Jr. (19). The wedding took place in Kingsville, Texas, at La Iglesia de San Martin, and the reception was at George's Hotel and Cafe.

Encarnacion saved the rent receipts that he paid to J.G. Vela for the Hill Street house. There were several receipts dated from January 10, 1943,[8] through April 8, 1943.[9] It's unknown if J.G. Vela was related to Margarita.

In September of 1943, Minnie started first grade at Breckenridge Elementary School while living at the Alazan Courts at 710 Colima Street.

On December 1, 1943, Leslie and Carlos del Moral had a boy, Juan Carlos.

Abel Gomez's aunt, Andrea Cadena de la Peña, lived at 524 Delgado and died on December 5, 1943. By December 28, 1943, the "Proof of Heirship" document was completed. At that time, Abel Gomez and his wife, Matilde Escobedo Gomez, obtained a loan from Eva Orvis for $725 for the purchase of the property. The monthly payment was $12, beginning on December 28, 1943 (and paid off on January 24, 1948). Matilde, Abel, Abel Jr., and Alejandro Escobedo moved from 719 Camada to 524 Delgado Street. It must have been a wonderful feeling for Matilde and Abel to have this house on a big plot of land.

On December 15, 1943, Abel and Matilde sold their house at 719 Camada Street to Enrique and Carmen.[10] Enrique, Carmen, and their four children moved into their house at 719 Camada Street. Although it was a small house, it was much larger than their apartment at Colima Street. It was built in 1941 and was less than 1,000 sq. feet. At last, their family now owned a home of their own. Their household included: Enrique (33), Carmen (29), Henry (9), Minnie (7), Irma (6), and Richard (3).

Sometime before December of 1943, Enrique had applied for two jobs, one at Kelly Field and the other at American National

Insurance Company(ANICO) at the same time.

"I received an offer from American National Insurance Company and an invitation to work at Kelly Field on the same day," Enrique later said.

He calculated that he could make more money at the insurance company. His two brothers (Canacho and Jesus) were already working for the insurance company. (Note: Encarnacion Jr. later switched to Reliable Insurance Company). Enrique also considered that he had a "3A" designation on his draft card. That designation meant that he had deferred status for dependency reasons, perhaps because he had children. After much consideration, Enrique decided to accept the Kelly Field job. Enrique said that he would get the training there, and if the government drafted him, he could use that experience as a soldier.

At Kelly Field, Enrique had excellent benefits, including paid time off, sick leave, and other benefits. Enrique left the Loteria and started working at his new job at Kelly Field at the beginning of 1944.

On February 1, 1944, Enrique received a promotion letter,[11] effective January 1, 1944. Enrique's income increased from $1,440 per annum, Grade CAF-2 to $1,500 per annum, Grade CAF-2.

Enrique was happiest when he was working as a bookkeeper and interacting with his clients. Surely, he told Carmen that he wasn't thrilled with his job at Kelly Field.

"It was boring. Not much to do," Enrique later said. He'd been in charge of the inventory of dangerous chemicals, acids in particular. Enrique kept track of how much acid remained in stock. He later said that it was in a way similar to bookkeeping because he had to carefully track the inventory in journals. Enrique was meticulous, so it was essential to account for each ounce of those caustic acids. His two brothers, Canacho and Jesus, still worked in the insurance industry, and he thought that he would enjoy that work much more than his job at Kelly Field. However, before the end of February 1944, Jesus was drafted into the Army.

Enrique continued to deliver the dried shrimp and spices in the morning to the bars and stores and then work at bookkeeping, and then go to the "Campo" (Kelly Field) in the afternoon at about 2 p.m. Enrique had three jobs at that time. Sometimes, Carmen's sister-in-law, Delia (wife of Jesus, Enrique's brother), helped Carmen pack while Enrique's brother, Jesus, was overseas. Enrique would usually get out of work (at Kelly Field) at midnight. One night, Carmen and Delia were up late, packing the shrimp. Suddenly all of the lights went out. Carmen said that they were alone late at night. She and Delia were scared, but Carmen remained calm. Carmen knew where the screw-in fuses were and simply replaced it. Carmen was always levelheaded in a crisis. Once the lights were back on, the laughter and chatter returned. After Delia went home, Carmen continued to pack. She and Enrique had agreed that any profits from the extra that she packed could be hers to do as she pleased. Carmen wouldn't spend it. Instead, she would hide it away for when the family needed it.

Minnie completed the first grade at Breckenridge Elementary School. In September of 1944, Minnie started second grade at Ogden Elementary School while living at Camada Street. She attended Catechism at "Christ the King" church. She had her sacrament of First Communion at that church.

Carmen remembered that her neighbor, Sra. Villalobos, told Carmen that she had noticed that the kids behaved very well. The neighbor said that she saw the four children play quietly outside, never being mean to each other, but instead laughing and enjoying themselves.

In 2019, Irma recounted a story about Sra. Villalobos, "When I was a little girl, I remember visiting Sra. Villalobos…" Irma talked about a beautiful, enticing doll collection that Sra. Villalobos had. She wanted so much to pick up one of the dolls and play with it. She believed that the dolls had belonged to Sra. Villalobos's daughter, who most likely had long grown out of them. Years later, Irma giggled as she remembered the dolls.

In 1983, Carmen smiled as she remembered her four small children in 1944 and said, "They were good children." She went on to say that the four kids never interrupted Carmen when she was talking. They would stand next to her to be acknowledged instead of interrupting her. Carmen would eventually ask them what they wanted, and then off they would go. She remembered she was talking to Tia Anita once. She told Tia Anita, "One moment while I see what the children want."

Carmen had so many happy memories from when they lived at the Camada Street house.

In 2019, Irma remembered living in that small house. She surmised that baby Richard slept in the bedroom with Enrique and Carmen. The other three children: Henry (9), Minnie (7), Irma (6) slept in the second bedroom.

Carmen said they had a goat at Camada, and she thought the milk was delicious in coffee (and also in chocolate).

"Junior [Henry] didn't like goat's milk," Carmen later said. "Or maybe it was one of the other children."

Carmen couldn't remember for sure which of her children didn't like the goat's milk.

One of her children accused her of using goat's milk in the chocolate.

"No, I didn't," she said with an affectionate smile. Perhaps, this little white lie was the reason that she couldn't remember to which child she had told this.

When the goat got loose from the garage, it did some damage to Carmen's roses, especially her beautiful white roses. She loved those roses. Years later, she said that she could never find another white rose bush like it. Not only did the rose smell beautiful, but so did the entire plant.

Henry, Minnie, and Irma only spoke Spanish when they started school. They each learned English as they integrated into the school system. Richard was still at home and began to incorporate English words into his vocabulary, thanks to his older siblings. Carmen and Enrique always spoke Spanish to the children, but they too expanded their English vocabulary as they further assimilated into the San Antonio bi-lingual culture.

As a young boy, one day, a bully from the neighborhood had come up from behind Henry and stepped on his heels. When he got home, Carmen saw that his heels were bleeding. She usually told her children that they should be patient and understanding with other kids and never hit them. But when she saw his bloody heels, it infuriated her. She said, "You should have hit him!"

Henry said, "No, then he would hit me even more."

Henry and Minnie went to school at Ogden Elementary School. One day, Minnie didn't wait for Henry and decided to walk home alone. She ended up walking towards downtown, instead of towards home. Not finding his little sister, Henry walked home alone. Dread likely filled Carmen's heart when she asked Henry where Minnie was.

He complained, "She doesn't wait for me!"

A short while later, a man brought Minnie home.

A relieved Carmen told Minnie to wait for Henry after school so that they could walk home together. Years later, Carmen said that Minnie got lost twice while they lived at Camada Street.

"Junior [Henry] really liked Richard," she said. When she punished Richard, Henry would object and tell her, "Don't punish him."

Enrique and Carmen would often visit Margarita and Encarnacion's family get-togethers at 219 Hill Street. The children usually played together while the adults would chat with each other. The children (there were many) would gather together and giggle and laugh with each other. One time, Arnold (Canacho's son) felt slighted because the other children excluded him from a game that they were playing. There were about seven or eight kids gathered around the game. Perhaps it was a game like marbles or something like that. An angry Arnold hit Henry on the head with a Nehi soda bottle. Probably Arnold had assumed the bottle would break like it did in the movies. Henry was not happy and likely had a bad headache from it.

About this time, Encarnacion and Margarita were told that their home at 219 Hill Street was scheduled for demolition to make room for a new highway. Encarnacion and Margarita had enough money saved away and went in search of a new house.

On April 7, 1944, Margarita and Encarnacion Mendoza bought a two-story house on the corner of W. Elmira Street and Camaron Street at 659 W. Elmira Street for $4,000.[12] She paid $1,500 cash and borrowed the rest ($2,500).[13] After they bought the house, the renters left, and Margarita had the inside of the house repainted, had repairs done to the structure, and repainted the roof.[14]

Just five months later, on September 25, 1944, Margarita made the last payment of $1,066.27 on the house loan.[15] The following day, the bank released the lien on her house. As was her habit, Margarita always paid their debts promptly.

On October 30, 1944, Margarita paid $675 to repair and repaint the outside of the house.[16] Once they completed repairs and settled comfortably into their home, they rented the upstairs apartments. Encarnacion and Margarita (and their family) lived on the first floor and in one room on the second floor. A lady rented the three bedrooms upstairs from them. There were three adults and three children that lived in those rooms. Times were good for Encarnacion and Margarita as they continued to invest in their family's future.

Margarita had always helped her community wherever she lived. She'd done this in General Terán at their church, in McAllen at Sacred Heart Church, and the Red Cross.

On July 7, 1944, Margarita donated $5 to the Hidalgo County

Chapter of the American National Red Cross.[17]

On November 14, 1944, Margarita donated $10 to the Brooks County Chapter of the American Red Cross in Falfurrias, Texas, for the United War Fund.[18]

On September 11, 1944, Margarita donated $5 to the Brooks County Chapter of the American Red Cross in Falfurrias, Texas, for the United Service Organizations, Inc. ("USO").[19]

Margarita believed in giving a portion of their income to charitable organizations. She continued her generosity by donating to the Red Cross as well as her local Catholic Church.

In January of 1945, Enrique was still working at Kelly field. His W-2 withholding receipt for the tax year 1944 showed that his gross wages were $1,813.37.[20]

On January 16, 1945, Encarnacion donated $10 to the Brooks County Chapter of the American Red Cross in Falfurrias, Texas.[21]

On January 16, 1945, Margarita donated $8.67 to the Brooks County Chapter of the American Red Cross in Falfurrias, Texas.[22]

On January 26, 1945, Margarita wrote a letter to Area Rent office to request that she be allowed to keep the rent on her upstairs apartment at $35 per month (instead of the authorized $15) to recoup the home improvements that she made to the property.[23] It's unclear what the outcome was of this request. However, Margarita had spent a considerable amount of money, making her improvements to the house and expected to receive a reasonable rental income from her tenants.

On January 27, 1945, Enrique received a promotion letter from San Antonio Air Service Command at Kelly Field.[24] It stated that his promotion was effective on February 1, 1945. His position changed from Jr. Storekeeper, making $1,500 per annum (Grade CAF-2) to Storekeeper, making $1,620 per annum (Grade CAF-3). That was about $0.78 per hour. In the year 1945, the United States minimum wage was $0.40 per hour. This is equivalent to $5.65 in

2019 dollars.

On May 9, 1945, Encarnacion and Margarita's children drafted the following letter[25] (Perhaps, they hadn't known that Encarnacion had sold the properties in Mexico back in 1932):

WHO CORRESPONDS, KNOW: HIDALGO COUNTY

We, the undersigned, residing in San Antonio, Texas UNITED STATES OF AMERICA, of legal age, and in good health, give full authorization to our mother, MARGARITA DE LA GARZA DE MENDOZA, a resident in San Antonio, Texas to that in our representation make the Claim of the properties of our parents, Encarnación Mendoza and Margarita de la Garza de Mendoza, located in General Terán, N. León Mexico. These properties consist of a Retail Store, Carneceria La Brisa, Panaderia La Alianza, and Teatro Juárez. According to the Primary Deeds of those properties, which were illegally sold by the person in charge. The Rent Collector, Mr. Gaspar Cantú de la Garza, has rented most of the properties to Mr. A. Rodriguez and Brothers residing in the City of Monterrey, N.L. Leon Mexico.

The collection was ninety-five pesos per month, collected by Mr. Gaspar Cantú de la Garza. These properties were illegally sold in combination with the Montemorelos Judge of Letters, N. León. Mexico, to Mr. Salomón Moya, and then they sold them to Dr. Joaquín Tova. Those collections were made since the Year of Nineteen Twenty-seven and the owners, ENCARNACION MENDOZA AND MARGARITA DE LA GARZA DE

MENDOZA, received no payment; and the property was sold the Year of Nineteen Thirty-one. Whose wording you will find in the files of the Court of Letters of Montemorelos, N. León. Mexico.

And for the legal purposes of this document, we sign this before a Notary Public, in Weslaco, Texas, United States of America on the Ninth Day of May of the Year of One Thousand Nineteen Forty-Five.

- Enrique Mendoza Garza
- Encarnación Mendoza Garza
- Virgilio Mendoza Garza
- Heriberto Mendoza Garza
- Jesus Mendoza Garza
- Margarita Elva Mendoza de Treviño
- Rube de la Luz Mendoza de Reygadas
- Leslie del Roble Mendoza del Moral

In July of 1945, Encarnacion, Margarita, and their grown children went to the San Antonio Zoo. Even though all of Encarnacion and Margarita's children didn't live with them anymore, they all continued to gather together for picnics, dinners, and other outings. One such outing was at the San Antonio Zoo in Brackenridge Park, where Encarnacion and Margarita stood proudly with many of their children and grandchildren around them. In the background, the zoo animals nonchalantly walked in their enclosures and ignored the large Mendoza gathering. Enrique recorded the whole event on color film using an 8mm camera that he had recently acquired. He later had the film processed and had several copies made. By this time, Enrique had taken hundreds (if not thousands) of pictures of the family. And, now, he was able to capture the moving images of his family on color film.

28 - Living 6/1945 to 2/1947

Carmen continued to save money whenever she could. By June of 1945, Carmen had accrued more than $200 savings from the dried shrimp and spices that she packaged for their home business.

About that time, Enrique had started to look for a new, larger house. He had an excellent job at Kelly Field and could afford to make mortgage payments. But he needed a down payment. Carmen gave Enrique $200, and he borrowed some more from his brother, Jesus.

Years later, Enrique's son, Richard, said that he remembered his father talking with a real estate agent about purchasing a new house. At that time, Richard was almost five.

Enrique found a bargain of a house at 139 Aganier Avenue. It had two bedrooms, a large screened back porch, a huge backyard, and tremendous growth potential. The Bell Telephone Company was next door, and a lumberyard was across the street. Coincidentally, the house in McAllen, where Enrique had once lived, was also across the street from a lumberyard.

Enrique sold their house at 719 Camada Street on August 4, 1945, for $1,750.[1] They had bought that house from Abel and Matilde Gomez on December 15, 1943, for $775.[2]

Carmen was sorry to move from the Camada street house. She had her beautiful garden of flowers there that she loved. Her favorite was the beautiful, aromatic white roses.

"Even the stems from that rose bush had a beautiful smell," she later said. "I loved that beautiful house."

Perhaps, she too loved that house because it had belonged to her sister, Matilde. It was also the first house that she and Enrique had owned. She also had developed close friendships with her neighbors there like Sra. Villalobos.

On August 9, 1945, Carmen and Enrique bought the house at 139 Aganier Avenue for $6,500.

Enrique, Carmen, and their four children Henry (10), Minerva (8), Irma (6), and Richard (4), moved into the Aganier house. Carmen was pregnant.

Enrique didn't want to sell the dried shrimp and spices anymore when they moved to the Aganier house. Perhaps he too thought it would smell up their new house. Also, Henry and Minnie didn't want to help to pack it anymore. The children wouldn't have enjoyed the pungent, lingering odor that had filled their last house. Carmen was disappointed that she had to give that up. She loved weighing and packing the spices on her porcelain-coated red table. Carmen liked her professional-grade scale that she used to weigh the spices too. The loss of the dried shrimp and spice business meant the end of the source of her extra income.

Although Enrique and Carmen were happy with their new home, they needed extra room for their growing family. Enrique wasted no time and converted the screened porch into a third bedroom.

Years later, Minerva said that Abel Gomez (Matilde's husband) might have been the person who replaced the wooden front porch with a cement porch at the Aganier house. He was a construction contractor.

The following September (of 1945), Minnie started third grade at Beacon Hill Grade School.

Carmen and Enrique had a beautiful collection of old films (American commercial movies). Enrique must have obtained them at a bargain from one of his acquaintances. Carmen loved to watch those movies. She later said (in Spanish), "The films were hilarious American films."

One afternoon, Carmen wanted to watch one of the films. She searched and searched and couldn't find any of them. When Carmen asked Enrique about them, Enrique told her that he had sold them to one of his cousins. Of course, she was disappointed. Even so, she figured that Enrique must have had a good reason to sell them. Enrique enjoyed buying things at a bargain price and then selling them at a profit. Those films would easily have given him quite a few extra dollars. Enrique would take any opportunity to earn extra money for his family.

"Enrique sells everything!" Carmen said, years later. "He even sold my favorite red table that I used to package the dried shrimp."

As Enrique continued to sell their things, Carmen had started to get annoyed. Often, Carmen noticed that something went missing from time to time. She surmised that Enrique had sold it. Back then, Carmen would never think to tell him to consult her before he sold one of their things. Even if he were to ask her, she would have said yes. During her interview in 1983, she looked over at Enrique, smiled, and said, "Now I have no problem saying no!"

Years later, Henry affectionately recounted a childhood memory when he was about ten years old. Leslie, Enrique's sister, would often visit Carmen and Enrique. Leslie was a heavy smoker and was visiting Carmen one day. Carmen was in the kitchen busily preparing some coffee and desserts. She looked over at Leslie, who was sitting on a stool next to the sink.

"Leslie, the coffee is about ready. Where's Enrique?"

Leslie looked out the kitchen door that led into the dining room. Henry was sitting at the table. She signaled to Henry to come to her.

Henry excitedly walked up.

Leslie asked, "Did you know that I can blow smoke out of my

eyes?"

"You can?"

She took a puff as Henry got closer and looked into her eyes. Her eyes widened. He impatiently squirmed as he waited for the smoke to flow out of her brown eyes.

When an ember from her hot cigarette lightly touched his arm, Henry howled. It was enough to cause discomfort but not to burn him.

Leslie burst into laughter as Henry looked at his arm and saw Leslie quickly pull the lit cigarette away.

She took another puff and laughed. She turned to Carmen.

"The kid thought that I could blow smoke out of my eyes."

Back at Elmira Street, Margarita continued to manage the household finances. On September 9, 1945, Margarita donated $15 to the Red Cross (Brooks County Chapter in McAllen). Maria N. Narvaez from that same chapter in McAllen wrote a letter to Margarita.[3] It stated that Margarita had donated about $1,500 in total to that chapter of the Red Cross. It also said that Margarita was temporarily retiring from that chapter because she didn't live in McAllen anymore. At the bottom of the letter, Padre Jorge (presumably a priest from Sacred Heart Church in McAllen, Texas) had written a message to Margarita. He said that Sra. Mendoza [Margarita] had regularly helped at the church, and he thanked her for that.

Margarita saved these positive references as usual to provide evidence that her family was in good standing in the community.

On October 4, 1945, Bell Telephone Company sent a letter[4] to Margarita, addressed to 219 Hill Street. Margarita had purchased the Elmira house six months before. In the letter, the telephone company told her that they were not yet able to provide phone service for her because of the war. It went on to say that they were back in operation and would provide phone service in "many months." It stated that they would let her know when they could install the phone at her residence.

On October 27, 1945, Encarnacion and Margarita signed a purchase/credit agreement from Joske Brothers for Joske Eagle Certified Jobs[5] with a purchase price of $675.00. Due in 36 monthly installments of $22.13, beginning December 10, 1945, at the rate of 6%. It's unclear what they purchased; however, they were financially in good standing with Joske's, a large San Antonio department store in Alamo Plaza. Things were going very well for Encarnacion and Margarita. Enrique would visit his parents often and, no doubt, told them that he had received a promotion at his job at Kelly Field.

On November 16, 1944, Enrique received an Installation Locality Wage Rates[6] letter. Effective December 16, 1945, Enrique Mendoza received a promotion from Storekeeper, making $1,620 per annum, Grade CAF-3 to Storekeeper making $0.92 per hour, Grade 7. That's about $1,913 per year. He worked at San Antonio Air Service Command, Kelly Field, Texas.

Encarnacion and Margarita were financially stable and were able to buy beautiful furniture for their home. They continued to make large purchases and responsibly pay them off. They were making a nice income from the Loteria and were renting the top floor of their home. When Encarnacion was at home, he sold fruits and vegetables from his Loteria tent outside for extra money.

On November 26, 1945, Margarita received a statement[7] from Flowers Furniture Company in San Antonio for $363.41 of furniture. The document showed three major purchases: October 4, 1945 (Bedroom Suite, Vanity Chest and Bench), October 23, 1945 (2 - Sealy Ace Turtles Mattresses and 2 - Pillows), and November 26, 1945 (Rose Wk. Mattress Tufted, Pillows, and Toast Bedroom Suite).

On January 26, 1946, Margarita Mendoza received a personal letter[8] from Maria N. Narvaez (the secretary at the Red Cross in McAllen, where Margarita had donated over $1,500). In the letter,

Maria Narvaez wrote that she was unable to write back with the letter that Margarita had requested due to a bout of influenza. At the end of the letter, she said hello to Encarnacion, Leslie, and Leslie's son.

Perhaps, Margarita had requested another letter of reference from the Red Cross. At this time, it appeared that only Margarita, Encarnacion, Leslie, and her son, Juan Carlos, were living at home at 659 W. Elmira Street. Undoubtedly, Lupe and her son were also there.

In February 1946, Margarita received a notice from the Army Service Forces, Office of the Fiscal Director, that the family allowance for Heriberto Mendoza stopped because Heriberto had separated from the service.[9] Margarita had prayed that her two children, Jesus and Heriberto, would return home safely from the War (WW II). And, Delia, Jesus's wife, prayed for Jesus to come home safely. God had answered both of their prayers. On February 1, 1946, Jesus, was honorably discharged from the Army. Margarita was happy that her two boys, Heriberto and Jesus, were safely home from the war.

Carmen's fifth child, Maria del Carmen ("Mary Carmen"), was born at Aganier in the front room (later converted to the office). She was delivered by a midwife (Sra. Gonzalez). Carmen said that Margarita occasionally took care of Mary Carmen.

On April 8, 1946, Enrique received a pay adjustment letter[10] that was effective April 14, 1946. His new title of "Warehouseman" earned Enrique a raise from $0.92 per hour to $1.00 per hour for days, $1.04 per hour for the second shift, and $1.06 for the third shift. That's at least $2,080 per year. He still worked at San Antonio Air Service Command, Kelly Field, Texas.

Encarnacion's heart dropped when his friend, who drove the truck for him, decided to move away. The Loteria was thriving, and he needed more workers and now someone to drive his truck (he never learned how to drive). Encarnacion and Enrique talked about what to do. About April of 1946, Enrique left his job at Kelly Field and went back to the Loteria to help his father. In addition to working the Loteria, Enrique drove the Loteria truck.

Carmen was disappointed that Enrique left his job at Kelly Field because the job offered paid sick leave, vacation, and other benefits. Enrique had long been unhappy with his job at Kelly Field even though he had been promoted each year that he was there. He had started at a Junior Storekeeper, earning $1,500 per year and ended at Warehouseman, making more than $2,080 per year.

Margarita used to take Minnie and Irma to the neighborhood Winn's Store to get candy when they were young children. In those days, Winn's Stores had the latest toys, the best candy, popcorn machine, clothes, and even fabric.

Irma and Richard attended private school at St. Ann's Catholic School. Henry and Minnie attended public school at Mark Twain Middle School. Perhaps, Henry and Minnie had remained in public school because that's where they had started.

On January 18, 1947, Enrique paid an insurance payment of $10 to S.P. Walker & Company for a National Cottage Trailer house.[11] The trailer was likely the one that Enrique used to travel with the Loteria. The trailer would be the place where Encarnacion, Margarita, or one of the family members might rest or sleep while at the Loteria.

On January 3, 1947, Encarnacion received a letter[12] from a manager at Sears, Roebuck, and Co. thanking Encarnacion for the on-time payments of his previous loan. The manager asked Encarnacion to reopen his account within 30 days with no down payment.

On February 3, 1947, Encarnacion received a statement[13] from the San Antonio Music company for a Bender Home Laundry Model B-310 washing machine. Encarnacion purchased the washing machine for $266.10. He paid $83.50 cash with $16.00 per month due beginning the following month.

On February 6, 1947, Manuel ("Méme") Garza (38), Enrique's cousin, filed a Declaration of Intention[14] to become a United States Citizen. At the time, his address was 2002 Ruiz Street, and he worked as a butcher. His wife was Maria de la Luz Sanchez, and they had five children (Hector Omar, Marta Elia, Guillermo, Luz Maria, and Manuel Humberto). According to the declaration, he had first entered the United States on February 1, 1926, via the Port of Laredo footbridge, Texas.

By February 1947, Enrique had left his job at Kelly Airfield and resumed working with his father at the Loteria. He joined his father at the Loteria because his father needed him. Working at the Loteria meant Enrique would be traveling out of town to other cities and leaving Carmen alone to care for the children during those absences. He and Carmen had now purchased a new, larger home that they were expanding to accommodate their five children. Enrique would continue to earn a good income, look for extra income opportunities, and capture and record memories in photos and film.

29 - It's Time - 4/1947 to 12/1948

Encarnacion (65) and Margarita (62) planned which nearby cities they could operate their Loteria. It was usually someplace that had a carnival. They secured the tax licenses as they traveled to each town in their itinerary. It appeared that they would sometimes go where Margarita's relatives lived. Margarita had many relatives peppered throughout Texas.

Some of the cities were nearby, and it was convenient to return home after two or three days of operating the Loteria and stock up for the next town. When they were at home, they frequently set up the tent next to their house and sold watermelons and their wares.

Henry (12), Enrique's son, and Fern (8), Canacho's son, were visiting their grandparents at their house on Elmira Street. Inside the house, Henry had seen the prayer kneeler where his grandparents would often pray. They went into the garage and climbed into the attic. They saw all kinds of glassware and gifts used as prizes for the Loteria. Henry said that there was no lock on the door. He figured that they didn't need a lock because his grandpa had two large German Shepherds to protect the prizes. One of the dogs had a brownish colored fur, and the other was white.

Henry spent quite a bit of time at his grandparent's house on Elmira Street. He had lived alongside his grandparents on Hill

Street until he was five (along with Enrique, Carmen, Minnie, Irma, and Richard). One time, Guadalupe's son, Jose Armando "Pepe" (16), got into trouble when he encouraged Henry to swing from a rope hanging from the tree, near the house. Henry let go too soon and fell back-first onto a rock. Pepe got a whipping from Encarnacion for prodding Henry to do that. Another time, Fern and Henry were playing "Cowboys and Indians" when Fern peeked out from behind something, and Henry shot an arrow at him. The arrow missed Fern's eye by inches. Henry got into big trouble for that. The cousins would invariably get into some sort of mischief from time to time.

When Encarnacion was ready to go on the road with the Loteria onto the next town, he would enlist the help of his sons or the hired help. They would load up the truck with the prizes and the tent (the frame, paraffin coated canvas, stakes, and everything that they needed to set up the tent at a carnival). They covered the back of the truck with a large tarp. The truck would be safe in the backyard until they were ready to leave early the next morning. Encarnacion liked that his two powerful German Shepherds kept his property safe.

"One of the dogs had bitten someone," Henry later recalled. "Maybe someone had been trying to steal some of the prizes that were in the truck. Maybe looking under the canvas that covered the Loteria prizes in the truck."

The next morning, Enrique or one of his brothers drove the packed truck pulling a trailer to the next town. Encarnacion and Margarita rode with him. The rest of the group followed in another vehicle. The trailer was a cottage trailer where they slept or rested when they needed to while at the Loteria.

Once the group arrived, they quickly set up the tent with the assistance of the hired help. They used a generator to power a radio that would play music while the Loteria operated. Henry couldn't imagine that they owned the generator and surmised that they rented it. However, it wouldn't have been out of the question if they did own it. Encarnacion had owned one in Monterrey when he ran the Loteria and his other businesses there in 1907.

Encarnacion obtained sales tax licenses for each of the cities and counties of Texas,[1] where they ran the Loteria. They took the Loteria to Charlotte and then Pleasanton starting on Tuesday, April 8, 1947. For the next Loteria, they traveled to Wilson County on Friday, April 25, 1947. Then they went to Karnes City and Kennedy, starting on Wednesday, May 7, 1947. After two or three days of running the Loteria in each of these cities, they would sometimes go home to prepare for the next town. Other times Encarnacion and Margarita would sleep in the trailer and then continue to the next city the following day.

Their multi-city tour had been very profitable. Towards the end, everyone was tired and worn out. Setting up the Loteria, operating it, and then dismantling it was grueling work. They packed up the tent and headed to the last town on their itinerary, the City of Sinton in San Patricio County. Margarita was fatigued more than usual, but she attributed it to the demanding work that was required to have a successful Loteria. She sometimes helped Encarnacion purchase the prizes. Margarita carefully picked the prizes and later helped pack them. She was developing a persistent and annoying cough that she treated, perhaps with home remedies or medications of the time.

During the trip to the City of Sinton, Henry and Pepe (Guadalupe's son) were riding on top of the cab of the truck facing backward. The makings for a very profitable Loteria filled the back bed of the truck: prizes, tents, and much more. All of that was under the tarp that Henry and Pepe had been resting their feet. Inside, Encarnacion, Margarita, and Enrique would have heard the two kids beating on the roof directly above their heads.

Suddenly, Henry and Pepe were both swatted down with a long branch that extended well over the road. It swept their backs and pushed them down onto the canvas-covered truck. They were lucky that it wasn't a much sturdier branch that might have tossed them off of the truck and onto the road and injured them.

Henry and Pepe brushed the leaves from themselves, and no doubt climbed back up to their precarious perch on the cab. It makes one wonder if Enrique had noticed the out-stretched branch, slowed down, and purposely drove close to it. It posed a relatively harmless remedy to get the two raucous boys off of the roof of the cab and onto the safety of the canvas-covered bed of the truck.

On June 1, 1947, they were operating the Loteria at a carnival in the City of Sinton in San Patricio County.

Henry had a lot of fun when he went out on the road with the Loteria. He enjoyed riding the Ferris Wheel at the carnival where the Loteria had a tent. The Ferris Wheel owner, a friend of Encarnacion's, would let him ride for free.

Encarnacion gave his favorite grandson, Henry, a starter gun. It was the kind that shot blanks that signaled the start of a competition. The 22 caliber gun was loaded with gunpowder and stuffed with cardboard. Not long after Henry got it, he pointed it at another boy in the far distance and fired it. The other kid told his father (or maybe the kid's father saw it happen). The father, a man with a strong foreign accent, rushed up to Henry, holding a real bullet in Henry's face and said, "You shoot at my son again. . . ."

Henry understood what the man meant, "you shoot at my son again, and I'll shoot you dead!"

While the Loteria was underway, Margarita certainly would have been tired. She was a very strong-willed woman. She had helped Encarnacion many times throughout the years with the Loteria. It was always a whole family affair. However, it was becoming more challenging for her. She could not so easily muster the energy she was used to wielding. Most of her children had commitments to their own families and their jobs too. She was grateful that, on occasion, her children helped them with the Loteria as their time permitted. The Loteria was much more vibrant and exciting when her children were running it rather than the hired help. The Loteria was still profitable, but not so much as it had been a year or two before.

She was so thankful that her sons, Jesus and Heriberto, had returned home safely from the war. It was a terrible, brutal war that ended on September 2, 1945.

She was thankful to her son, Enrique (37), who had left his job at Kelly Field on April 8, 1946, to help with the Loteria. He had five children, and his wife Carmen was pregnant.

Margarita's children had long ago left to start their own families. Although Leslie and her son Juan Carlos still lived with them.

Margarita couldn't see how she and Encarnacion could continue to operate the Loteria without their children.

Enrique was quite close to his mother. Of course, she loved all of her children, but of all the boys, she seemed to favor Enrique. At least that is what it seemed. This may have to do with the birth of Margarita's and Encarnacion's first son, Jose Enrique Mendoza. He was born on March 20, 1909, and he died soon after. It must have been devastating for both parents.

It was indeed a joyous event for her to be expecting again the following year. Perhaps, God had answered her prayers. Enrique was born on July 8, 1910. His baptismal name was Jose Enrique Mendoza, the same name as her first child. She would forever be grateful to God for the miracle. Neither Enrique nor his younger brother, Canacho, would have known this. Canacho might have felt less favored than his brother Enrique.

Margarita wasn't feeling well enough to even think about any sibling rivalry that may or may not have existed between her two oldest children, Enrique and Canacho.

Instead, she would have been contending with a persistent cough. She might have thought that she had caught some sort of respiratory illness, perhaps from working so hard the last few months. Maybe, she thought that she was getting the flu as she felt pain in her chest, back, or even her shoulders. She had to have known that something was wrong. She'd begun to lose her appetite and have a shortness of breath when she exerted herself.

Fortunately, she could rest in the trailer. During the day, it was hot and stuffy inside the trailer. Sometimes a gentle breeze would blow in through the small windows. Rest for her in the middle of a hot summer day was almost impossible. And even if the weather had been cooler, her persistent cough would not allow her any peace. Her cough exacerbated the pain in her ribcage as her body expelled the unwelcomed invader from her lungs.

When she discovered blood in her handkerchief, she knew something was seriously wrong. Her son, Enrique, had begun to complain about severe back pain. Margarita immediately sent for Carmen. Margarita knew that she couldn't care for her son in her condition.

Back in San Antonio, Carmen (33) received a telegram from her mother-in-law, Margarita (62). The Loteria was in San Patricio County. Carmen was familiar with that area. Some of her fondest childhood memories were born there. She grew up on a farm near there. San Patricio was near to where her Uncle Guillermo had lived too. In the telegram, Margarita said that Enrique was ill, and she was unable to care for him. Margarita said that Carmen should come right away. At the time, Carmen was pregnant. Carmen took the four older kids and toddler Mary Carmen to tend to Enrique at the Loteria.

When Carmen arrived at the Loteria, she found that Enrique had hurt his back. Years later, Enrique said that he had some sort of kidney issue.

Carmen saw that Margarita was very ill too. Margarita had a persistent, chronic cough and looked tired.

Years later, as Carmen remembered seeing Margarita at that time, she said, "She was already very sick . . . ."

Carmen had become alarmed when she saw how ill Margarita was. Carmen would have seen speckles of blood in Margarita's handkerchief. She noticed that Margarita's illness looked similar to the symptoms that her sister, Maria Luisa Garcia, had. Maria Luisa Garcia had died from tuberculosis on October 8, 1941.

Soon after, they all left for home with Margarita, Encarnacion, and Henry in the same vehicle. Presumably, the other family members were following in other vehicles (or stayed behind to pack up the Loteria).

On the way home, Margarita felt better. Perhaps she felt relieved that she would soon be resting in her bed. It was a Sunday as they headed to San Antonio, probably via Bandera Road.

Margarita saw a church.

"Stop!" she yelled.

She insisted that they stop so she could get to the church. She wanted to pray. Given her grave condition, she would have wanted to pray to have the curse of her illness lifted from her.

"But this is not a Catholic church," Encarnacion said.

"It doesn't matter. Stop here anyway!" Margarita said.

Years later, Henry said, "We stopped at the church. She always got her way."

She went in to pray.

She likely prayed to be healed of her illness. Her God was powerful enough to work his miracles through any church.

At the time, Margarita was not aware of how ill she was. A deadly cancer was creeping into her lungs.

By October of 1947, Margarita was spending most of her time recovering from her illness in bed. Carmen may still have thought that her mother-in-law had tuberculosis. Carmen took Henry to the doctor to have him checked for tuberculosis in October of 1947. She received the following letter from the doctor's office:[2]

"Señora Mendoza: The fluoroscope exam does not show any

tuberculosis in Henry's lungs. We would like for him to come back in three months, and his appointment is for January 22, 1948, Thursday at 8:00 a.m."

Carmen was relieved that her son was tuberculosis-free. Although, she would have to return to the doctor on January 22 to know for sure. Carmen would later find that Margarita did not have tuberculosis. She learned a few weeks later that Henry did not have any illness when he returned for his next appointment with the doctor.

It had been several months since Enrique, Encarnacion, and Margarita had operated the Loteria. Enrique and Carmen had five children to care for and one on the way. Enrique needed a good-paying job. With his mother ill and his father not wanting to leave her side, Enrique could not rely on the Loteria for income for his growing family. Two of his brothers had already worked for either American National Insurance or Reliable Insurance companies, and it was good work. He applied for a job at American National Insurance Company, and they hired him. Soon after, Enrique took the job because he needed the money. On December 3, 1947, Enrique started working at American National Insurance Company (ANICO). He handled the checks working as the treasurer ("Tesoro"). While he awaited approval to become an insurance agent, his employer assigned him to head the grievance committee for the district office.

A few days later, Rosa Maria Mendoza ("Rose Mary") was born. Carmen was thrilled with the birth of her sixth child. She was born at home on Aganier Avenue in the second room (the room next to the dining room). The same midwife (Sra. Gonzales) that delivered Mary Carmen delivered Rose Mary. Both Carmen and Enrique felt blessed with their newborn baby girl.

On December 29, 1947, Encarnacion rented a hospital bed[3] for $7.50 for 30 days. Margarita had been bedridden for more than two months already. Encarnacion wanted to bring as much comfort as he could to his suffering wife. It took every ounce of strength for Encarnacion to endure the sight. She was wasting away, and her appetite had all but vanished. She was no longer able to get out of bed. He was losing her.

On January 1, 1948, Encarnacion obtained a store license[4] to conduct sales at his home (659 W. Elmira Street). It was valid until December 1948. Encarnacion had regularly sold watermelons and other items from his property to supplement his income. Now that he was no longer operating the Loteria, he needed to continue his home sales. He also had income from his tenants that rented the apartments on the second floor.

Encarnacion wasn't alone taking care of his wife. Leslie may have been there with her son, Juan Carlos. Guadalupe was still living with them. Guadalupe had lived with them as their housekeeper when they lived in McAllen, Texas. And when they moved to San Antonio, Guadalupe stayed with them. Encarnacion and Margarita had unofficially adopted her as their daughter when they lived in McAllen, Texas. Her son, Jose Armando ("Pepe"), also lived with them.

On Monday, January 5, 1948, Enrique received a notice that he had been approved by the "Home Office" to be an agent for American National Insurance Company.[5] Enrique was thrilled with the change in his status at his work. As an agent, he would be able to earn quite a bit more money selling insurance policies to the customers on his assigned route. His financial worries were disappearing. He had six children, including a newborn infant. He knew that his mother would be proud of him.

Two days later, at 8:00 a.m., on Wednesday, January 7, 1948, Margarita de la Garza Mendoza labored as she took her last breath. Her suffering was over. She had succumbed to carcinoma of the lung at the age of 62 years. Encarnacion's wife had been stolen away from him. His raw feelings had moved painfully deep inside of him. Only his tearful eyes betrayed his true feelings. He had married Margarita on April 28, 1908, and in just a few more months, they would have been married forty years. He loved her and drew much of his strength from her. Encarnacion and Margarita were such a close couple that genuinely worked together as a team. While Encarnacion was a successful businessman, he depended on Margarita for the bill paying, home renovations, purchases of furniture and appliances, and running the house. They depended on each other. Encarnacion was now alone after forty years together, and the loss of his wife devasted him.

Carmen loved her mother-in-law. Margarita had comforted her when her mother, Estefana, had died.

"I never knew her [Margarita], to say any "tonteria" [silly nonsense]," Carmen later said.

"She [Margarita] was very involved in the charity bingo games held at her Catholic Church. She always gave money to those in need. Margarita never got to meet [her new granddaughter,] Rosa Maria. It was too cold to travel with such a young infant."

Carmen paused and then said. "Rosa Maria looked a lot like Mama Margarita."

Canacho made arrangements with Joe Ortiz Funeral Home to provide the complete funeral service for his mother.[6] The total cost was $525. The siblings would have more than likely shared in this expense.

On January 9, 1948, Margarita (b. February 22, 1885, d. January 7, 1948) was 62 years, ten months, and 16 days old.[7] Forty-five family members and over eighty-five friends attended Margarita's funeral service that day. Margarita was much loved and respected by her community. Family and friends who were farther away weren't able to participate in Margarita's funeral. Encarnacion received many telegrams and letters expressing their condolences.

On January 10, 1948, Encarnacion purchased two grave plots at San Fernando Cemetery No. 2, in Section 1, Block I N, line 9, Lot 233, Grave No(s). A & B.[8]

On April 20, 1948, Encarnacion purchased a large, ornate grave headstone for he and his wife from Texas Memorial.[9] Encarnacion paid it off on May 27, 1948.[10]

On June 17, 1948, Encarnacion's ten children legally transferred ownership of 659 W. Elmira Street to him.[11] Originally, the house was in Margarita's name, leaving Encarnacion without legal ownership. His children did the transfer to ensure his rights.

The rest of 1948 was a quiet year for Encarnacion and his children. Enrique had lost his beloved mother, Margarita. His mother had been the matriarch of the family. She was kind, generous, smart, and hard-working. She was dedicated to her family and the Catholic Church and had donated to various charities for decades. Enrique now had six children and had a new job as an Insurance Agent that would provide a good living for his family and had the potential to become his lifelong career.

Resident Alien's Identification Card for Margarita (a U.S. Citizen). She was not able to obtain her U. S. birth certificate and had to register as a Mexican citizen.

30 - The Pace of Life - 2/1949 to 12/1953

Enrique had his doubts as to whether his father would continue with the Loteria. Enrique renewed his commercial driver's license on June 2, 1948,[1] anyway. The license listed his vitals: date of birth was July 8, 1910; brown eyes, 160 lbs., black hair, height of 5'5" and he lived at 139 Aganier Avenue, San Antonio, Texas.

On February 26, 1949, Enrique purchased a Clary Electro Adding Machine for $81.25, payable at $20 per month.[2] He most likely purchased this expensive equipment to meticulously record the accounts of each of his customers on his insurance route.

Encarnacion was still recovering from the loss of his wife. He wasn't operating the Loteria. However, he did receive income from rent for the second floor at Elmira and for the watermelons or other produce he sold at his home.

About June 29, 1949, Encarnacion bought a major appliance on credit for $223.75 from James Kerr Appliance Company on Broadway street. It's unclear what appliance Encarnacion bought, but perhaps it was a television set. Years later, Henry remembered that his grandfather, Encarnacion, had owned a television. It was about this time that television sets appeared in the Sears catalog.

Minnie attended 7th grade at Mark Twain Jr. High School ("Mark Twain") in September of 1949.

On January 16, 1950, Encarnacion purchased a water heater on credit from Sears for $89.95.[3] Jesus Mendoza had signed the receipt, listing his address at 118 Ruiz Street. Encarnacion Mendoza also signed the receipt and wrote his address at "659 W. Elmira Street, City."

On January 22, 1950, Encarnacion purchased a Kirby Vacuum cleaner on credit for $75.60.[4] Encarnacion seemed to be buying quite a few appliances on credit.

Encarnacion may have now felt a little freer to purchase major appliances on credit. He had the money to purchase these items, and he always paid his debts promptly.

Henry had gone to Mark Twain for 7th, 8th, and 9th grades and dropped out before he finished the 9th grade at age 16. In those days, it was acceptable for a son to drop out of school and seek employment to help the family.

In an interview, years later, Henry surmised that vision might have been the reason that he wasn't able to do well in school. Although, he'd taken a seat in the front of the class, which seemed to help. However, when he had one day asked the teacher too many questions, she became annoyed with him. She failed to recognize his inquisitive nature and moved him to the back of the class. This punishment, of course, made it more difficult for Henry to see the blackboard.

By this time, Minnie was in 8th grade at Mark Twain. Irma and Richard were attending St. Ann's Catholic School ("St. Ann's"), and Mary Carmen and Rose Mary were still at home.

One time, Carmen and Enrique went out to visit with Leslie. Henry surprised them with dinner when they returned home. He had used a whole box of rice to make the rice. Mom smiled as she remembered, "Aye, si! [Oh, yes]. We were at Leslie's. We had rice for weeks after that."

As a teenager, Henry had a small allowance. Years later, Carmen remembered that Henry's allowance was either a nickel or a dime. Enrique said that he provided for all of the children with everything that they needed, like clothes, food, etc.

Enrique added, "I gave them money so that they could buy things that they wanted that was all of their own."

When Henry would go to the store, he would always bring back something for his mother even if it was a little box of matches.

On October 11, 1950, Encarnacion received his Mexican identification card. It indicated that he was 72 years old [he was 68 years old according to his birth affidavit from 1918], a widow, and a merchant. Encarnacion was 5'1" in height and had dark skin, brown eyes, and gray hair.[5] His uniquely identifying feature was that he had a mole on the left cheek. And lastly, his birthplace was General Terán, Nuevo Leon, Mexico. [Note: Other sources stated that Encarnacion was born in Monterrey.] It further stated, "The undersigned, Consul General de Mexico in San Antonio, Texas, certifies that Encarnacion Mendoza Garcia is a Mexican Citizen, as stated in the document he has presented at this office, and from which is noted in the respective Registration Book. October 11, 1950." Encarnacion had to keep his identification card updated throughout his time in the United States because he was a Mexican citizen.

On January 22, 1951, Leslie Mendoza received a receipt for a payment of $7 she made to American National Insurance Company.[6] It was signed "J. Mendoza." This receipt verified that Jesus was working at American National Insurance Company at the time. There is a picture of an insurance company Christmas party with Enrique and his brother Jesus standing in the back row. Jesus's daughter, Yolanda (5), and son, Jesse (11), were in the front row along with Enrique's son, Richard (11).

On July 30, 1951, Enrique sent $50 to Francisco ("Paco") Treviño in Roma, Texas, via post.[7] This payment appeared to be for a loan that Paco and Margarita Elva had made to Enrique. The family still supported each other and would often help each other when they could.

Migrants: Exploring the Colors of my Family History

A month or two later, Ramiro ("Ramie") was born in the hospital. Carmen wanted Ramie to be born at home, by her side. However, Enrique's insurance would only pay if Carmen delivered in the hospital. Enrique worked at American National Insurance Company. The cost of the delivery was $50. Carmen regretted that she hadn't demanded that Ramie be born at home. But she said that in those days she obliged her husband and did what he told her to do.

In September 1951, Minnie started 9th grade at Mark Twain, which would be her final year there. Irma and Richard continued at St. Ann's, and Mary Carmen and Rose Mary were still too young to enter school.

On September 14, 1951, Jesus Mendoza (son of Encarnacion) purchased the bedroom set and the Cedar Closet/Cabinet from Encarnacion.[8] Encarnacion was probably selling the furniture that his wife had bought before she died.

On December 11, 1951, Encarnacion paid $21.78 for the property taxes for his home. The tax notice indicated that the property was worth $2,500, and Encarnacion owed $21.78.[9]

Rose Mary and Mary Carmen shared a bedroom. Carmen said that often, at bedtime, she heard Rose Mary murmur something to Mary Carmen, and then Mary Carmen laughed raucously in response. The back and forth would go on until they would fall fast asleep.

Carmen had always been sentimental. She loved to save every photograph and document about her children. She'd often put them on display for all to see. Carmen usually used her private savings to buy these sorts of things and expected Enrique also to contribute some money for these things. On April 10, 1952, Enrique paid off the balance for an "Our Baby" album with a plastic cover for $8. Carmen had put a down payment of $3 a week or two before.

Enrique added a large room that was as wide as the house and was located right after the kitchen. Enrique told her that this room would be for the children to play in.

Carmen said, "No!"

She wanted more bedrooms to accommodate all of her kids. Enrique finally agreed and redesigned the big room into two separate living spaces. Carmen had continued to insist that Enrique accept her input when making big decisions that impacted the family. Carmen was becoming a powerful force of reason in their relationship.

On August 6, 1952, Enrique formalized a contract with IG&N Lumber company to extend the house for $1,034.82.[10] The new construction included two rooms (next to the kitchen) with a footprint of ten feet by thirty feet and an outdoor covered porch (just beyond the two new rooms) that was ten feet by thirty feet. This addition turned out to be the "Cuartito" (where the washing machine was) and a fourth bedroom.

On November 6, 1952, Encarnacion paid $20.34 for the property taxes for his home.[11] The tax bill indicated that the property was worth $2,500. The bill was for $38.75, but after a discount, the balance due was $20.34.

At the time, Henry (about 17) was working at Kelly Field in San Antonio as a Jr. Warehouseman. It was interesting that he had a similar job to Enrique years before. It was quite a trek to travel there by bus each day. It may have taken Henry about an hour to get to work and get home.

On March 26, 1953, Encarnacion received a letter[12] from the United States Department of Justice Immigration & Naturalization Service with his Alien Registration Receipt Card. It stated that he was admitted to the United States on March 2, 1927. It further said that he was born on March 25, 1874, had gray hair, brown eyes, and was 5'2" in height. Note: The birth year indicated on this card differs from his birth affidavit[13] dated May 1, 1918, that stated he was born on March 25, 1882.

Migrants: Exploring the Colors of my Family History

On March 28, 1953, Enrique bought a 1952 Chevrolet, four-door Styleline Deluxe Sedan for $2,031.21.[14] It had two-tone paint. He received $295 for his 1939 Chevrolet Tudor Sedan as a trade-in from the dealer.

In 1953, Minnie was going to Fox Tech High School, and she also had volunteered at the courthouse for two or three days a week for free. Her supervisor was so impressed with her efficiency, he asked her to work more hours. They told her that they would pay her for the extra time. She made 50 cents an hour for the additional days that she worked.

In December of 1953, Marie Nilda, daughter of Jesus, and Minnie went to McCrory's Department Store in downtown and got hired for the Christmas rush. Minnie was 16, and Marie Nilda was 15 at the time. They hired Marie Nilda, but they were hesitant to hire Minnie because she seemed to them to be younger than 16 years old. They never questioned Marie Nilda's age. Eventually, Minnie convinced them that she was indeed 16 years old, and they hired her too. Minnie never revealed Marie Nilda's actual age to their employer.

When Carmen and Enrique traveled to Monterrey, Mexico, to visit family, Carmen said that Minnie would clean the house from top to bottom. They forgot to mention that Irma helped, but she had.

On July 22, 1953, Encarnacion paid $39.65 for the school tax portion of the property tax receipt for his property but didn't pay the city tax portion of $75.60.[15] Perhaps, Encarnacion had overlooked it. The property tax bill for the previous year was much lower than this one. For some reason, his property tax bill was about three times higher than what it had been the last year. Maybe he thought the tax office had made a mistake.

Enrique and Carmen's 21st wedding anniversary was fast approaching. Enrique knew what to get Carmen. He would probably have briskly walked into the department store and smiled as he thought how much she would appreciate a gift that would make her life more comfortable. Enrique wanted a gift that would be practical too. He loved shopping for a good deal and knew where every item sat in that store. Once home, Enrique hid the package from Carmen. He probably had one of his daughters, Minnie or Irma, wrap the large gift. Fortunately, the manufacturer had conveniently included a pretty card attached with a lavender string where he could write in the "To" and "From" areas. He wrote: "To Carmen, From Enrique; On our 21st Anniversary of Happy Marriage 7-24-53." Inside the card, the manufacturer wrote the following: "The PRESENT with a FUTURE."

On July 24, 1953, Enrique was grinning from ear to ear as he presented the perfect gift to his wife, Carmen. She opened it and was elated when she saw that it was a Coffeematic coffee pot. Carmen loved it. The card had a beautiful lavender colored flower on the front and inside, she read about its many features: the flavor selector, the cold-water pump, the Redi-lite, and no bowls to remove. It was very romantic. She kept the tag[16] amongst her mementos.

On August 12, 1953, Encarnacion drafted his final Will.[17] The lawyer charged $25, and Encarnacion paid it off in two payments.[18]

Last Will and Testament of Encarnacion:
STATE OF TEXAS
COUNTY OF BEXAR

Know all men by these present, that I, ENCARNACION MENDOZA, of the County of Bexar and the State of Texas, being of sound and disposing mind and memory, and desiring to so provide for the disposition of my estate, that there may be no confusion concerning the same after my death, do hereby make, declare, and publish this, my last will and testament, hereby revoking all wills and codicils by me at any time heretofore made.

1. I will and direct that at the time of my death I will be given a Christian-like funeral, suitable to my circumstances and station in life and that my just debts, including funeral expenses, and expenses of my last sickness, be paid by my Executor, hereinafter appointed, as soon after my death as can conveniently be done, without the unnecessary sacrifices of any of the properties of my estate.

2. After the payment of my just debts, funeral expenses, and expenses of my last sickness, I will, give, and bequeath to my children, and to my grandson, Juan Carlos del Moral, all my property, both real and personal in the following shares of percentages:

- To my daughter, LESLY M. DEL MORAL, 12-1/2% of my property.

- To my grandson, JUAN CARLOS DEL MORAL, 12-1/2% of my property.

- To my son, ENRIQUE MENDOZA, 12-1/2% of my property.

- To my son, ENCARNACION MENDOZA, JR., 12-1/2% of my property.

- To my son, HERIBERTO MENDOZA, 12-1/2% of my property.

- To my son, JESUS MENDOZA, 12-1/2% of my property.

- To my daughter, MARGARITA M. TREVIÑO, 12-1/2% of my property.

- To my daughter, RUBY M. REYGADAS, 12-1/2% of my property.

3. It is my will that the share of income from my

property, or, if the said property is sold, their share of the proceeds from same, which belongs to my grandson, Juan Carlos del Moral, shall be placed in trust in either the West Side Bank or the Frost National Bank and not to be turned over to him until he reaches the age of 21 years.

4. I hereby nominate, constitute and appoint my son, ENRIQUE MENDOZA as my Executor of this my last will and testament, and I direct that no bond or other form of security be required of him as such, and that the courts take no further action hereon than to admit this will to probate and record and to cause a return of an inventory, appraisement, and list of claims, as provided by law.

In testimony thereof, I have signed my name hereto, in the presence of E. G. Garcia and Jesus Morales, my attesting witnesses, who at my request and in my presence, and in the presence of each other, sign their names hereto on this the 12th day of August 1953.

[Signature] Encarnacion Mendoza [Testator]

The above instrument was here now subscribed by ENCARNACION MENDOZA, the testator, in our presence, and we, at his request and in his presence, and in the presence of each other, sign our name hereto as attesting witnesses on the above written.

[Signature] E. G. Garcia; [Signature] Jesus Morales

On October 21, 1953, Margarita Elva (Enrique's sister) and Paco Treviño sent a postcard to Enrique and Carmen from Roma,

Migrants: Exploring the Colors of my Family History

Texas.[19] The picture on the front of the postcard was Falcon Dam in Falcon Heights, Texas. Enrique and Margarita Elva stayed in close contact, even though they were hundreds of miles apart. Margarita Elva and Paco would visit for several days when they came to San Antonio. And, Carmen and Enrique and their family would often visit Margarita Elva at their home in Roma, Texas. Enrique filmed many of his family's visits. There was an 8mm film with Minnie and other family members walking at the Falcon Dam.

On November 2, 1953, Encarnacion received an overdue notice for his property tax[20] for the property at 659 W. Elmira Street. The property value was $3,360. The tax statement indicated that this was for City Taxes only. The property land value was $990; the improved value was $2,370. City Tax due was $75.60 with a penalty and interest of $7.56, for a total of $83.16. Encarnacion immediately paid it in full on November 2, 1953.

On December 9, 1953,[21] Encarnacion received a notice for the City of San Antonio, notifying him that there was a change in the assessed value of his property at 659 W. Elmira Street for 1953.

Last year's assessed values Land: $990; Improvements: $2,370; Total $3,360.
New assessed values Land: $1270; Improvements: $2,810; Total $4,080.

San Antonio's property values were increasing as the city was growing at that time. Encarnacion's expenses were increasing, and he couldn't imagine what would come next for him.

By the end of 1953, Enrique now had six years with American National Insurance Company as an insurance agent. Carmen and Enrique celebrated 21 years of marriage and had seven children. Their Aganier house was again under construction to add more bedrooms. Everything was going well for Enrique and Carmen.

31 - Peace at Last - 1/1954 to 9/1954

On February 12, 1954, Enrique filed his 1953 Income Tax Return.[1] Enrique and Carmen had listed five dependents: Minnie, Irma, Mary Carmen, Rose Mary, Richard. Enrique worked at American National Insurance Company. His yearly income was $4,608.07. When Enrique worked on his taxes, he proudly considered his five children to be his dependents. Henry filed his own income tax return and was no longer Enrique's dependent.

On March 12, 1954, Encarnacion bought a lawnmower from Sears, Roebuck, and Company on credit for $23.15.[2] Perhaps, Encarnacion figured that he would occupy his time with cutting the grass that grew in the front and the side yards. Years before, he would direct one of his sons to do such chores. But now all of them were grown up and had families of their own. Soon his daughter, Leslie, and her son, Juan Carlos, would move away once Leslie married Pete M. Rivera. And then none of his children would be living with him.

On March 18, 1954, Encarnacion purchased a Kelvinator refrigerator from Leslie's soon-to-be husband, Pete M. Rivera, for $75. He paid $25 immediately and later paid the remaining $50 balance. On the back of the receipt,[3] Pete M. Rivera had signed it as paid in full. Incidentally, Pete listed his address as 202 Crescent Avenue on the back of the receipt.

Encarnacion seemed to make it a habit of paying his debts off quickly. It's the sign of someone who has a relatively steady income and can responsibly manage his money. At this point in his life, he had very little, if any, debt. His mortgage on the house was paid, his expenses were minimal, and his rental income was steady. There was a modest balance in his bank account and a few dollars in the trunk under the stairs. Sometimes he'd squirrel away a few dollars in that trunk. But, mostly, he used that trunk to store his essential papers and journals. Encarnacion had a journal where he kept some of the recipes for the "reposteria"[4] and other bakery goods that he made back in the 1907 and 1908 (when he lived in Monterrey, Mexico). His Will was stored there too. Perhaps his wife's purse was in there stuffed full of papers that were important to her. Whatever was in that trunk was important to Encarnacion.

On March 25, 1954, Encarnacion celebrated his 72nd birthday. He'd been having trouble with his eyes. He went to see Dr. E. D. Dumas, M.D. "Eye, Ear, Nose, and Throat" doctor. The doctor charged him for the office visit and prescribed medication for his eyes.[5] Encarnacion paid the doctor $3 and promised to pay the rest later. For a day that was supposed to be full of celebration and joy, it turned into one of doom and uncertainty.

Years later, Enrique and Carmen said that Encarnacion thought that he was going blind. He was developing cataracts. He had spent many years outside in the bright UV rays of the sun. His work at the Loteria had finally taken its toll on his vision.

Some progressive doctors who found the illness in its early stages might have prescribed a vitamin regimen that included high doses of vitamins like C, E, and sometimes A. Encarnacion received such a prescription when the doctor told him about his condition. The prescription was for "Pulv. Vitamins Cebetium Original." It is unclear precisely what was in this compound, but it is clear that it was for a vitamin compound of some sort.

Perhaps the doctor had found that the cataracts were in their very early stages, and he had hoped that he could reverse their damaging effects through vitamin therapy. In any case, this was awful news for Encarnacion. Indeed, he would have encountered friends or relatives who had become blind after succumbing to cataracts. He knew that Margarita's relative, Tia Anita, was blind. Encarnacion had never needed to wear glasses before. For someone as independent and self-sufficient as he was, this condition would have been a devastating prognosis.

A week later, on April 2, 1954, Encarnacion received a letter from his cousin, Antonio, from Monterrey, Mexico.[6] Antonio had sent condolences for Encarnacion's loss of his wife, Margarita. The tone of the letter was somber and depressing. Antonio spent most of the letter expressing how horrible it must have been for Encarnacion to lose his wife. Antonio had typed the letter and signed it "Antonio." Antonio had sent the letter a full six years after Margarita had died. After reading a letter like this, it would undoubtedly have brought Encarnacion back to the day that he had seen his wife lose her fight to cancer. It was not a comforting letter.

On May 1, 1954, Pete M. Rivera (40) married Leslie Mendoza (31) in Seguin, Texas. Leslie and her son, Juan Carlos, had been living with Encarnacion on Elmira Street. She moved to her husband's house at 202 Crescent Avenue. Now, Encarnacion was living alone with his adopted daughter, Guadalupe, on the first floor. His tenants rented the rooms on the second floor. Leslie likely kept her room on the first floor for a while longer.

On May 26, 1954, Henry (19) signed up for the United States Air Force.[7] Henry's enlistment may have been bittersweet for Encarnacion. He was undoubtedly proud of Henry but would have missed one of his favorite grandsons.

In May of 1954, the United States Immigration Service began "Operation Wetback." It was a program to "manage" the illegal border crossings and illegal aliens over-extending their stay in the United States. Encarnacion might have felt threatened with the

Migrants: Exploring the Colors of my Family History

program and the fear of deportation.[8]

By June of 1954, Henry's first assignment was at Lackland Air Force Base in San Antonio, Texas. His family was happy that Henry was nearby. Lackland was on the far west side of San Antonio, where the new airmen started their training.

Enrique and Carmen wasted no time in visiting Henry at Lackland Air Force Base. The whole family (Enrique, Carmen, Minnie, Irma, Richard, Mary Carmen, Rose Mary, and Ramie) piled into their 1952 Chevy. Enrique drove out U.S. Highway 90, headed to Lackland Air Force Base. Carmen brought her Brownie box camera. It was the kind that you held at waist level and looked down into its large viewfinder. Enrique brought his camera too. Henry greeted them when the exuberant bunch arrived. He was proudly dressed in his khaki uniform and wearing his hat. Perhaps, three-year-old Ramie was the most excited to see the monstrously sized propeller planes up close. Enrique posed for a picture while holding the tip of an enormous propeller blade that was more than twice his size. They took quite a few pictures: Carmen standing with Henry, Enrique standing with Henry, Ramie standing solo with Henry's hat, Carmen and Enrique with Henry, and so many more, including one with Henry saluting as he looked straight into the camera. Enrique took a picture of Minnie taking a picture of Carmen and her children, all standing together at attention. The photograph that Minnie took showed Carmen and the children smiling with their arms relaxed at their sides. It was fun and exciting for the whole family to visit with Henry at Lackland Air Force Base. Before Enrique and his family left, Richard took a picture of the family under the enormous propellers of the aircraft that were on display. And then Richard took one last picture of Enrique standing next to his 1952 Chevy with the family loaded and waiting inside of the car.

In June of 1954, Encarnacion and his children's families gathered together at a park in or near San Antonio. They posed for a group picture where the adults stood in the back row and the children in the front. In the back row, from left to right, Jesus held his son (Joe), Pepe, Lupe, Encarnacion, Carmen, Enrique, Fernando, Canacho, Enriqueta, and Delia. In the front row were Yolanda, Mary Carmen, Rose Mary, Maria Enriqueta (daughter of Canacho and Enriqueta), Ramie, Richard, Gilbert, and Arnold (the latter two, sons of Canacho and Enriqueta). The families got together often for picnics.

As the years passed, the value of Encarnacion's house continued to rise, as did the property taxes. He was able to pay the taxes easily enough. His income was primarily from the rents he collected from his upstairs tenants. He'd retired from the Loteria shortly after his wife died back in 1948. However, he most certainly had a ragtag collection of prizes and artifacts of his once-thriving Loteria stored in the garage. He could still sell some of that if he wanted, and occasionally, he did. He had given some of the canvas that he had used for the Loteria tent to Enrique. Enrique had installed it on the back porch of the Aganier house to shade the porch. No matter. Encarnacion's income had decreased after he retired from the Loteria. His only expenses were for a small loan from Alamo National Bank and the upkeep of the Elmira house.

When his Loteria was active, Encarnacion enjoyed the success of the Loteria. He knew the business well and knew where the Loteria would perform best. He knew the carnival circuit well too. During that time, his wife was alive. Now that he was a widower and the Loteria was a fading memory, he had time to spend with his children and grandchildren.

On the Fourth of July of 1954, the family got together for another picnic. Henry joined the family at the celebrations. He arrived at the Aganier house first as they prepared for the picnic. He was dressed in his khaki uniform and posed for the camera with Leslie, who was wearing a beautiful pearl necklace with matching earrings. They stood on the sidewalk next to the whitewashed walls of the Bell Telephone Company building.

July 1954 - Leslie and Henry pose in front of the phone company (300248)

Meanwhile, in the backyard, Carmen watered her plants while her children, Rose Mary, Mary Carmen, Ramie, and Minnie, stood by. Perhaps, the younger children were anxiously awaiting the trip to the park. As Carmen watered the plants, she paused to admire a corn stalk that had grown much taller than her. Perhaps, she had planted it in remembrance of the life she had loved on the "Ranchitos" where she had grown up. A second one, barely two feet tall, was growing three feet away from the first one.

The real fun started later at the picnic, recorded on film and pictures. The children waved little United States flags in excitement. Perhaps they had learned in school that the celebration of freedom was what the flag represented. They ran around waving their flags for the fun of it. Yolanda had her arm around Rose Mary as they stood next to Ramie and Mary Carmen. At the picnic table, Delia, Jesus, Joe, Carmen, Jesse, and Marie Nilda ate and drank from the aluminum tumblers. Later, Rose Mary and Yolanda stood waving a flag in their left hand as they held their right hands firmly over their hearts. Perhaps, the children had learned the significance of Independence Day and about patriotism.

On July 6, 1954, Encarnacion made the last payment on a loan. He wrote, "El Ultimo Pago" (The Last Payment) on the back of a receipt from Alamo National Bank.[9] It was an installment payment of $10.46 per month, with the last one in the amount of $10.50. He seemed relieved to pay off this loan that started two years before. It looked like he was getting his affairs in order. Another translation of "El Ultimo Pago" could be "The Ultimate Sacrifice."

Encarnacion had completed his Will eight months before (on August 12, 1953).

Encarnacion did not drive. He would often walk or take the bus to one of his children's houses. When he went to Enrique and Carmen's house, they would enjoy a leisurely time having coffee and desserts. Encarnacion knew all of Enrique and Carmen's children up until Ramie. He knew all of his grandchildren that were born through 1954. The young ones enjoyed it when Encarnacion reached into his pocket and gave them a piece of candy. He always had candy in his pocket for just such an occasion.

The rest of Encarnacion's children became aware of their father's concern about going blind and subsequently being unable to care for himself. It's unclear how they became aware of it, but once they knew, then it fell to them to decide what to do with their father. In the past, they had always agreed on a course of action for significant life-events as a family. That's how they decided to move to San Antonio back in 1932.

Encarnacion's children had been trying to decide who would take care of their father. Their solution, which they thought would be simple: Encarnacion would stay with each family for a short time and then move on to the next. They would all share in their responsibility of looking after their father. From their point of view, this was a generous solution, especially since most of Encarnacion's children's families were still growing. And each of his children worked hard to provide for their own families. Taking on the responsibility as their father's caretaker was daunting for them.

On September 2, 1954, Encarnacion was at one of his son's house. It appeared that many of Encarnacion's children had gathered there. Later that day, there was a heated argument at the family gathering. Encarnacion left in a huff. He was angry and upset.

Years later, when Enrique was recounting the story to his son, Rogelio, Enrique wouldn't say what specifically the disagreement had been about, but that his father had left upset and walked home. Enrique seemed slightly agitated as he said, "it wasn't that far, but —"

It must not have been easy for Enrique to recount what had happened that day, 35 years before.

Encarnacion walked alone to his house, which was a few blocks from his son, Canacho's house. Encarnacion's vision was not bad enough to keep him from finding his way back to the safety of his home at 659 W. Elmira Street.

While he walked home to his house, what had he been thinking? Would the walk home have calmed him down, or would he have been getting angrier and angrier as each step brought him closer to his house? Had he become resigned to an imagined fate?

There may have been much bigger questions looming before Encarnacion: "How can I take care of myself now that I am going blind? What will I do? How can I live with this burden?"

For a fiercely independent person, this was a big deal.

His wife, Margarita, had died six years before. She had been his rock - his reason for being. Both Encarnacion and Margarita were strong-minded and independent people who worked together to provide for their children. If Margarita were still alive, she would have squelched his fears. But now, it seemed to him that he would have to face his blindness alone. Could he have possibly thought that he was becoming a burden to his children too?

When he arrived home, did he chat with anyone, or was he alone? Perhaps the tenants that lived upstairs hadn't heard him come home.

Encarnacion had a prayer kneeler where he would kneel and pray. Had he used it that night?

He probably wouldn't have been able to sleep that night. How could he sleep with the weight of the world resting solidly on his shoulders? A good night's sleep might have staved off his dark feelings. Perhaps closing his eyes might have reminded him of what he thought was coming for him - eternal darkness.

He made his way to the closet under the stairs that led to the apartments where his tenants lived.

Inside was a trunk where he kept his valuables and important papers. He had $45 in there. He did not lack money.

He walked into the closet beneath the stairs and sat on his large trunk, with his important papers and cash. He had a handgun in his hand. It was heavy.

He took the gun, pointed it to his head, and shot.

If Lupe were asleep, she would have jumped from her bed from the thunderous explosion that sounded and surely shook the walls. Lupe would have called out to Encarnacion and would not have gotten an answer.

On September 3, 1954, at about 6:00 a.m., Encarnacion, patriarch and father, died. He died from a self-inflicted gunshot wound to the head.[10]

Encarnacion was 72 years old. Encarnacion's children may have felt some guilt over just having a disagreement the day before. The family would be grieving probably for years to come.

Encarnacion Mendoza, Alien Registration Receipt Card

32 - Aftermath - 1954

Little Mary Carmen (8) answered the phone on the morning of Friday, September 3, 1954.

"Hello," she said innocently.

On the phone, she heard her Aunt Leslie's whimpering tone. She'd never heard Leslie speaking softly like that before. Usually, when Leslie called, she spoke with a loud, quick pace interspersed with puffs on her cigarette. But this time she was speaking slowly and softly. Nevertheless, Mary Carmen recognized Leslie's distinctive voice.

"Let me talk to your Papa," said Leslie, her voice quivering.

Mary Carmen turned from the phone.

"Pop, it's for you," she yelled out.

Mary Carmen could hear Leslie crying.

Enrique picked up the phone.

Mary Carmen could see the shock in her father's face as he nodded and said an occasional, "Si, Si."

He hung up the phone, his eyes swollen with sadness.

When he told Carmen that his father had died, Carmen gasped.

"Aye, Dios mio [Oh my God]!" she said.

Enrique's adrenaline forced him to focus beyond the unthinkable. He rushed to his father's house.

Carmen recounted later, "I wish I knew that he was suffering that much. I would have said that he could live with us."

Carmen stayed home with the children. She always stayed home with the children. She hadn't worked at a job outside the house for nearly twenty years, since 1935 when her son, Henry, was born. Enrique had wanted her to stay home to raise their son.

Enrique and Carmen had received Encarnacion to their home often over the last few months. He'd often take the bus since he never learned to drive. He was retired from the Loteria. He would have coffee and some sort of dessert. He had owned a bakery in Weslaco, Texas, and also in Mexico, where he had made a delicious assortment of pastries and candies. He most definitely enjoyed a sweet pastry while he chatted with Enrique and Carmen.

Carmen had said that Encarnacion had told her that he was going blind. Of course, she didn't think that it was true. Carmen knew about the advances in eye care. She'd read about it in the newspapers and most certainly discussed it with Tia Anita, who would also visit now and again. Tia Anita was blind. Encarnacion had told Carmen about the medicine that he took for his eyes. She knew that he was still lonely from the loss of his wife. Carmen, too, missed her mother-in-law, Margarita. She had thought of Margarita as her mother after Carmen's mother, Estefana, died. Carmen noticed that Encarnacion had seemed more somber than usual the last time that Carmen had seen him. He was always a serious person, at least as long as she'd known him. She didn't know him that well, not because she didn't care to, but rather because Encarnacion was a private person. He always portrayed the face of a proud, successful businessman.

Carmen had always been closer to Margarita than to Encarnacion. She'd never heard Margarita utter a swear word in her presence. She couldn't say the same about Encarnacion. Of course, she still cared for him and prepared the coffee and dessert when he came to visit. Carmen was busy taking care of her seven children, cleaning the house, cooking dinner, and performing other housekeeping duties. Enrique spent more time with his father than she ever did.

Enrique had told her stories about his parents. However, most of those stories revolved around him. Even so, she'd always been curious about his family. Perhaps it was because she knew virtually nothing about her father and had no way of learning anything more about him since her mother was already dead. Her mother had told Carmen that her father, Canuto Garcia, had gone off to the war and had never returned. She'd always been curious about who he was, but she thought it not proper to ask her mother about him. If her mother had wanted to tell her, she would have. Perhaps it was a secret her mother purposely chose not to reveal to spare Carmen the humiliation of the scandalous truth about her father. Had Estefana chosen to tell Carmen the truth about Canuto Garcia, she might have told Carmen that he was married and living in San Patricio, Texas with his family.

Perhaps Carmen was motivated to learn more about Enrique's family because she didn't want to know the truth about unpleasant things from her past. Her uncle, Anselmo Longoria Sr., who had died in 1936, knew the truth about Carmen's father. Scandalous rumors had circulated about Anselmo too. Carmen found those rumors distasteful and preferred to focus on the more positive aspects of her and Enrique's lives.

Years later, Carmen seemed to remember more about the history of Enrique's family than he did. Of course, she enjoyed talking to all of his sisters and his brother's wives. They, too, would tell her stories about their past. The Mendoza siblings were a tight-knit family. They would always get together at each of their homes. Often, the men would be playing some game, maybe poker, and the women would congregate nearby having coffee and dessert as they chatted about the goings-on in the family. Carmen had a sharp memory and remembered everything that they discussed.

Enrique arrived at his father's house. The police were there conducting their investigation while Enrique, Leslie, and other family members were a short distance away. Perhaps they were sitting at the table in the dining room where they had often had family gatherings. No matter, they were within earshot of the police.

Leslie was crying at the loss of her father. She was the youngest of the family.

"I killed him! I killed him!" she said between her tears.

Enrique was alarmed. His eyes were wide with shock.

"Be quiet. The police will hear you," whispered Enrique.

Of course, she didn't kill her father. But she may have had words with her father the night before. Or perhaps she'd felt guilty when she moved out of Encarnacion's house just three months earlier when she married Pete Rivera.

After the police left, Briggs-Dubelle Funeral Directors removed the body. They had arrived there soon after the police. The funeral company was only five blocks away (125 W. Elmira Street), so it would make sense that they would come so quickly. Perhaps the police had called them. In any case, Enrique and his brother Jesus handled the funeral paperwork, although other family members might have participated in the details regarding the funeral services. Both Enrique and Jesus signed the paperwork. In it, they had agreed to pay $425 for funeral services for Encarnacion Mendoza, which included a casket, preparation of remains, and complete funeral services. They also agreed to pay for a "12 Gauge Steel Vault" for another $175.

Note: The steel vault was a heavily fortified, sealed container into which the coffin was placed. Once in the ground, the vault (or grave liner) protected the casket and ensured that the earth above wouldn't sink due to the weight of the ground. Although rarely required by law, most cemeteries required that a steel vault to be used to preserve the aesthetics and reduce maintenance costs of the lawn above.

Enrique and Jesus agreed to pay the total amount due of $600 by September 15, 1954.[1] Five days later, Enrique paid the $610.[2] This cost included $10 for an extra car. Encarnacion had a large family: Enrique (44), Canacho (43), Heriberto (41), Jesus (38), Margarita (35), Ruby (33), Leslie (32), and Virgilio (48).

The funeral company was quite efficient. On the unruled side of a 4 inch by 6-inch index card they wrote:

BRIGGS-DUBELLE
Funeral Directors
123 W. Elmira Street
　Name: Encarnacion Mendoza
Passed Away Friday Morning
Remains are at Briggs-Dubelle Funeral Home, 123 W. Elmira Street.
Rosary will be Sunday Night at 7:30 at the Funeral Home.
Mass will be Monday Morning at 8:00 at the San Fernando Cathedral, and Prayers will be said at 7:30 morning at the Funeral Home before going to the Cathedral.

The evening of Encarnacion's death, the family wasted no time in notifying the relatives about the terrible passing of their beloved father. They compiled a list of all the relatives who should know of Encarnacion's death.[3] They listed them as Teran (General Terán), Monterrey (Mexico), Texas, and Ciudad (City). On a scratch piece of paper, they also had written a list of people under the heading of San Antonio. Presumably, the San Antonio relatives and friends could be contacted immediately by telephone or in-person.

Carmen or Enrique contacted the Red Cross, and they notified

Henry at Scott Air Force Base in Illinois. He'd been there just a few weeks. He was very close to his grandfather. Henry arrived a few days after the funeral. Henry signed the "Journal of Funeral Attendees." He stayed for a few days to pay his respects and then left for McGuire Air Force Base in New Jersey.

The Funeral service provided a lovely guest book called "Cherished Memories.[4]" In its first few pages it contained the following:

"In Memory of Encarnacion Mendoza, born in Monterrey, Nuevo Leon, Mexico, on March 25, 1879, and died on September 3, 1954, at the age of 75 years, 5 months, and 9 days."

This birth date contradicted his birth affidavit that he had filed in General Terán, Nuevo Leon, with the Mexican government on May 1, 1918.[5] There he stated that he was born on March 25, 1882.

Father Joe Gutierrez presided over Encarnacion's funeral mass at San Fernando Cathedral at 8:00 a.m. on September 6, 1954, in downtown San Antonio. Encarnacion was buried at San Fernando Cemetery No. 2, next to his wife, Margarita Garza Mendoza. The headstone had lovely pictures of each of them. It was healing to the family that Encarnacion and Margarita were happy and together at last.

Western Union telegrams of condolences arrived on September 7, 1954, from the families of Arthur C. Maldonado[6] and Jesus Garcia Guajardo.[7] Both of them were from Monterrey, Mexico. There were enormous outpourings of love from the multitude of relatives and friends. Encarnacion relatives and friends in Monterrey, Mexico, where he grew up, respected him. His life changed direction when he met the love of his life, Margarita Garza, who was from General Terán. In 1908, they married in Montemorelos and then began their life together in General Terán, where they had their family and had grown his businesses. Some say that Encarnacion had even been Mayor of General Terán at one time.

Under the threat of death, he and his family had fled to Texas in 1927. There he started a bakery and operated a traveling Loteria. He was quite resourceful in his life. Never had his family suffered through the hardship of poverty. He was quite gifted at navigating through life with his keen sense of family and his stellar entrepreneurial skills. Both he and his wife had left their children with everything that they needed to thrive and grow in the United States.

Encarnacion and Margarita had sacrificed much to bring their family to the United States, where they would all be free to live without the imminent threats of extortion and even death threats that they'd grown accustomed to in Mexico. The one thing that neither Encarnacion nor Margarita could do was to protect their children from prejudice. Instead, they taught their children to endure the discrimination, for it was far less harmful to them than the harm that had threatened them in Mexico. Encarnacion's life was over; the lives of his children were not.

33 - Rebuilding - 1954 to 1955

Carmen might have had reservations when Enrique had told her that he was the Executor of his father's estate. Enrique would have no trouble creating the financial accounting to capture the state of Encarnacion's finances and distribute them equitably among the eight heirs. Carmen might have thought about the Elmira house. Would they sell it right away and distribute the proceeds? Would they keep the house and share the collected rents from the tenants who lived upstairs? Carmen might have wondered how a family of competitive, business-minded siblings might feel about Enrique managing their father's estate.

Had Encarnacion named his son, Enrique, as the Executor of his estate because Enrique had excellent accounting skills and would be able to distribute his estate equitably? Or was it because he was the eldest son, and that was who usually handled these matters in a family? Whatever the reason, Encarnacion had trusted Enrique to carry out his wishes.

As part of his duties, Enrique prepared an account reconciliation for his father's estate on September 23, 1954.[1] On that reconciliation was a line item for $20 to an Eye Specialist. When Enrique saw that line item, he most certainly remembered how his father had been acutely distressed about losing his sight. Enrique found that Encarnacion had paid up all of his loans. Encarnacion managed the budgets of all of the businesses that he had, including the Loteria. He was an astute businessman. However, Margarita had managed their home finances until she died in 1948. Being a very responsible person, Encarnacion would not have wanted to leave his children with any financial burden. The Elmira house was worth $5,000, and its tenants were: Homero Garza, Manuel Saldaña, Santos & Carmela Acevedo, Mrs. Rosa H. Valdez, and Miss Clayton, who was renting the garage. Guadalupe Galvan (mother of Jose Armando "Pepe" Galvan), was living on the first floor.

On October 7, 1954, the heirs (Enrique, Canacho, Heriberto, Jesus, Ruby Mendoza Reygadas, Ernesto Reygadas, Leslie Mendoza Rivera, and Francisco "Paco" Treviño) signed a document in which they promised to pay $500 to each, Guadalupe Galvan and Virgilio Mendoza, upon the sale of 659 W. Elmira Street.[2] The heirs agreed that Virgilio and Guadalupe should receive something from the estate. [Note: Paco was the husband of Margarita Elva Mendoza].

All of Encarnacion's children had been working at their jobs, earning a respectable salary, and raising their families. By the end of 1954, Enrique (44) had earned $5,530.75 while working at American National Insurance Company (ANICO). Enrique had been working there since December of 1947, just a few weeks before his mother died. In January of 1955, he prepared his income tax return.[3] He listed he and his wife, Carmen (40), as well as their six dependents (children): Minnie (17), Irma (15), Richard (14), Mary Carmen (8), Rose Mary (7), and Ramie (4).

Enrique's oldest son, Henry (19), was stationed at Palm Beach Air Force Base in Florida for training. Henry had sent his mother, Carmen, a postcard on January 14, 1955.[4] In it, he told her that he would be leaving on February 2, 1955, to McGuire Air Force Base in Trenton, New Jersey. He wanted to make sure that his mother had his correct address since she had sent him a letter with five dollars to New Jersey when he was in Florida. The letter had found its way to him, nevertheless. He had needed that money sooner than he had received it.

Henry sent another postcard on February 5, 1955, from McGuire Air Force base in Trenton, New Jersey.[5] He proudly told them that he had just arrived there and that his title was "Passenger and Operations Specialist." He went on to say that he worked six days on, then two days off. As he integrated into life in the Air Force, he had found a world where he could exploit his passions. It was a healthy distraction from the loss of his grandfather; he missed him dearly. Encarnacion, who had always been very protective of Henry, would have been very proud of him.

The government deducted a small sum of money each month from Henry's paycheck and sent it to his mother. Carmen would squirrel it away in one of her many hiding places. She was frugal and saved such money to use whenever it was necessary. From time to time, Henry would call home, asking for cash for unexpected expenses.

Henry would reciprocate with cash and gifts when he had the funds. He had bought a tape recorder for his father. Henry had a tape recorder also and thought it would be an excellent way for Henry and the family to "chat" back and forth instead of using the costly telephone service (or the very slow mail). Enrique was testing the recorder when Enrique had called Henry. Enrique had the recorder set up with the microphone right next to the phone. Carmen spoke first as Enrique sat beside her.

The recorder had trouble picking up Henry's side of the conversation as Carmen held the telephone tightly against her ear. Occasionally, she would pull it slightly from her ear, and it was easier for the tape recorder to pick up parts of his conversation.

Henry asked, "How much money do you have?"

Carmen hesitated.

"I have the $25 that you sent for the machine," she said as she looked at the tape recorder that was recording their conversation.

Henry asked, "I need $50. Can you send $50?"

Carmen hesitated as alarm crept into her voice.

"Why do you need the money?" she asked. She was suddenly concerned that something was wrong. Henry explained the reason, and she said, "Oh, I see. That's too bad. Why don't you talk to your father? Okay. Here he is."

She abruptly passed the phone back to Enrique.

Enrique listened as Henry explained why he needed the money.

"I don't have any money. Maybe your Mama . . . I can send you $25 tomorrow," said Enrique.

Henry explained further, ". . . $50 . . ."

"Well, I can send you $25 tomorrow and the rest we can figure out. You can't pay it over time?" Enrique asked.

". . . No . . ."

"Well, I'll send you $25 or $30 tomorrow. Well, goodbye, son," said Enrique dismissively. He didn't like giving up money.

Henry said goodbye. Enrique hesitated as if he wanted to say something more and then hung up the phone. It was the kind of phone that when you put the phone back on its cradle, it would end the call. Enrique admired his new recorder briefly and stopped recording. Carmen and Enrique discussed the matter a while longer, and then Enrique went back to fiddling with the tape recorder, and Carmen went back to her chores. Carmen had seen Minnie and Irma working on their schoolwork.

At the time Minnie was attending San Antonio College ("SAC") and Irma was attending Ursuline Academy. Irma was quite knowledgeable, and had a knack for drilling deep into her studies. She had quite a gift to be able to absorb details efficiently about the subjects that interested her. If she didn't know the answer, she would do fastidious research. That was one of her many strengths. She was quite the intellectual and a veritable font of knowledge in a wide variety of topics. Occasionally, when Minnie struggled to solve one of her homework problems, she would ask Irma. Of course, she could count on Irma to help her out. But, in Minnie's estimation, it would come at a price. The answer would come with the details that would support Irma's response. Irma would provide references that supported her answer. She would explain more detail than Minnie had wanted. Irma just wanted to be thorough.

Carmen later said, "Minnie didn't like that. She just wanted a concise answer."

Enrique continued to work on his father's estate and was excited that his siblings had agreed to sell the Elmira house.

On July 22, 1955, Enrique wrote up a contract and got all of his sibling's signatures except for his sister, Margarita Elva.[6] Perhaps he got her signature later because she lived in Roma, Texas. In the contract, it stated that Enrique could sell it to a real estate company for $10,000 or more and pay 5% to the real estate company. That was twice the property tax appraised value of the Elmira house. Maybe they hoped a commercial buyer might pay that much. In the mean time, Enrique continued to perform his executor duties. He continued to collect the rent from the Elmira house and pay the utility bills and hoped for a buyer.

On July 24, 1955, Carmen, Enrique, Carmen's sisters, Matilde, and Marcolfa, and most of their children had a family get-together at San Pedro Park. At the time, Enrique and Carmen had seven children Henry (20), Minnie (18), Irma (16), Richard (14), Mary Carmen (9), Rose Mary (7), Ramie (4) and one on the way. Matilde Gomez had five children, Abel (16), Rudy (12), Olga (10), Humberto (5), and Jose Angel (2). Marcolfa had seven children, Claudio (15), Victor (14), Marcolfa (12), Dorotea (10), Jesus (8), Yolanda (6), and Alicia (5). It was a rare treat for Carmen and her sisters to be together. Carmen often visited with Matilde but rarely with Marcolfa because Marcolfa lived in South Texas. Carmen loved her sisters dearly. When Marcolfa came to town with her family, Carmen excitedly coordinated an outing.

Enrique loved to film these family get-togethers. He always kept his wife centered in the frame with the rest of the family tightly around her. Carmen's bright red hair brought vivid life to his films. And the children brought warmth with their exuberant playfulness. Enrique filmed them as the group walked together toward him. Enrique had directed them to walk together for his film production. Although, with so many children having fun and running here and there, they would come in and out of the frame. Enrique always kept a few rolls of film handy for family events like these.

A couple of months later, Enrique filmed the family as they celebrated Ramie's fourth birthday. Ramie got a six-shooter toy gun that had a very long barrel and was waving it around excitedly. It was the kind that held a paper ribbon of caps filled with minute amounts of gunpowder. The gun had a trigger just like a real gun and even a hammer that would retract when a finger pulled the trigger. The motion of the hammer would complete when it hit down hard on the cap against the metal plate. It was exciting to hear the cap pop and then to smell the ignited gunpowder. A little while later, Ramie sat on the front lawn with a large present. He tore the wrapping paper. He laughed as he pulled out an inner package and held it up for all to see. As he peeled back the neatly wrapped present, he saw a tiny propeller. Instantly he knew what his birthday gift was and pulled the toy seaplane from the packaging. It had two floats where wheels would typically be on a regular plane. Ramie was anxious to take a nice long bath and play with his new toy.

By August 30, 1955, Carmen was pregnant and was expecting to give birth any day. Enrique and Carmen had made the last payment on the loan that they had used to add the two rooms just past the kitchen. The first room was next to the kitchen and had a large empty area in the middle, and on the right was the laundry room. It was called the "cuartito." The second room was across from the "cuartito" and was Enrique and Carmen's bedroom. On that day they received a letter from the bank. It was a "Release of Lien[7]" to

Enrique Mendoza and Carmen Mendoza for the loan that had covered the house addition made in 1952 in the amount of $1,034.82. With six children at home (Henry was away in the Air Force), Carmen would likely have wanted more space in their house for bedrooms. Enrique would have excitedly wanted that too. He loved to spend money on such projects. He only spent money when it meant that he would end up with something of significant value. In this case, the room addition would increase the value of their home. Carmen was more practical. She simply needed more room for her growing family, and the expense was well worth it. She had already calculated, long before, that they could afford it. Carmen was anxiously looking forward to the birth of her next child.

Enrique had told Carmen that the insurance would only pay if the baby was born in the hospital.

Carmen said, "No!"

She didn't want her next baby to be born in the hospital, even if the insurance paid for it (Ramie had been born in the hospital). The doctor told her that he could instead deliver her baby in the clinic, and the insurance would still pay. Carmen stood firm and refused to allow her baby to be born anywhere outside of her home.

On September 6, 1955, Enrique and Carmen's eighth child, Rogelio, was born. He was born in the bedroom adjacent to the laundry room ("cuartito"). Once Carmen and her baby were presentable, the other children came to visit their new baby brother. All were thrilled. Ramie (4) leaned over the edge of the bed and looked in bewilderment at his mother and then to his new baby brother. Rogelio was lying peacefully next to Carmen and sucking his thumb.

Years later, Carmen said that unlike the rest of her children, Rogelio was a chronic crier. None of the other children had cried or screamed as incessantly as Rogelio. Not even the doctor could find a cause for his persistent wailing.

Minnie (18) was working part-time at Acme Engraving as a secretary (she was also going to college). The business was on Market Street caddy-corner from the San Antonio Main Library. She worked on one of the higher floors in the building. As she entered the building, next to Tandy Leather, she turned right and took the stairs to where her desk was. She kept her office desk neat and orderly. She had a typewriter where she could quickly type up error-free memos. She also answered the phone.

Minnie's boss at Acme Engraving created the birth announcement for her younger brother, Rogelio. It was a cute birth announcement with a picture of the newborn baby on the left side. The text was on the right side of the postcard and read:

> Hi folks,
> I'm a **BOY** BABY! They call
> me ROGELIO MENDOZA.
> I came here Tuesday Sept. 6,
> 1955 on the 1:10 A.M. Stork,
> And landed at 139 Aganier Ave.
> Tipping the scales at an even 8
> pounds. My father was a
> little nervous, but mother is
> doing fine. Come on over
> and let's get acquainted.
> So long for now.

Minnie enjoyed working there. She was a fast and efficient worker that took pride in her work. Soon the owner of Acme Engraving played an indirect part in steering Minnie towards a young man named Eddie Alejandro (20).

Eddie Alejandro and his business partner were painting murals for nightclubs. They needed enough space to create the large, several foot-wide canvas signs or the stencils they'd use to create the signs. Eddie's partner, while searching for a space in downtown San Antonio, found that the owner of Acme Engraving had a room off to the side that would be large enough to hold a large table. Eddie must have been thrilled with the prospect of his partner and him having their very own space to work their creations.

Eddie was quite a gifted artist. He had a knack for precisely positioning the letters on the large signs. He could just as easily create the smaller signs too. His eye for perspective and color also translated to much smaller artwork like oil paintings and pencilwork. Eddie possessed a similar skill to that of Leonardo da Vinci, with his scaled drawings and precise measurements that captured the relationship between elements of his subjects in a scene.

The owner of Acme Engraving agreed to rent a room where Eddie and his partner could produce their signs. They set up the workspace that included a sizeable eight-foot-wide table. The owner also told them that they could take phone calls there. If a phone call came for Eddie or his partner, it was Minnie who would call him to the phone or take a message. Later, when Eddie and Minnie met, they discovered that they had quite a few mutual friends.

Already two months had passed since Enrique's siblings had consented to sell their father's house at 659 W. Elmira Street, and Enrique was unable to sell it. Enrique continued to collect the rents from the tenants at the Elmira house, pay the utilities, and perform the other duties required to maintain the property. Also, he meticulously recorded all of the financial details of his father's estate. He charged the estate $15 per month while he did that job.

Enrique was disappointed that he wasn't able to sell Elmira. But then Paco suddenly agreed to purchase the Elmira house. Enrique felt optimistic about his finances. Enrique was relieved that his obligations as Executor would soon be over.

When he first became the Executor, he was very excited about managing the Elmira house. He was very good at both bookkeeping and property management. But he hadn't expected that some of his siblings would become impatient with his handling of the estate.

"He was fair," he thought.

"Not fair enough," they thought. "We want our money."

Enrique was hopeful that the discord would heal once the house sold.

Enrique was thrilled that he would soon complete his obligations as Executor. He started making plans to buy a new car right away. When the deal came along to buy a 1955 Mercury at a bargain, Enrique couldn't resist. He needed about $500 cash and was able to trade in his 1952 Chevy for $1,900. His monthly car payment would remain the same as it had been before with the Chevy.

Even though he had already borrowed $300 a few months before from Paco and Margarita Elva, Enrique borrowed another $500 from them. Now he owed Margarita Elva and Paco $800. Enrique had already calculated that each of the eight heirs would receive about $600 from the sale of the Elmira house. After the property sold, Enrique would end up owing Paco and Margarita Elva about $200. He had already agreed to pay them $25 each month, and he would pay off that obligation within eight months.

Life continued happily for Enrique and Carmen's children. Minnie was working. Irma, Richard, Mary Carmen, and Rose Mary were in school, and Ramie and Rogelio were at home. Henry was away in the Air Force. Before he had left, Henry had stored his model airplane that had a three-foot wingspan up in the rafters of the garage to keep it safe. Sometime after that, someone had taken the plane from the garage. Sixty years later, Henry saw photographs of that time with his airplane in the background of one of his father's pictures. Perhaps, Richard had taken it down from there and hadn't realized that Henry might one day see his siblings playing with his model airplane in the family photographs.

In November of 1955, Enrique bought a brand new 1955 Mercury Montclair automobile. Enrique's son, Richard (15), was very excited about the new car and would later tell Henry in a tape recording a couple of months later, "It's a Mercury 55. It's two-tone, four-door. On top, it's black, a dark black. On the bottom, it's sort of a yellow. Something like a light yellow. . . . And remember what you were telling me when you were over here vacationing, about the Chevrolet that it didn't have enough power - that the Ford had more power. Well, now what do you think about the Mercury? After you take a ride in that, you'll be going zero to fifty miles an hour in two seconds at take-off."

By December of 1955, Eddie had asked Minnie if she would do him the honor of going to a Christmas dance with him. Minnie was flattered. But she would have to find out if her parents would allow her to go, and Eddie would have to wait for her answer.

Minnie asked her father for permission to go to the dance with Eddie. Enrique and Carmen would have a bit of hesitation for his daughter to go to the dance with Eddie Alejandro. Minnie was persistent, and her father eventually gave his permission for her to accompany Eddie to the dance. That's when Eddie met Minnie's parents. Although Minnie and Eddie went to the dance together, it would be a few more months before they would become more than just friends.

By December 31, 1955, Enrique had created a detailed report of the estate of Encarnacion Mendoza.[8] He listed every detail of the estate from September 1954 through December 31, 1955. The grand totals for Encarnacion's estate during this period were: Rents received $2,234.66; Expenses paid: Utilities $246.94; Insurance 78.76, Taxes $148.83; Administrative fee $240.00; Legal fees $198.00; and Maintenance $242.40. The Rents received, less the expenses, yielded a net rental income of $1,079.75. Added to that was $93 from Furniture sold, and another $45 found in Encarnacion's safe that brought the total net cash assets to

$1,222.68. Subtracting the $833.00 cost of the funeral and the $320 cash disbursement to the eight heirs ($40 each) left a cash balance of $69.68 in Encarnacion's estate. Some of Encarnacion's children might have taken note that Enrique had earned $240 in administration fees plus his inheritance of $40. In contrast, the others (Canacho, Heriberto, Jesus, Leslie, Ruby, Margarita, Juan Carlos) had each received only $40. Perhaps, if they sold the Elmira house, they would each receive one-eighth of its $5,000 plus worth, about $625 each.

Some of his siblings were growing frustrated with the execution of the Will. Encarnacion's huge two-story house still had renters. Ill will was seeping surreptitiously between the family members. No longer was their mother, Margarita, or their father, Encarnacion, there to mitigate misunderstandings or the growing suspicion that the disposition of the Will might be inequitable. Perhaps some of the family members needed the money for their growing families.

Whatever the reason, some of the children of Encarnacion and Margarita had begun to splinter. It wasn't by a lot, but even a tiny crack had the potential to grow. Enrique was still working at American National Insurance Company and continued to complete his duties as Executor of his father's estate. The women of the family were strong and would have played a considerable part in keeping the families together. These women were Leslie (Encarnacion's daughter), Carmen (Enrique's wife), Enriqueta (Canacho's wife), Imelda (Heriberto's wife), Delia (Jesus's wife), Margarita Elva (Encarnacion's daughter), and Ruby (Encarnacion's daughter).

Encarnacion's children had families and other responsibilities of their own. Additionally, Encarnacion and Margarita's children would be grieving the loss of their father for a very long time. None of them could move forward and completely heal until they sold the house. But not all of them could easily let go of the pain of the loss of their father. However, those that worked through the pain and grief of losing their father followed a path of healing.

Perhaps there was a glimmer of hope for Encarnacion's heirs when Paco and Margarita Elva had decided to buy the Elmira house. But only if they could agree on a fair price.

34 - The Recorder - 1955 to 1956

On New Year's Eve, Saturday, December 31, 1955, Carmen spent most of the day cooking, cleaning, and taking care of baby Rogelio. Perhaps she'd snuck in a nap or two while baby Rogelio slept. Enrique too customarily took a nap in the afternoon on his days off. Both Carmen and Enrique had been invited to Jesus and Delia's house and were looking forward to spending time with them.

Later that evening, Enrique, Carmen, and their children drove over to Jesus and Delia Mendoza's home. It had been a beautiful day, and the evening looked like it was going to be just as lovely.

That day was neither hot nor cold, and the humidity had been relatively low. It was such a pleasant day. Carmen felt that it would be safe to bring baby Rogelio to Delia's house. He would be four months old in just six days. Enrique and Carmen had brought the whole family to Jesus and Delia's house to celebrate the coming New Year. Enrique's sister, Ruby Reygadas, her husband Ernesto, and their children were there too.

As midnight drew near, they went outside. At least one of the family members had a pistol. As the clock struck midnight, someone shot their gun into the air. Several others in the neighborhood did the same. None of them realized the danger involved in this New Year's tradition.

Migrants: Exploring the Colors of my Family History

All three families (Enrique, Jesus, and Ruby) welcomed the new year, 1956. Enrique (45) and Carmen's (41) family included Minnie (18), Irma (16), Richard (15), Mary Carmen (9), Rose Mary (8), Ramie (4), and Rogelio (4 months). Jesus (39) and Delia's (36) family included Marie Nilda (17), Jesse (15), Yolanda (9), and Joe (3). Ruby (33) and Ernesto's (42) family included Ernesto Jr. (14), Victor (12), Ruby (11), and Margarita Elva (6).

Carmen said, "The day was beautiful, and so was the night. There was no cold. We were so content with Delia and Chuy ("Jesus"). And Ernesto and Ruby were there too and the children too."

As Enrique and his family got ready to go home, already well past midnight, he saw what looked like a small dent on the hood of the car. It was dark and hard to see, but when he looked closer, he noticed that the dent, although small, was well pronounced. His heart sank. The car was barely two months old, and it had its first dent.

"It must have been from a bullet," Enrique had said that night to Carmen.

A few days later, Carmen would tell her son, Henry, on a tape recording, "That's what he thinks. But who knows what it was [that caused the dent]? Maybe it was something else. But we'll see if it can be fixed."

Richard (15) explained it to Carmen in Spanish, "On New Year's, like everyone is shooting their gun up in the air. And the bullet, with its force . . . It doesn't have enough force that it will go up only so high, then it will come down with a force. Maybe even greater because of friction. Then when it hits the car, it makes a dent."

Carmen had smiled at his explanation.

On Monday, January 2, 1956, Enrique received a package from his son, Henry (20). Henry had made an audiotape recording from his barracks at Scott Air Force Base in New Jersey on December 27 and December 28, 1955. Enrique excitedly opened the package. He set up the tape recorder and gathered the family.

He carefully threaded the fragile tape from reel to reel in his new tape recorder and hit the play button. The family listened breathlessly as Henry's voice came loudly through the speaker.

"I'd like to have that tape, two reels, 1200 feet. And Minnie, appreciate it if you send me that address and Richard, I appreciate hearing from you. Mom, Dad, and all of you. I hope you had a Merry Christmas and a Happy New Year. I've been having a pretty good time down here."

Music was playing on the radio in the background as Henry continued.

"[I] don't go off the Base much, but [I] always got something to do. Right now, I'm working on a projector - a tape recorder, fixing a couple of radios. I got enough books to read if I ever get bored, and it never does get boring around here."

Henry talked about how odd it was to be speaking to the tape recorder all alone by himself.

"Why don't y'all send me a nice long tape with all of you all on it - even Ramie. He could at least cry on it or yell or something. He knows how to talk."

There was a brief pause on the tape. Carmen got teary-eyed as Henry continued.

"Well, I'm getting pretty close to the end, so I'm gonna send you all my love, Mom and Dad. [I] hope you have a nice New Year to come or a happy one."

The tape recorder was making a clicking sound, and Henry had brought the microphone closer to it to reveal the annoying clicking that the spool was making as it turned on its spindle. He continued.

"That's about it, I guess. That's all I have. Now, as soon as you can, send out the tapes. Send down a nice long tape along with the rest of the tapes [that I asked for]. And, Minnie, the address. And if you want anything recorded, the music, tell me about it. I'll record it for you. And Richard, I'd like to hear from you, Irma, Ramie. Bye, you all."

Side one of the tape ended. Enrique turned the tape over, and the family anxiously awaited more. It almost seemed magical how Henry was talking to them. It was exciting for all of them. Carmen was touched and missed her son very much and prayed for him often. Enrique pressed the play button, and Henry's almost New Jersey accent continued.

"This will be for Mom, Dad, and all of them... By the way, yesterday was the 27th [January 27, 1955], and today is the 28th [January 28, 1955]. I wanted to say thank you to you all. I'll get you something [Christmas presents] later on in the year. I can't now. There is something called [a] lack of money. Anyway, thanks a lot. I came home—"

On the tape, Henry was about to tell the family something about the last time that he came home.

Then Henry asked again for the two 1200-foot roles of recording tape and then added another request for an 8mm roll of film if they had it. He asked again for Minnie to get that address for him.

"Oh yeah, I asked Minnie to get me some address the other day when I called - not the other day, I called months ago. Anyways she didn't do it. At least I haven't received no address. I wish she'd send it to me. It's never too late. Please do, Minnie; Send me the address cause it ain't the same old address I understand she's at . . . That's all the stuff I got, except that it's cold up here. We had some snow about a week ago."

He had wanted the address of an old girlfriend.

Henry continued, "By the way, Minnie, this may interest you. Down at the library down here, we got a record library on the Base. I can get all the Glenn Miller music or anybody . . . as long as it's recorded. I went down the other day and recorded an hour and a half. Now anytime we have some time off, I sit down and relax and listen to [my recorded music]."

On the tape, Henry addressed Richard directly. Richard perked up, grinning.

"Hey Richard, you there? I was talking the other day [to the guys] about you, kid. What have you been doing? Any [electrical] shocks lately? Two guys were working on twelve-hour grave shifts from 8 o'clock [at night] to 8 o'clock the next morning."

Enrique and the family listened to the rest of the tape. Then Enrique told the family that they should immediately record a new tape and send it quickly to Henry.

Richard (15) was excited to get that project started. However, he had to wait for a new tape. Richard got a little impatient and recorded over the tail end of one of Henry's tape. Perhaps he'd been testing the recorder while he waited for a fresh new tape. He'd recorded Rose Mary (8) reading a story about Jonathan Starbuck, a young boy. Rose Mary got the cue from Richard to start reading. Rose Mary obliged as she began to read a story, no doubt, from her schoolbook. She spoke in a delicate, articulate manner.

"Jonathan's Buffalo. In April 1846, a wagon trail started westward from Independence, Missouri. Of the hundreds of Pioneers in it, none was happier than fifteen-year-old, Johnathan Starbuck...," said Rose Mary as she continued reading. And a few sentences later, Rose Mary stopped, and a commercial started for a popular ointment for burns. Richard had planned this interruption. He wanted it to sound like a radio broadcast, complete with commercials. After the commercial ended, Rose May read on.

Richard had a profound interest in many of Henry's hobbies. Henry had given Richard an old Motorola Radio. Richard had tinkered with the radio and found that it had many hot tubes inside. When he turned it on, he'd wait a minute or two while it warmed up. Henry had also left behind his photography processing equipment. Richard enjoyed taking pictures and had begun to experiment with photography. Richard enjoyed filming with his father's 8mm film camera too. He especially liked taking pictures. His newest hobby included playing the reel-to-reel tape recorder.

Richard enjoyed playing with his train set, although not as often as he used to when it was new. It was a Lionel train set that had a bountiful assortment of bridges, crossings, a smoking engine, and a dual transformer. The transformer had two separate arm-like levers that controlled the speed of the train. There were enough tracks to create many different layouts. The train also came with a small bottle of "pills." After dropping a pill in the smokestack of the locomotive, it produced a realistic stream of smoke as the train ran through its laps. Any fifteen-year-old boy would have been thrilled to have this high-end train set like Richard's.

On Sunday, January 8, 1956, Enrique started a new recording for Henry.

"Hello, Junior. How have you been, Son? I don't have any more news except I bought a Mercury 55. It turned out well for me. They gave me a good guarantee. They gave me $1,900 for my car - the Chevrolet 1952. All of us here have been well. The baby [Rogelio] is very big, very fat, everything is fine. Right now, Alejandro [Carmen's brother] is here. He'll speak in a moment to say a few words, and don't forget to tell us when you are going to come home," said Enrique.

Enrique brought the microphone closer to Carmen's brother, Alejandro Escobedo.

Alejandro spoke slowly and deliberately into the microphone.

"Hello, Junior. How you been? I'm over here visiting and like to say Merry Christmas and Happy New Year to you. I'd like to say it right now and. . . . How you been up there? Very cold? How do you like staying in the Army?"

Alejandro paused as Enrique (or someone) whispered something to Alejandro.

"In the Air Force? Well, [I] haven't got much to say, and I hope you be home soon. Bye," said Alejandro.

Minnie sat close to the microphone.

"Hi Henry, this is Minnie. How have you been? I hope you've been okay. How is the Air Force treating you? Hey, about that address you wanted, it's 106 Hannasch, and I had a little bit of trouble getting that address, but I finally got it. Finally! And about recording a little something for me. What I like is progressive jazz. I'm sure you like it too. Anything, Dave Brubeck or Stan Kenton or anything - Glenn Miller is alright too. Let's see what else? I hope you haven't been working too hard. When are you gonna get another leave? I hope you come soon. And I've been working pretty hard as you probably know. I always work hard. No," said Minnie with a giggle. "Well, anyway, I guess that's all. I'll be seeing you. Bye."

Rose Mary stepped up to the microphone.

"Hello, Henry. How are you? When are you coming home? I'm in the third grade in school. I like school so much, but," said Rose Mary. She sighed loudly and then continued. "I don't - sometimes I can't - uh - do any answers in my school. How have you been? Alright, bye."

Mary Carmen was next.

"Hello, Henry. How you been? I'm Mary Carmen. I passed the fourth grade, and I got a mixer for Christmas and a dress and some shoes and some other things. Goodbye, Henry. I went to Mass this morning. It was real cold. I had to wear a coat and sweater, and this was our - so long, Henry," said Mary Carmen. Someone told her to move on so that the next person could speak.

Irma spoke next.

"Hi, Henry. How have you been? What have you been doing? I'm still going to Ursuline. Everybody is okay over here, and so you have snow over there? Huh? Did you make a snowman? Today is Sunday, in case I haven't told you. It's Sunday the eighth [January 8, 1956]. Did you have a good New Year? And a good Christmas? What do you do over there? And tell us all about it. And send us

Migrants: Exploring the Colors of my Family History

another reel [tape recording] real soon. We wanted to make this sooner, but we couldn't. So you try to make it real soon."

Carmen sat with baby Rogelio. He was making baby cooing noises.

"Did you hear that noise? It was Rogelio. He's playing with a little toy. I don't want to take it away from him. Otherwise, he'll start screaming," said Carmen.

Enrique was nearby watching, and Carmen asked him to take the toy so that Rogelio might make some noises for Henry. Enrique took the toy and offered the microphone to Rogelio instead. Rogelio was reaching for it and couldn't quite get a hold of it. His fingers slipped across the microphone, and it got recorded as a loud scratching noise. Eventually, Rogelio cried out, annoyed. He had tried to pull the microphone to his mouth but couldn't.

Carmen giggled as Rogelio got more annoyed. He noisily reacted but didn't quite cry. Carmen whisked him away before his screams started. She knew that once he started screaming and crying, there would be no satisfying him - at least for a while.

Enrique took the microphone. Ramie was with him.

"Do you want to go to H.E.B.?" asked Enrique.

"Yes," answered Ramie.

"What do you want there?"

"Cake, Pie, Ice Cream," said Ramie.

Enrique whispered to Ramie for him to repeat into the microphone, "How are you today?"

"How are you today?" Ramie said obediently. He wanted the Cake, Pie, and Ice Cream.

Irma spoke up.

"What did Santa Claus bring you?" asked Irma of Ramie.

"A truck," said Ramie in Spanish.

Enrique stopped the recorder and then started it again. The family, including Alejandro, were seated around the recorder. Enrique was holding Rogelio as he asked Alejandro, "How have you been doing, Alejandro? What's new?"

"Right now, I have much new," said Alejandro.

"It's been cold today," said Enrique, not realizing that Alejandro had just said that there was "much new" with him. Alejandro had been thrilled about starting a new job.

"Yes," said Alejandro as if nothing was new for him.

Suddenly Rogelio stiffened up, and he slipped out of Enrique's arms. Rogelio hit his head on the chair's armrest, which had stopped him from falling to the floor. Enrique brought Rogelio closer to him to comfort him.

One of the girls giggled.

Richard's mouth fell open.

"What happened? He just had the baby and let him fall," said Richard as he pointed to his father.

Rogelio wasn't crying after hitting his head. He was dazed, and he started to smile.

Enrique continued.

"What were you doing that your head hit the chair. What? He's very anxious, this baby. He's standing very straight. Now do a little murmur," said Enrique as he wondered why Rogelio wasn't crying. Perhaps Enrique was relieved that baby Rogelio was not doing his usual wailing.

"What happened?" Enrique said affectionately to Rogelio. "Why don't you scream like you usually do every day? Huh? One little scream. Come on, just a little shout."

Rogelio murmured.

Enrique continued, "The baby just turned four months old the day before yesterday. On the sixth, he turned four months, and right now, he's laughing and laughing. Let's see if he wants to let out a little scream for the microphone. A little scream so that your brother [Henry] can hear."

Enrique continued to encourage Rogelio to make some noise for Henry to no avail.

Richard took the microphone and brought it over to him and Alejandro while Enrique continued to try to get Rogelio to scream. Richard most certainly knew that once Rogelio started his loud, annoying screaming, it would not end until much longer than he or anyone could stand.

Richard looked over at Alejandro.

"Let's get back to Alex. Where are you working now?" asked Richard quickly.

Alejandro smiled kindly. His first language was Spanish, and when he spoke in English, it was still slow and deliberate. He continued to talk more energetically than before.

"Well, not working right now. I'll be working tomorrow morning, and I think I have a steady job," answered Alejandro patiently. His new job was Alejandro's exciting news that he would have told earlier.

"What kind of job?"

"Well, it's maintaining, painter, handyman, and all-around man."

"Not easy, is it?" asked Richard.

"No. It's pretty hard, but it's still a job."

"Hey! Did you know Abel gave me four pigeons?" Richard asked excitedly. Abel was the son of Abel Sr. and Matilde Escobedo Gomez (Carmen's sister).

"No, I didn't know it until now. When you told me."

Richard said, "He told me about it a while ago - four or five hours ago. He said if I wanted some pigeons. First, I said no. But then I said yeah. So I got four pigeons out in the backyard, and they're going to be pretty tasty after a while."

"That's pretty good, and I hope you're gonna have more pigeons," Alejandro said more slowly than before.

"No! I'm not gonna have more pigeons. I'm gonna have some stew. If you're lucky, you might get some. Come on, say something else," said Richard.

The sound of Rogelio gurgling in the background was getting

louder. Enrique was still sitting next to the recorder with Rogelio on his lap. Richard was getting annoyed with the distraction.

"This is Rogelio again. He's gonna tell you something," said Richard.

Enrique brought the microphone closer to Rogelio.

Enrique said, "Say something to the microphone. A scream at least. He doesn't want to talk. Rogelio doesn't want to right now. He's very content. But sometimes he just gets to screaming and screaming, and sometimes he seems like he's about to cry like when he's hungry. But now he's content. He's not hungry."

Enrique finally gave up and left with Rogelio. Rogelio would probably wait to cry sometime in the middle of the night when he was hungry, and Enrique and Carmen were fast asleep.

Richard asked Alejandro several questions so that Henry "could get familiar with their voices." Alejandro said that he was living with Matilde (his sister) and Abel (Matilde's husband). Matilde's house was about nine blocks away from the Aganier house. Although, to Richard, Matilde's house was on the Westside and the Aganier house was not. At the time, most of Enrique and Carmen's relatives lived within a mile or two of each other.

Richard asked Alejandro about crime in San Antonio, drugs, curfews, highway deaths, drunk driving, etc. Alejandro courteously answered Richard's questions and explained that crime was all over San Antonio and that it is not just limited to the Westside of town.

Alejandro ended the interview by talking directly to Henry.

"So long, Henry, keep your nose clean and excuse my English," said Alejandro.

The train blasted its horn as it rushed by. The train tracks were behind the lumberyard that was across the street from the Aganier house. Inside, Enrique and Ramie were chatting into the microphone. They were both conversing in Spanish.

"What is passing by right now?" asked Enrique.

"The train," said Ramie.

"Do you enjoy watching the train?"

"Yes."

Enrique and Ramie chatted a little longer before Enrique shut off the recorder. The entire family had taken their turn speaking to Henry on the audio recording. Soon the tape would reach Henry in the Air Force Base in New Jersey. In his room, on an identical recorder, Henry smiled and laughed as he heard the voices of his family, who had included him in the family's holiday celebrations.

35 - Day in the Life - 1956

The next day, Sunday, January 8, 1956, Carmen, as usual, spent a bit of time in the kitchen where she prepared breakfast for the family, and after everyone finished, she washed the dishes. And then later, she had made lunch, and after they ate, she washed those dishes too. Then Carmen did the same for supper.

In her kitchen, she had a double-wide sink with two basins. At the sink, Carmen could look out the narrow window to the garage entry to the Bell Telephone Company next door. It wasn't the best of views out that window, but at least she could see the sun shining on the concrete driveway leading into the garage next door. In between her "cooking and dishwashing duties," she would tend to the baby when he interrupted her every so often. When that happened, Carmen would just grab a towel and dry her hands and then rush to baby Rogelio before he would change from crying to screaming. Once the baby was taken care of, she would return to her unending work. Along with the housework and child-rearing, Carmen found time to sew her children's clothing.

Later that evening, Enrique had left for his sister Ruby's house. There, Enrique would visit with his siblings (who would also go) and usually play a card game or other game of chance. Carmen would almost always stay home with the kids when Enrique went to one of his siblings' houses to play cards.

Carmen was at the sink and grinned and shook her head when she saw Richard waddle awkwardly past her with the recorder as he headed to his room. Richard's bedroom was entirely private. He loved having a room to himself. That room had once been Henry's room. On one side of the room, he had his train tracks set up. On the shelf, he had a Motorola AM radio that Henry had left for him. A khaki uniform was hanging next to the closet.

It's not clear if Richard had permission to move the tape recorder to his room. Perhaps, Richard had gotten permission from his father before his father had left. After Richard placed the recorder on the small table in his room, he plugged it in. When he turned it on, he smiled as the indicator lights illuminated. He brought the microphone near to him and started the recorder.

"Hello, Henry. This is Richard again, and this time I'm in my room with Ramie all alone. Just with Ramie and you been hearing me talk a lot, but now you want to hear Ramie sing. Well. You said Ramie will sing. I told him I was going to give him balloons if he sings. That's the only way I got him to sing. So, what are you going to sing, Ramie?"

After a brief back and forth, Ramie started singing, "Sixteen tons and what do you get..."

Richard chuckled. "Okay. Have you sung enough?"

"Yes," said an expectant Ramie. He wanted the balloons that Richard had promised him.

"Well, do you know who we're talking to?" asked Richard.

"With who?"

Richard laughed.

"Well. He's [Henry] going to hear you. He's going to hear you when he puts the tape in his recorder of his. When he's in his own room, and he's going to tell everyone because you are a great singer! Did you know?"

"Yes!"

Richard smiled and said, "Tell Henry, hello."

"Hi, Henry."

"Tell him where you live. Where does Henry live?"

"Where do you live, Henry?" asked Ramie.

"That's what you're going to tell him?"

"No."

"What are you going to tell him then?" asked Richard, not sure what Ramie might say.

"To come home."

"When?"

"Tomorrow," said Ramie assuredly.

Richard and Ramie bantered a bit as Richard giggled. Richard turned back to the tape recorder.

"Okay! Alright! Now you heard Ramie. I hope you're satisfied because you wanted him to yell, and he did more than that. You know the radio that you gave me? The Motorola? It's still working, you know. It's not broken or anything. That's the background music you're going to be hearing. Hey Henry! In school, we already have ROTC, and I'm taking it. Well, I guess when you come home, I'll be just marching around here showing myself off to you, and well, that's all there is new at school besides homework. We get plenty of that every day. Well, I don't think this is the last time that I'll say goodbye. I've already said goodbye three times, but I'm gonna say so long on just one side of the tape. And probably tomorrow everybody is gonna talk on the other side [of the tape]. In case you haven't heard it before, when I was talking to Alex, I have four pigeons, and I have them in a cage back there. A cage I tried to make anyway. And one of them laid an egg on the first day. I tried to fix a nest for it, so it'll hatch."

Richard turned back to Ramie.

"What is your name?"

"Ramie," said Ramie without hesitation.

"Ramie? Ramie, what?"

"Mendoza!"

"Ramie Mendoza?" asked Richard.

"Yes," said Ramie with a giggle.

"How do you spell that?"

"M-O-U-S-E," said Ramie laughing hard.

Richard was surprised and laughed affectionately. He turned back to the microphone.

"Hey, Henry! In case you're still talking about me like you said in the tape you sent me, you talking about me to some guys, well, I hope you're saying nice things about me because most of the people don't say nice things about me. That'd be a compliment," said Richard. He paused for a few seconds. "Let me see what else could I talk about. Hey, next time you send a tape, ask some questions. You see? Like, I'll ask you a question and— Look, it's almost ending! So, turn it around. Huh?"

The tape ended abruptly. Richard turned the tape over and started to record again.

"Henry, I finally got the radio fixed. You see. I didn't have it on. I had it on, but I didn't have it on the right station. I have it on KAMC — that's San Antonio if you'd like to know. I always listen to it. I always have music. Hey, I was going to tell you more about ROTC on the other one. I thought that I'd put it in, but now that I have the whole rest of the tape to go, I'll tell you more about it. So far, it hasn't— We haven't learned very much. But you see all we've been doing is having inspections. That takes about an hour for about a hundred guys. And then—"

A dog barked loudly.

"That was Skipper. He's barking outside. He's barking at some old hoodlum. Ah, you never know about these guys. Anyway, all I've learned is standing, right-face, left-face, about-face, forward. But we haven't marched yet. We're thinking of marching next year if we ever get there. Now you see. All we've been doing is having inspections. What's the use of having that [if] all you're going to do is have inspections?"

Richard grimaced and said, "Well, that was a dull subject!"

Ramie was skulking around in the room next to Richard's train set and then asked Richard if he could play with the train.

"What?" asked Richard.

"I want to play with the train," asked Ramie.

"When?"

"Right away," Ramie said.

"Why?"

"Because I want to play with it," Ramie said a little louder.

"With what?"

"With the train," Ramie said with certainty and a little frustration.

"And why do you want to play with the train."

"Because I like it a lot," said Ramie, now pleading.

Richard didn't want to let him play with the train. Perhaps it was too late in the day.

"What did you get Junior for Christmas?" asked Richard trying to switch the subject. The family sometimes referred to Henry as Junior.

"Nothing."

"You didn't give him anything?" Richard asked Ramie in a scolding manner. Richard turned back to the microphone and said, "Well, I don't mind anyway, because I didn't get you anything anyways."

Ramie said something softly. Richard ignored Ramie.

"Oh! That reminds me, Henry. I didn't get you a Christmas gift. You see, I didn't have any money either like you said. You had 'lack of money,' and I had 'money lacks!' Oh, you know how it goes. No money, no dough, no presents, no nothing. Well, anyway if you go Christmas shopping sometime next February for us, don't get anything for me because it wouldn't feel right that you get something for me, and I'll be so cheap that I won't get nothing for you. So, if you don't get me nothing, it's alright. Of course, if you want to get me something, you could always get me a nice Cadillac or something."

Richard's eyes widened as he remembered something that he'd meant to tell Henry.

"Oh! Let me tell you now about Pop's car. He bought it last year."

Richard told Henry all about the car and then paused pensively for a second or two.

"Listen, I've been talking to you in English with a Spanish accent. Now I'm going to talk to you in Spanish with an English accent. Okay?"

Richard started to speak in Spanish, "It's better this way because if some American is listening to this, they aren't going to know what I'm saying. And later, you can tell them that I'm saying that you are really good. And they'll believe it. And that you are really big [famous] over here! You know. All of that stuff."

In the background, Ramie asked again to play with the train.

Richard slipped back into English.

"It's nine o'clock, and Ramie wants me to put on the train."

Richard switched back to Spanish.

"What do you think that I should do? Put on the train for this [in English] monstrosity? Or, I give him his balloons and throw him out."

Richard slipped back into English.

"Tell me in the next recording. I'll be waiting for it. Oh! I'm supposed to talk Spanish with an English accent. But you know how it is in America, you just can't get used to it. Ramie's trying to pull the cord [and unplug the recorder]. And I can't let him do that, because I'm too good to go to waste without [recording to this tape (if the recorder loses power)]. . . . So that's how come I can talk so much because I know that I'm talking to you, I think. Well, it better be you because I don't like to be calling you Henry if you're not Henry. You know. It don't sound right, calling you a different name. So, if you're not Henry, give this to my brother."

Suddenly a loud knocking came from Richard's locked door.

"Somebody is banging down the door, so I better go!"

It seemed like Richard had displeased one or more of his siblings by moving the recorder into his room. Somebody had tattled on Richard. Enrique was still not home, so it fell to Carmen to settle things. But first, she had put baby Rogelio to bed, and now that he had fallen asleep, she was ready to deal with the "situation."

After a quick "Did you get your father's permission?" lecture, Carmen sat down next to the microphone in Richard's room. She was tired, but she wanted to make sure that she recorded something more for Henry.

"Hello Junior, how have you been? Have you been well? Here everyone is fine, thanks to God. I hope that you are fine too. Just now, I came to Richard's room, and he asked me if I wanted to record. And I told him yes. I haven't had time. And the baby just went to bed, and I thought that now that he's sleeping, I'll catch up. Otherwise, he doesn't let me— He screams a lot and cries too. You know. If you extend your arms to him, he stands up really well. He's very strong. He says, "Ma" and "Pa." He does a lot of babbling. I don't always understand him. I just tell you. And we were alone because your father went off to the card game at Ruby's house. And no one is here to tell us to stop [and go to bed]."

Carmen looked over at Richard with an affectionate half-smile. And then she continued.

"Although, your father wants us to record ever since your tape arrived. And he wanted us to quickly record, and you know how it is. Time passes, and we haven't had the time. Richard knows how to use the recorder. He knows very well."

Richard smiled.

She continued, "I have so much to tell you, but now that I'm here, I don't remember any of it."

She hesitated as a memory suddenly came to her.

"Last night, Ruby, Ernesto, Queta [Enriqueta, Canacho's wife] were here. And Queta's daughter [Maria Enriqueta] has crutches. She was in a wheelchair for one month and could move around where[ever] she wanted. And now she's on crutches and hopefully she'll do well. Queta says that sometimes [her daughter] is happy, other times sad. It looks like she's going to have a little bit of a problem with her leg. But the girl seems happy, not like before. And she just turned six years old, I think on December 2nd. She is really beautiful."

She remembered something else.

"Leslie and Pedro were here last night too."

Carmen paused for a second.

"I hope you come home soon so that you can ride in the car. Because you know how to drive, but your mother can't," Carmen laughed.

Richard said, "Hey, Mom! Why don't we play a game? Like I'm Henry, and I ask you a question, and then you answer it. You see? And he gets the feeling that he's asking the questions. That way, he thinks he's talking to you."

Carmen sighed and then chuckled as she said, "No."

Richard forged on and said, "Like if I ask: How is Matilde?"

"Aye! Matilde is doing really well. Today, I spoke with her, and we talked so much. And your father is upset too with the question of the [Elmira] house. You know. They are never content. And Paco was going to buy the house, then yesterday, he called and said that he wasn't [going to buy the house anymore]. And before, since Paco was going to buy the house, Enrique had borrowed another $500 from Paco. And with Enrique, instead of the $300 that he used to owe Paco, now he owes him $800. Well, now he's [Enrique's] going to be left with that obligation. He asked for that loan so that he could pay off the house and buy the car. Well, he said that they gave him a really good deal on the car. He'd have the same payment as he had with the other car. But now, he will have the obligation to Paco too. Instead of paying $25 to Margarita, it will be $50 each month. We'll see how he's going to do it. Well, for that part, he's been troubled. I told him that he should pass the management [of Elmira] to one of the other siblings. You know, all the things that management entails: collect the rent, keep the books, etc. He's hoping that Paco will buy his part of the inheritance. That will leave him owing Paco only $200 since he loaned him $800. So, who knows if Paco wants your father's portion of the Elmira house? That is if Paco even wants it. That way, all that is left is the automobile loan. I don't think that I'm going to talk anymore, because I'm getting hoarse. We'll see if maybe a little later or tomorrow I can talk more. Because everyone here likes to talk a lot."

She turned back to the recorder and said, "Well, then bye and hope you come soon."

Carmen rushed back to the kitchen before the baby would wake up. She had dishes to wash. Carmen would have gone to bed exhausted, and would probably have gone to bed that night pondering the issues like the Elmira house, the doubled car loan payments, and when her screaming baby would awaken.

36 - Memorial - 1956

Several days passed without recording anything on the tape they'd started on the 8th of January. But then on January 18, 1956, the recordings continued. The recorder was back in the dining room, where everyone had access to it. Jose "Pepe" Armando (Guadalupe's son) and Licha (Pepe's wife) were visiting the Aganier house along with Ernesto Reygadas and his wife Ruby Mendoza Reygadas (Enrique's sister) along with their sons Ernest (Jr.) and Victor. They all wished Henry well and hoped to see him soon.

Richard talked again about his pigeons.

"Remember me telling you that I had four pigeons? Well, they seemed to have flown the coop. Really, the cat got them. They're dead! I think. I hope. Cause I don't want to be flying after them!"

Irma walked into the room.

"Hey, Irma! You wanna talk?" said Richard.

Irma got close to the microphone.

"Hi, Henry. How's everything? When are you coming home? Your next leave?"

Richard jumped close to the microphone, interrupted Irma, and said, "Hey, wait a minute! Wait a minute! Henry, this is Irma."

Irma grimaced and laughed as she said, "Yeah! I'm your sister. Remember?"

Richard interrupted again and told Irma to wait until a new song started on the record player. Richard had stacked four records at a time to play on the spindle of Minnie's record player.

Irma didn't wait.

"Well, anyway. Richard was just telling you about his midterms, and we're having them too. Except they're different than his, besides the grades. As long as we get through with the test, we can leave the school. We might get out at twelve or might get out at two instead of 3:40. What's really good about these tests is that you can get out earlier. And that's about all except that Ramie is here just sitting and just listening to me. Want to say anything, Ramie? Tell him what Santa Claus brought you."

Richard interrupted again and said somewhat sarcastically, "You want to let Mom talk?"

"Sure, I want to let her talk!" Irma said.

Richard yelled out to the kitchen, "Come on, Mom!"

Carmen said something, and then Irma said into the microphone, "She's busy right now. She doesn't know what to say to you [right now]."

Richard grimaced and said, "She don't know… Alright, let's talk some more!"

Eventually, Irma continued, and Ramie was making funny noises in the background.

"Oh, did Richard tell you. Richard loves Algebra, and he hasn't taken it in school yet. I was teaching Richard some Algebra yesterday. I tried to [trick] him with some problems, but he got them."

"Better than her," said Richard snidely.

"Huh?" Irma grimaced.

Minnie walked in from outside.

Richard spoke up, "Hey Henry, here's Minnie. She just came from the job."

Minnie smiled at Richard and came closer to the microphone.

"Hi Henry, I just got home. Richard just told you. Boy, is it cold outside! It's about 40 degrees or something, and they say it's going to be 44. They say it's going to be 28 tonight. Boy, is it cold! We haven't had any snow, but it rained last night around 12, 12:30—thunder, rain, and everything. And uh. What else?"

Next, Carmen sat down with Rogelio in front of the microphone.

"Hi Henry, it's your mother. I'm here with Rogelio. We'll see if he wants to let out some little screams. It's been two weeks since I talked to you last on this tape. And we haven't had time because we've been really busy with the baby because he's so needy. I wanted to tell you not to worry about Christmas presents. The only present that I want is that you behave well and that you are well. That's all we need for gifts."

Carmen smiled at baby Rogelio on her lap and then continued.

"The baby had a little fever, and I gave him a tiny bit of aspirin, and he is fine today. Except he doesn't want to do his little screams. He makes a lot of noises like he's talking. He says agua (water), Mama, Papa. And he eats now - practically a half a bottle of carrots. He eats peas and peach[es]. He's very big already, completing four months. And he'll be turning five soon. Méme's (Manuel Garza, Enrique's cousin) son is going to get married, and the fiancé is going to have a party on Sunday. The kids are invited. And what else was I going to tell you? I remember while I'm working, and then when I sit down, I forget it all."

Baby Rogelio started to make gurgling baby-talk for well over a minute while Carmen laughed with delight.

"Okay, tell him bye," said Carmen to baby Rogelio.

The tape was coming to an end, and a few family members said their goodbyes.

"It's Mary Carmen. I just wanted to tell you that I have a bank book, and I have fifteen cents left over. And I just got a letter that they're going to have a party at the cafeteria, at 7:45, January 30. I have to be there, but I don't know if I'm going yet. And, uh, I didn't go to school today. I was too sick. But anyhow, we're almost running out of tape, so I have to go and let someone else talk. So long, Henry," said Mary Carmen.

"Hello, Henry. This is Rose Mary. Have you been working pretty hard? Well, we had a science test at school today and tomorrow is a holiday. And uh. The science test was pretty hard. But I didn't do some of them right. But I did it. Goodbye, Henry."

"Well, son. This is your father. Many good memories here. You take care, son. Don't forget to write. Just in case you want to tell us something, you can send it in a recording. Hopefully, that they give you some vacation time soon. I'm working on the accounts, and I'll be finished soon. I'm looking at your baby brother, and he's wearing a red hat. He's very nice. And he's a very loud crier. Maybe you've already heard him scream. Well, son."

"This is Richard again. It's the last time that I'm going to talk to you on this tape. So, I'm going to say so long for this tape. And send us another tape as quick as you can so we can hear your voice again. Here's mother."

Carmen spoke up, "I'm so glad to send you this tape. And don't forget to go to Church on Sunday. I hope you'll be alright."

In the background, Irma whispered something to Carmen. Without missing a beat, Carmen continued, "Did you receive the missal that Irma sent you for Christmas? Let us know if you did and I hope to see you soon. Come home very, very soon. Well, Henry, I will leave you, and I await your . . . to hear from you. Also, Bye."

The tape recording was carefully packed and sent to Henry.

On February 20, 1956, Enrique filed a Fiduciary Income Tax Return[1] for Encarnacion Mendoza. It showed that the rental income from 659 W. Elmira Street. (Encarnacion's house) for 1955 was $1,663.78. According to the return, Enrique had made no financial distribution to any of the family members. Receiving no money from the estate was another frustration for Enrique's siblings. The siblings might have agreed to keep the house for rental income, either because they couldn't sell the house or simply didn't want to. They each saw their inheritance from afar, except for Enrique, who was managing the interests of the estate.

Enrique worked at American National Insurance Company where they regularly sponsored dances, picnics, or other family-oriented gatherings for its employees. In April of 1956, they were having a dance at La Villita, a small historic venue located between the river Walk and the Alamo in downtown San Antonio. As usual, Enrique invited all of his family and friends. His sister, Leslie Mendoza, was there with her husband, Pete Rivera. Carmen's brother, Alejandro Escobedo, and his wife, Julia, were there too. Alejandro was dancing up a storm with anyone that would dance with him. He was quite a dancer. Of course, Minnie was there with her boyfriend, Eddie Alejandro. For the first time, Eddie was able to meet a much larger medley of Minnie's relatives than before. Soon, Eddie would learn that the Mendoza family and its relatives were part of a much larger, loving tribe that connected through laughter, love, dancing, and so much more.

Reliable Insurance Company where Enrique's brothers worked also had similar celebrations. Between the two insurance companies where Enrique, Jesus, Canacho, and likely Humberto were employed, they had enjoyed numerous family gatherings that strengthened their interpersonal relationships. However, the children of Encarnacion and Margarita were equally skilled and gifted entrepreneurs. They all had an eye for making money.

By September 3, 1956, the children of Encarnacion had a Memorial Mass for their father, Encarnacion Mendoza, at the San Fernando Cathedral in San Antonio, Texas.[2] Despite the frustrations, the extended families attended the Mass and then later gathered at San Fernando Cemetery No. 2 to pay their respects to both of their parents. Enrique used an 8mm film camera to record the family gathered in loving homage to their parents. The film showed the grandiose, double-wide headstone with flowers, wreaths, and ferns that surrounded the stone structure. Several of the women tended to the flowers along with Leslie, who watered them with a large bucket of water. Children were running after each other. Ruby and her family walked towards the camera as Enrique filmed them arriving at the site of the celebration. In the background, Delia (wife of Jesus) ran after her son Joe who reluctantly went back with her.

Soon after, the whole family: Ruby, Margarita Elva, Leslie, Lupe, Virgilio, Canacho, Minnie, Delia, Jesus, Heriberto, etc., [too many to list], sauntered towards the camera. Still later, Rose Mary, Ramie, and Mary Carmen walked up holding hands. Many large vehicles from the mid-1950s parked along the edge of the cemetery's road. Later, the families gathered outside of the San Fernando Cathedral in downtown San Antonio. It was quite amazing that so many relatives gathered lovingly to pay homage to Encarnacion and Margarita Mendoza. It was a short film, but it was evident that the families continued to be close to each other. In spite of their closeness, they each still had a concern about their inheritance.

On October 8, 1956, Marie Nilda (daughter of Jesus) entered a contest to meet Elvis Presley in San Antonio, Texas. It was the start of his career. She addressed the postcard to "The Meet Elvis Presley Contest" c/o K.T.S.A. Radio Station. On the back of the postcard, she'd written a poem to Elvis. She was selected as the winner of the contest and attended his show. Marie Nilda's family was there with her to enjoy the excitement. One of the talented artists, who worked where she did, created a large-sized replica of the postcard. At the press junket, Elvis Presley signed her replica. He wrote, "To Marie, My Very Best to You, Love ya, Elvis Presley."

Enrique Mendoza continued to work for the American National Insurance Company. He enjoyed that kind of work where he could exercise his salesman skills and utilize his bookkeeping education. He had the flexibility to adjust his schedule whenever he needed to.

Part of the day, he would spend at his office and other parts of the day he would be driving on his route where he would be collecting payments or signing up new customers. On occasion, he would travel to insurance conventions where he would meet other agents and attend a conference or two. On December 2, 1956, Enrique attended a convention in Galveston, Texas. He sent a postcard to Carmen from there.[3] In it, Enrique told Carmen that they arrived the day before (Saturday) at 10:30 p.m. It was short and to the point but, considering that he'd been driving for hours, he still wanted to let her know that he was okay. It was similar to the postcards and letters that Enrique would send to Carmen in 1930 as he traveled with his family with the Loteria in distant Texas cities.

Enrique and Carmen were thrilled that their son, Henry, had come home on leave from Maguire Air Force Base for Christmas of 1956. That is when Minnie had forewarned Eddie, her boyfriend, that Henry possessed a kind of humor that might be a little difficult to handle. When Eddie met Henry for the first time, Henry was quick to offer him a beer. It was evident to Minnie that she needn't have worried about them meeting. Soon, Eddie and Henry had left in search of Bunny, a friend of Henry's (perhaps a girlfriend). They were gone for quite a while. Years later, Minnie said that she was not upset that they'd been gone so long, leaving her behind. Eddie seemed to suggest otherwise. Perhaps, it was guilt that had suggested to Eddie that Minnie had been upset with his extended absence.

All of Enrique and Carmen's family were together for Christmas that year. After a few weeks, Henry headed off to his next base assignment in Casablanca, Morocco. Carmen (42) was pregnant with what would be her ninth child. She continued to cook the meals, wash the dishes, clean the house, and take care of baby Rogelio.

37 - Ghost of Plutarco - 1957

Enrique continued to manage his father's estate. It was his obligation to stick with it even though it had become somewhat of a burden for him. He had hoped that he would have been able to sell the Elmira house by now, but buyers in San Antonio likely found much better deals on other nearby homes.

On February 1, 1957, Enrique filed a Fiduciary Income Tax Return for Encarnacion Mendoza.[1] It showed a rental income of $1,635 from 659 W. Elmira Street. (Encarnacion's house) for 1956. It also stated that Enrique distributed $95 to each family member in 1956.

Often, Enrique used his compact 8mm movie camera to record his family at home, his American National Insurance Company Conventions, and any events important to him. He loved directing his subjects to move just right when he filmed them. Enrique always kept several fresh film cartridges ready for his trips.

He had a knack for recording his family history using film. Carmen had a near-photographic memory and remembered quite a bit about her past. Enrique had a good memory for most things, but he preferred to remember numbers and balance sheets. He was a good talker too; he remembered amusing stories from his past, recited funny jokes, and enjoyed having fun with his family.

Sometime in 1957, Enrique took a quick trip to General Terán with his cousin, Manuel ("Méme") Garza to visit relatives for a few days.

As they drove down the well-maintained highway through the mountains of Mexico, Enrique sat in the passenger seat and filmed Méme as he drove. He pointed the camera at the dashboard and then out the window. Off in the distance was a vast, neatly arranged orchard of citrus trees. The growing brush along the side of the highway seemed to fly past the window as the camera recorded the beautiful landscape.

As they came closer to General Terán, Enrique continued to film. Méme slowed the car and exited from the highway and drove through the paved roads that led to General Terán. On the left was a man dressed in white riding his horse through the brush. Further down, Enrique filmed two dozen or so men dressed in white clothing, each wearing a tan, straw hat. Elements of a small town came into focus as they drew near to the town where Méme and Enrique had grown up. They drove up to Hacienda Soledad de la Mota owned by the Calles family.

They parked the car and got off to see the building where citrus fruit from the orchard was processed. Enrique filmed inside the building. The oranges moved in tight rows on a gigantic conveyor belt that hurried them along to the washing station. There were at least a dozen men moving crates of oranges and loading them into the machine. Méme picked up an orange from the conveyor belt and posed for the camera. He jokingly dropped his hat on the conveyer belt and then swooped it up before the machine could eat it up.

A few minutes later, Enrique filmed a group of three men standing outside of the building. The camera zoomed in on one of the men who had a thick mustache and smiled as he looked straight into the camera. The man was photogenic and looked like Aco, the son of the former Mexican President Plutarco Elias Calles. Enrique zoomed in close on him, and then the camera indicated that it had come to the end of the film roll. Enrique fumbled with the camera. He held the camera close, to keep stray light from exposing the film and turned the film cartridge over. Enrique continued to film. He filmed another man; this man was somewhat overweight and looked like he was in charge. The man seemed comfortable being on-camera. He too had a mustache but was different than the man that Enrique had filmed before. Méme stood off in the back, smiling, and two other men stood behind the "comfortable" man with their arms tightly crossed against their chest, and they were not smiling. The comfortable man seemed confidant and in-charge like the manager of the plant would be. Later, after Enrique had the film processed, he labeled it "PLUTARCO."

When the trip was over, the two of them, Enrique and Méme, left back to San Antonio to join their families. Enrique still had film left in his camera and wanted to get the three film cartridges processed as soon as they got home. Each film held about three or so minutes. He filmed Méme driving, the dashboard, Méme's polished, tan shoes, and playfully spun the camera as he pointed it at Méme.

It was ironic that the Calles' family was the reason that Encarnacion's family had to flee Mexico back in 1926/1927. Enrique and Méme had been visiting the very plant that was owned by Aco. Thirty years before, Encarnacion might have visited that same plant. What a difference thirty years had made.

Enrique and Méme had likely stayed with their relatives in General Terán. Perhaps they stayed with their cousin, Salomon de la Garza. Or maybe they stayed with one of Méme's relatives on his mother's side of the family.

Méme's father (Juan Garza) was the brother of Margarita (Enrique's mother). Méme's mother was Juana Sáenz. It's interesting to note that the wife of Aco (Plutarco Elias Calles Jr.) was Elisa Sáenz. Elisa Sáenz and Juana Sáenz both lived in the small town of General Terán. The mother of Elisa Sáenz had a surname of

Garza. Was the family of Elisa Sáenz related to Méme's family?

Back in San Antonio, on Monday, March 25, 1957, Enrique filmed his children having a grand time in their front yard. Ramie (5) was riding his white Fire Chief peddle-driven toy automobile. He raced down the sidewalk next to the phone company and headed towards the Aganier house. He turned the corner rapidly and rode up the walk to the house steps. Later he rode up into the telephone company driveway. Their gate was open, and there were no workers in sight, not even Jesse, who was a very kind black man who worked there. He was probably inside of the building.

Years later, Mary Carmen shared her memory of Jessie, "[He] worked next door at the phone company. He'd take care of the trucks, pump gas, and was a really sweet, respectable, and a very nice guy. Jessie would always ask Mom if [he] could have some of her beautiful roses to take home to his wife. Mom always happily said yes. We all liked Jessie! Richard said that Jessie had an Engineering degree and couldn't find a job in engineering. I was never aware of the struggles that Jessie may have experienced, but he was well liked and respected by our family." Mary Carmen went on to say, "Jessie had a heart of gold, as did Richard."[2]

With the coast clear, Ramie rode up the driveway just past the gasoline fuel pump, where the company sometimes fueled its trucks. Ramie turned back and headed back to the sidewalk where Irma was.

Irma was wearing a long dark green dress with sleeves that barely passed her elbows. She was wearing a black hat that smartly hugged the top of her head as she walked assuredly down the sidewalk with a hand-held black leather purse. Then, Skipper, the family dog, ran down the driveway and wrestled a husky white dog to the ground. There was no blood, so it was probably innocent, rabble-rousing fun for them. While Ramie (5) rode his car, Richard (17) sat awkwardly on Rogelio's (2) tricycle. Irma (18) helped Rogelio as he tried to ride the tricycle. Later, Rogelio stood on the sidewalk, turning counterclockwise, following his left hand as if trying to capture it. He paused now and then, getting dizzy, and then he continued to turn around in circles. Enrique continued to film his family.

Later that day, Heriberto (Enrique's brother), his wife Imelda, and their kids arrived. They stood in the front yard of the Aganier house. Mary Carmen (11) was sitting on top of Ramie's little toy car with her legs barely able to reach through the small opening intended for a five or six-year-old child. She was using her tiptoes to propel the little car as she steered the car down the walk. Irma stood next to Carmen and grinned with excitement at the site. However, Carmen began to cross her arms as she looked at her daughter, Mary Carmen. "Your too big for that thing," Carmen seemed to tell Mary Carmen with her eyes.

The Mendoza children from Enrique's family, as well as Heriberto's family, were enjoying themselves in the front yard of 139 Aganier Avenue. Carmen looked very much ready to give birth to her next child.

After a lovely visit, Heriberto and his family left. Enrique changed the film cartridge in his camera and continued to film.

In the film, it looked like Henry was getting into the passenger side of a car that was parked far into the driveway. A friend of his was in the driver's seat. Enrique continued to film as the car backed out of the driveway. Carmen came rushing past Enrique and went up the driveway toward the back of the house. She disappeared around the corner.

Enrique corralled the children into the living room to watch cartoons on their Philco black and white television. He planted them there to keep them entertained while Carmen and the midwife were in Carmen's bedroom, preparing to welcome Enrique and Carmen's ninth child.

A while later, Enrique set up his bright lights on a tripod in his and Carmen's bedroom. Carmen was in bed with her newborn baby, Roberto ("Bobby") lying next to her. The room was clean and fresh.

Enrique set up his camera and then left to get his children so that they could come to see their new baby brother. The children had gone back to play in the front yard. Ramie, Rogelio, Mary Carmen, and Rose Mary walked up to the front steps. Rogelio seemed hesitant to climb the first step. He looked worried. Eventually, they all went inside to discover what or who was waiting for them inside.

Bobby was born in the bedroom next to the "cuartito" (laundry room) - the same room as Rogelio. Carmen said that Bobby was born at 10 o'clock.

Carmen now had an 18-month-old toddler and a newborn infant to care for along with her other children. She so deeply loved her family and especially loved her newborn.

Enrique continued to complete his obligations as the Executor of his father's estate. In July 1957, Enrique completed a final reconciliation statement of the estate of Encarnacion Mendoza dated from September 3, 1954, to May 31, 1957.[3] It appeared to have been meticulously prepared with an additional entry to cover expenses for June 1957. It stated that the eight heirs received $135 each for a total of $1,080. The other entries included the rents for the apartments at 659 W. Elmira Street as well as the expenses (utilities, repairs, insurance, property taxes, and salaries). His salary for all three years was $495.

At long last, there was a buyer for the house. His sister Leslie and her husband Pete had agreed to purchase the home for $5,500. On July 10, 1957, Leslie and Pedro Rivera purchased 659 W. Elmira Street from the estate of Encarnacion. In a 2007 interview, Margarita Elva (daughter of Encarnacion and Margarita Mendoza) said that she received her portion of the proceeds from the sale of the house and used that money to put into her business in Roma, Texas.

On July 24, 1957, Enrique and Carmen celebrated their 25th

Wedding Anniversary. It was exciting for them to celebrate their silver anniversary, especially now that the Elmira house was sold. They were happy. Enrique's brother, Jesus, sent a telegram[4] congratulating them on their wonderful day.

Life was a bit hectic as the family grew, and everyone was well. Skipper, the family dog since 1947, was a big part of the family. He was a beautiful dog. He had a black patch of fur on either side of his head with white between his eyes. On his side and back, he had more black splotches staining his beautiful white hair. He loved the family unconditionally and was especially close to the children.

On December 26, 1957, Enrique borrowed $3,500 from Texas Savings and Loan[5] to add another bedroom to the back of the house at 139 Aganier Avenue. Enrique bought the lumber from Leesch Lumber company that was located directly across the street. Perhaps they discovered that the house was not large enough to support a family of eight children from the youngest, Bobby (9 months) to Minnie (20). (Henry was away in military service.)

Carmen (43) suspected that she was pregnant again. She smiled from her usual optimism.

38 - Family United - 1958

Enrique continued to film family get-togethers with his 8mm film camera. About March of 1958, Enrique filmed Eddie Alejandro's parents and their family when they came to visit Enrique and Carmen at the Aganier house. At the time, Eddie's mother, Ernestina, was pregnant with her soon-to-be-born son, René Alejandro. Carmen was pregnant with her next child. Enrique, Guadalupe (Eddie's father), and Eddie were all dressed in suits, as was the custom back then. Richard wore a long-sleeve blue shirt and khaki pants. Perhaps he was wearing his uniform from ROTC. Minnie, Rose Mary, and Socorro (Eddie's sister) each wore dresses with puffy petticoats. Carmen was wearing a navy-blue dress with short, loose sleeves. Right below her collar were four two-inch round buttons that decoratively adorned the middle section of the top half of her dress. The navy-blue dress accentuated her bright red hair.

They were all stepping down from the front porch when Carmen sat down on one of the concrete benches that sat on either side of the stairs. A few minutes later, Richard and his sister Minnie were playing ball on the front lawn, and Carmen and Eddie's mother, Ernestina, went back inside to talk.

Both Carmen and Ernestina seemed energized as they sat chatting on the living room couch. They were laughing and giggling as Enrique filmed them on his 8mm film camera. Outside, the Mendoza children and the Alejandro children continued to play. They had a lovely time together as Enrique filmed the two families. After a pleasant visit, Guadalupe and Ernestina Alejandro and their children left.

Carmen and Bobby joined the rest of the children outside along with a birdcage with their two pet parakeets. Enrique continued to film them. Rogelio (2-1/2) and Bobby (1) were playing on the porch. The birdcage was sitting on the porch at Carmen's feet. Bobby quickly fixated on the parakeets. He reached for them, and the two parakeets (one yellow and one blue) squawked in terror. He affectionately beat on the top of the cage as the parakeets jumped chaotically from perch to perch. Carmen quickly picked up the cage as Bobby raced towards the edge of the concrete porch. Carmen almost dropped the cage unceremoniously down on to the top step. She grabbed Bobby by the arm, just in time to keep him from falling down the concrete stairs. Rogelio was next to them, not paying attention to his mother and Bobby. Rogelio was throwing a softball down the stairs and then rushing down to retrieve it. When he returned to the porch with the ball, he threw it down again, and again. Rose Mary was standing by the front door, apparently uninterested in the goings-on with the birds, Bobby, Rogelio, and her mother. It looked like the youngest two children, two boys, were quite a handful for Carmen.

Minnie and Eddie decided to get married and started to make plans for their special day. Unexpectedly, Eddie got drafted into the U.S. Army, and their wedding plans were put on hold. On April 18, 1958, he was stationed in Lawton, Oklahoma. Eddie and Minnie were quite serious about marriage, but Eddie's obligation to serve in the military had preempted any plans that they might have had for a wedding - at least it would have seemed so.

Minnie and Eddie often talked by phone over the next few weeks. One time, Eddie had found a way that he could take some time to get married.

"Let's get married in July," he told her. "Do you think you could be ready in three months?"

Of course, Minnie said yes. The plan would be that Eddie would get leave, they'd get married, and then have a beautiful honeymoon. Minnie had the seemingly impossible task of planning the wedding of her dreams in a fraction of the time anyone would have expected.

Minnie went to work quickly to prepare for the wedding. Enrique had already made sure that his bank account would pay for the grandest wedding for his much-loved daughter. No doubt, Carmen had too insisted that they make Minnie's wedding day as beautiful and memorable as Carmen's had been. Carmen remembered, her mother-in-law, Margarita, had spent $25 on her wedding dress. In those days, in the middle of the depression, that was an enormous amount of money. Carmen's wedding dress alone was the most beautiful gown indeed that she had ever owned.

Enrique and Carmen most certainly stood in awe at how Minnie had meticulously planned every detail of her and Eddie's wedding. She selected a wedding photo and wrote a wedding announcement and gave that to The San Antonio Light, the local paper in San Antonio.

In June of 1958, Minnie's aunt, Leslie, had a bridal shower for Minnie at the Elmira house. Many relatives gifted her thoughtful household gifts.

A few days before the wedding, Minnie sat in her bedroom, unpacking her wedding shower gifts. She unwrapped the gifts, there were towels, dishes, and much more. She carefully placed each item inside of her Cavalier Cedar hope chest that sat at the foot of her bed. By 11:00 a.m., Minnie had stowed all of the gifts in her hope chest. Minnie walked into her room, carrying a hard-sided purse that resembled a candy box with a beautiful handle. Minnie wore a long-sleeve, puffy blouse and a brown skirt that extended stylishly below her knees. Her brother Richard had filmed her and, no doubt directed her in the film.

Minnie was in her bedroom, getting ready for her second bridal shower that Eddie's family had planned at their house. She went to the mirrored dresser and picked up a letter, opened it, and smiled as she read it. It was from Eddie. She put the letter away and then got her purse and walked out of the room with a spring in her step. Soon after, she drove to Eddie's house for the shower.

Later she entered her soon-to-be in-law's house. Some of the people there were Delia Mendoza (wife of Jesus), Yolanda (Delia's youngest daughter), Marie Nilda (Delia's daughter), Socorro Alejandro (Eddie's sister), Ramie, Rose Mary, and Mary Carmen with Rogelio. Mary Carmen was affectionately petting Rogelio's head. It looked funny. Maybe she was trying to comb his hair with her hands.

Both Minnie and her favorite cousin, Marie Nilda, had stylish dresses with large petticoats, Minnie's was white, Marie Nilda's was yellow.

Of course, Richard was filming (and directing) when Eddie arrived at the party. Richard probably told Eddie and then Minnie, "Eddie, you go back outside and then come in. And then Minnie, you look surprised when Eddie shows up because he's not supposed to see you on your wedding day."

Eddie was on leave from the Army. He was dressed in his khaki uniform and had his cap in his hand as he entered the room. Minnie covered her eyes as if it were forbidden to see the groom on that day. The loveseat behind them was empty, and they both sat down, posed briefly for the camera, and then turned away and chatted.

Weeks before, Minnie had sent the wedding invitation as follows:

Mr. and Mrs. Enrique Mendoza, Sr. request the honor of your presence at the marriage of their daughter Minerva to

Mr. Eddie Alejandro, son of Mr. and Mrs. Guadalupe Alejandro on Saturday, the fifth of July nineteen hundred and fifty-eight at ten o'clock in the morning at St. Ann's Church, 210 St. Ann St., San Antonio, Texas.

On July 5, 1958, Minnie (21), the eldest daughter of Enrique and Carmen, married Eddie G. Alejandro (23) at St. Ann's Church, presided by Father John W. Yanta.[1] Richard likely filmed the wedding and then later the reception. Mr. and Mrs. Guadalupe Alejandro were proud of their son. According to the San Antonio Light, from July 7, 1958, the wedding gown was described as follows (authored by Minnie):

The Chantilly lace bodice of the bride's gown was fashioned with a jeweled Sabrina neckline, long sleeves, and V-waistline. The peas de sole skirt featured a lace panel which cascaded to a cathedral train.

A crown of orange blossoms held her fingertip veil of illusion edged with lace. She carried lilies of the valley centered with a white orchid.

Her Maid of Honor was her sister, Irma Mendoza. The Bridesmaids were Socorro Alejandro (Eddie's sister), Marie Nilda Mendoza (Jesus's daughter), and Elva Rosa Treviño (Margarita Elva's daughter). Melba Alejandro (Eddie's sister) was the flower girl. Ramie (Minnie's brother) was the ring bearer.

The Best Man was Joe Esquivel. The Groomsmen were Oscar Lopez, Jesus Mendoza Jr. (Jesus's son), Jesse Cantu, Joe Rodriguez, Alfred Joe Garcia, and Richard Guerra.

Minnie and Eddie's wedding reception was at Beethoven Hall, originally built in 1895 as a concert hall. A full orchestra played music. Enrique and Carmen paid for the wedding reception, and Eddie's parents provided the food. For Enrique and Carmen, this was a grand, momentous event. Their first baby girl had grown up and had gotten married. Enrique was quick to point out that Minnie was the first grandchild of Encarnacion and Margarita to get married.

At the wedding reception, there was a double-decker cake adorned on top with an 8-inch tall groom and similar sized bride with a lavish dress that seemed to flow over the entire top tier of the cake. Eddie and Minnie stood in front of the cake, admiring it. Not far behind them was a pregnant Carmen holding baby Bobby with Rogelio at her feet. Enrique was standing nearby, admiring the cake.

Both Minnie and Eddie held the knife as they cut into the cake. Leslie (Minnie's aunt) came rushing in and hugged the groom before they could put the first cake piece onto a plate. Leslie whisked Eddie and Minnie both to their seats.

"Take the baby," Carmen told Enrique as she handed Bobby off to Enrique. Rogelio also stayed with Enrique.

Carmen walked awkwardly down the step and then towards the cake. She expertly cut the cake and handed the first piece to Minnie. It was a large piece. Minnie took it and put it squarely in front of her and Eddie. Carmen continued to cut smaller pieces for the rest of the guests.

Eddie cut a smaller piece of their slice with his fork and offered it to Minnie. It was apparent that they were blissfully happy as they both partook of the delicious wedding cake.

After the reception, they drove off on their honeymoon to Corpus Christi in the 1955 Mercury sedan that they borrowed from her father, Enrique. When Minnie and Eddie arrived safely in Corpus Christi, Minnie got a copy of the San Antonio Light newspaper and quickly turned to the wedding announcement section. She found her wedding announcement right in the middle. Minnie was disappointed because they had placed a picture of an older woman with a caption below it that said: Mrs. Eddie

Migrants: Exploring the Colors of my Family History

Alejandro. She hadn't noticed that on the top right corner was an eye-catching picture of her. It was quite beautiful in its monochromatic, dithered format. It stood out like a photograph from a famous Hollywood actress that conveyed both power and beauty. She was quite striking with her gorgeous earrings as she looked straight into the camera. The caption below Minnie's picture: Anita Madrid.

Many congratulation letters came from the families who had not attended the wedding. One such letter came on July 15, 1958, from Arturo G. Maldonado in Monterrey, Mexico.[2] Enrique and Carmen had recently vacationed in Monterrey and visited with Arturo's family.

Just a couple of months before, Irma had graduated from Ursuline Academy (high school) in San Antonio, Texas.[3] Richard was attending Jefferson High School. Mary Carmen, Rose Mary, and Ramie were at St. Ann's Catholic School. Rogelio and Bobby were nestled at home.

Margarita ("Margaret") was born at the Aganier house in the front room. Years later, in an interview, Carmen pointed out that Margaret was the only child born on a queen bed. After Margaret was born, Carmen prayed that she be allowed to live until Margaret was sixteen years old. Maybe the plea was from her memory of losing her mother when she had barely turned 17 years old.

Canacho and his wife, Enriqueta Chapa Mendoza, couldn't have been prouder of their firstborn son, Fernando ("Fern") Mendoza, when he married the beautiful Beatrice Galindo on September 13, 1958. They sent out the following wedding invitation:[4]

Mr. and Mrs. Indalecio Galindo, Jr. request the honor of your presence at the marriage of their daughter Beatrice Lucia to Fernando Mendoza, Airman, United States Navy, son of Mr. and Mrs. Encarnacion Mendoza, Jr. on Saturday, the thirteenth of September Nineteen hundred and fifty-eight at ten o'clock in the morning at Saint Ann's Catholic Church, San Antonio, Texas.

The joyous event was recorded on 8mm film by Enrique Mendoza. The film started with Beatrice in the middle of the frame. She was wearing a beautiful lacy dress with her veil pulled back from her face. Atop her head was a beautiful white, modest crown also made of the white, lacy fabric.

She was radiant as she held Fernando's arm as they walked out of the church. Fernando lovingly pressed his hand against hers. They continued out of the church and stepped down the stairs, still embracing, as a hundred or more family and friends cheered the beautiful couple.

The 8mm film clip captured their excitement as they posed for wedding pictures. The camera panned around and showed the crowds of loving family surrounding Beatrice and Fernando. Some of the families that were there were Canacho, Enriqueta (Fernando's parents); Jesus, Delia, and their children: Marie Nilda, Yolanda, Joe; Heriberto, Imelda, and their children: Sylvia, Gloria; Virgilio and his wife, Genoveva; and so many more. It was a wonderful occasion. Of course, Beatrice's family was there too. It was a beautiful, loving day.

On November 11, 1958, Enrique (48), Richard, and Irma traveled to Lawton, Oklahoma, to visit Minnie and Eddie Alejandro. Eddie Alejandro was in the Army and stationed in Lawton, Oklahoma. Enrique and his son, Richard, drove the family car. It was a 1955 Mercury Montclair 4-door sedan with a black top and a light-yellow body. Soon after arriving, the whole group (Minnie and Eddie included) traveled to Mount Scott and climbed huge boulders. From the very top, the 8mm film showed a landscape that included a beautiful blue lake surrounded by soft, rolling hills. It must have been chilly on top of that mountain because both Minnie and Irma had heavy, woolen coats. Enrique and Richard wore jackets too. Richard's jacket was dark, navy-blue with a six-inch-wide red/white pattern that traveled horizontally across the upper chest part. The design adorned each of the sleeves on the upper arms.

The day appeared considerably warmer when, a few hours later, they returned to Eddie and Minnie's home. Richard and the family had a bit of fun in filming. Richard pointed the camera at the car and yelled, "Action!" Next, he filmed his father, Enrique, as he exited his car as if he had just arrived. Enrique walked up to the porch, where Minnie and Eddie rushed out the door to hug him. Irma followed closely behind Enrique and continued with the ruse. Both Enrique and Richard enjoyed using the film camera to tell little stories like these. Later, the whole group posed for the camera and then continued with their goodbyes, while Richard loaded the suitcases into the trunk. It was undoubtedly Richard's idea to film the earlier "arrival" sequence.

In an 8mm film from December of 1958, Carmen held Margaret safely nestled in her arms. At that time, Carmen (44) had bright red hair in a distinctive 1950's style that rested just above her shoulders. In that same film, just a few feet away from Margaret, Ramie struggled to cut the cake. The cake slid back and forth as Ramie pushed down hard on the knife. Irma or Rose Mary reached across and stabilized the cake as it came precariously close to the edge of the table. Ramie was still dressed in his white suit and thrilled that his family had gathered together to celebrate his Holy Communion. Carmen looked on proudly at Ramie as she held her sleeping baby Margaret.

Carmen had given birth to her tenth child. She was happy that she and Enrique now had ten healthy children. Carmen loved children, especially babies. "I had five boys and five girls," she said proudly years later.

39 - Future

By January 1, 1959, Carmen (44) and Enrique (49) had ten children. The oldest, Henry, was in the Air Force, and the second-oldest, Minnie, was married and living in Lawton, Oklahoma, with her husband, Eddie. The children living at home were Irma, Richard, Mary Carmen, Rose Mary, Ramie, Rogelio, Bobby, and Margaret (almost four months).

Who picked the children's names?

Enrique said that he had created a list, and they would both decide on the name.

Carmen said that they both wanted names with the "R" sound. In Spanish, the letter "R" had a beautiful rolling "R" sound ("erre").

Enrique said he picked Mary Carmen's name ("Maria del Carmen") because it was Carmen's name.

Enrique said that Carmen picked Henry's name (Enrique Jr.) after Enrique. But Carmen quickly said, "No!" She said she picked it because it has the "R" sound. Enrique insisted that Carmen picked Henry's name (Enrique Jr.) after him. That's when Carmen grimaced.

Carmen named Irma and Minerva after two of her close childhood friends. They were "chulas y lindas [pretty and beautiful]," she said. That's why she picked those names, and the names both had the "R" sound.

"Suene el nombre con el erre," Carmen said. "The names with "R" resonate.

It was probably a coincidence that Carmen's best friend, Leonor, in 1930, had a brother named Rogelio Padaz, who was just a year older than Carmen. Carmen had said that a boy had written her a letter that she had never answered. And the Padaz family lived in a house directly behind her. Could Rogelio Padaz have been that boy?

Enrique used to sing a little song when he was younger and Carmen said that Chuy (Jesus, Enrique's brother) loved to sing that song:

"Erre" con "Erre" Cigarro
"Erre" con "Erre" Barril
Rapido rueda los carros del ferrocarril...

The sound of the names of each of their children were En-rrrr-ique, Mine-rrrr-va, I-rrrr-ma, Rrrr-ica-rrrr-do, Ma-rrrr-ia del Ca-rrrr-men, Rrrr-osa Ma-rrrr-ia, Rrrr-ami-rrrr-o, Rrrr-ogelio, Rrrr-obe-rrrr-to, Ma-rrrr-ga-rrrr-ita.

In April of 1959, Eddie Alejandro's parents, Guadalupe Alejandro (45) and Ernestina de la Garza Alejandro (41), came to visit Enrique (48) and Carmen's (44) family at the Aganier house. Eddie and Minnie had driven from Oklahoma. Richard and Eddie walked towards the house; Eddie was swinging his keys happily around his right hand. Eddie's parents, Guadalupe and a pregnant Ernestina, and their children followed close behind. Guadalupe affectionately supported his wife as they climbed the stairs to the porch.

Inside, the table was arranged lengthwise across the narrow width of the dining room. Perhaps it was arranged this way so that the camera could easily view the family eating together. It was like the "Last Supper" painting by Leonardo da Vinci. No doubt it was Richard's idea to arrange the table like this. Near the head of the table on the left was Carmen, and on the far right, facing the camera, was Guadalupe and Ernestina. Minnie stood next to her mother, Carmen, presumably because Enrique was serving coffee to everyone from the Coffeematic coffeepot that he had gotten Carmen for their 21st wedding anniversary on July 24, 1953. Eventually, Enrique sat at the head of the table opposite Carmen, and then Minnie sat down next to Carmen. Of course, the mood was excitement and loving camaraderie as the children ran in and out of the scene. Ramie sat briefly and then left. Rose Mary sat on the piano bench behind Carmen in her pretty pink dress. Irma, dressed in a stylish, shiny, blue dress, held Bobby as he munched away on a snack.

Later, Eddie and Minnie posed briefly for the camera - Eddie in a formal suit and Minnie in a pretty, light fabric dress that reflected the jolly activities. Eddie's brothers and sister smiled and excitedly laughed as they enjoyed the festive occasion. Mary Carmen and Rogelio were somewhere in the background. Richard was wearing a blue and white, long-sleeved, striped shirt and khaki pants. He got a quick bite and then got his pet alligator from his room and proudly showed it off to the Alejandro children. Ramie and Rose Mary looked on as Richard reveled in the excitement of letting the children touch his pet alligator.

The alligator had grown considerably since he'd gotten it as a pet. Enrique and Carmen became concerned since the alligator would soon grow much too large to keep as a pet. The alligator disappeared one day. Years later, Richard suspected that someone had taken the alligator to the zoo or someplace.

On July 10, 1959, Enrique bought a Chevrolet Kingswood 8, four-door station wagon, two-tone (green/white).[1] It was listed for $4,143.35, Enrique paid $2,956.00. It had ample room to hold the whole family on long trips. There was room to seat nine passengers. One time, the family had gone to Fed Mart (2514 S.W. Military Dr.), a big box store on the southside of town. When they returned home, Enrique backed his car into the driveway, and the children unloaded the groceries. Enrique forgot to set the parking brake, and the car rolled slowly at first down the driveway and picked up a little speed as it plunged into the large gate belonging to the lumberyard directly across the street. The gate crumpled at its center but held firm to the two posts that held it. The gate had been held tightly by chains and was rarely used to enter the lumberyard. The main (and only working) entrance to Leesch lumberyard was on Ashby Street. There was no serious damage to his car.

For years afterward, the lumberyard gate remained tied to chains on either side, although it was a bit crumpled from the impact of the Chevrolet Kingswood 8, four-door station wagon.

Just like the gate of the lumberyard company, the families related to the Mendoza's withstood the weight of the world and its sometimes cruel impositions. Although, the Mendoza families continued to grow despite those assaults. That drive, deep down at its core, sustained the family through tough times.

Around this time, Henry got his first pair of glasses while in the Airforce. He was shocked that he was able to see so much detail when he first put them on. Likewise, the children of Encarnacion and Margarita had begun to see through the haze that resulted from their grief. Life slowly came into focus as the pain and grief of losing family lessened. Their need to nurture and support their families grew; life became sharper and clearer. The families kept the lives of their lost loved ones in their hearts and their prayers. The children of Encarnacion and Margarita were grown now and responsible for the lives of their children. There future had arrived and was sharply in focus. The memories of their lost ones faded, ever so slightly, into the background. The next generation was about to come into existence.

The first grandchild of Enrique and Carmen was born in Oklahoma. Cynthia Alejandro (Cindy) was born to Eddie Alejandro and Minnie Mendoza Alejandro. She was the first great-grandchild of Encarnacion and Margarita Mendoza.

Shortly after that (about August 1959), Enrique, Carmen, and the children traveled to Lawton, Oklahoma, to visit the family. They drove there in their Chevrolet station wagon. They stopped alongside the road to watch a large herd of buffalo. Richard took his camera and jumped the fence to get a closer look at them. He took pictures with his camera as he walked dangerously near to the herd. In retrospect, he was very fortunate that the buffalo ignored him.

Fernando Mendoza and his lovely wife Beatrice celebrated the birth of their first child, Richard ("Ricky") Mendoza. He was the first grandchild of Canacho and Enriqueta Chapa Mendoza. He was the first great-grandson of Encarnacion Mendoza Sr. and Margarita Garza Mendoza.

The family had never fully resolved the Mariana Ybarbo property. On November 3, 1959, Jesus Mendoza (Encarnacion and Margarita's son) attempted to reclaim the property located in Nacogdoches, Texas area that had belonged to his grandmother, Mariana Ybarbo (Margarita's mother). The attorney filed the legal paperwork for Jesus Mendoza in Rusk County and Anderson County in east Texas.[2] Mariana's brother, Vital Ybarbo, had also attempted to reclaim the property on December 11, 1902. At that time, her brother, Vital Ybarbo (served as Mariana's attorney and had power of attorney for her), her brother, Benjamin Ybarbo, and her husband, Juan de la Garza, had quit-claimed the 2,302 acres of the property. The original property from the Juan Jose Ybarbo grant was much more extensive. It appeared that those who took the land from the Ybarbo property had done so through questionable means. They used the money that Juan de la Garza and Mariana Ybarbo de la Garza received in December 1902 to move to General Terán. In 1959, Jesus did not succeed in reclaiming the Ybarbo property.

On December 16, 1959, Ofelia Montalvo Vda. de Longoria,

Anselmo's wife, died at the age of 59 years, eight months, 23 days. She died at 9:50 p.m. in McAllen, Texas.[3] Her death announcement listed her surviving children: Chemo, Delia L. Jones, Elida L. Davila, Ofelia L. Clark, Heron, Jose Eduardo and Alicia L. Contreras.

Carmen, who had been her housemaid for a while, said a prayer for Ofelia. Perhaps Ofelia had happily reunited with her husband, Anselmo Longoria, who had tragically died in a car accident in 1936.

Chemo, who was a very close cousin of Carmen, continued to visit her in San Antonio. Perhaps, he had recognized the kind heart and the ambitious mind of his father, Anselmo, in Carmen. Carmen had met all of her mother's siblings, except for Matilde Longoria, Luisa Longoria, and Benjamin Longoria. She was understandably the closest to her uncle, Anselmo, who had rescued them from certain poverty in San Benito after Crisanto Escobedo (Carmen's stepfather) had died.

In a sense, Anselmo had also saved the Mendoza's who had come to McAllen, Texas, to seek refuge after fleeing for their lives from Mexico. It was Anselmo's property where the Mendoza's had lived on 15th Street in McAllen, across the alley from Anselmo's home on 10th Avenue (later renamed Houston Avenue). It was Anselmo's Phoenix Lumber Company that supplied the lumber for the Loteria. And later, it was the hinges that Enrique bought at Anselmo's burned out lumberyard that modernized the Loteria tent construction. It was also on Anselmo's property where Enrique met Carmen. The children of Encarnacion and Margarita began their journey of integrating into a culture that was not always welcoming. All of them persevered, and all of them succeeded despite the culture barriers.

Enrique's brothers and sisters became citizens of the United States. They thrived in the future that their parents had made possible for them. Each of them used their skills to become proficient in profitable areas like sales, insurance, retail, engineering, accounting, bookkeeping, garment production, and so much more.

The ancestors of the families of Mendoza, Longoria, Garza, Garcia, Escobedo, Ybarbo, (and others) would be in admiration of how wonderfully their sacrifices had rewarded their descendants.

These ancestors created an incredible future full of fantastic opportunities through their life choices for their descendants.

They would have wanted their descendants to likewise forge a path of opportunity and prosperity into the future for the generations that followed.

We are grateful!

The ultimate test of a man's conscience may be his willingness to sacrifice something today for future generations whose words of thanks will not be heard.
- Gaylord Nelson.

THE END

Meet the Family

The Longoria Family Tree

Alejandro Longoria Sr. married **Estefana Martinez**
—— Guillermo Longoria
—— Luisa Longoria
—— Matilde Longoria
—— Benjamin Longoria
—— Estefana Longoria
—— Anselmo Longoria, Sr.
—— Alejandro Longoria, Jr.
—— Cristobal Longoria

—— **Anselmo Longoria** married **Ofelia Montalvo**
—— —— Anselmo "Chemo" Longoria, Jr.
—— —— Delia Longoria
—— —— Elida Longoria
—— —— Ofelia Longoria
—— —— Heron Longoria
—— —— Jose Eduardo Longoria
—— —— Alicia Longoria

—— **Estefana Longoria** and Manuel/Canuto Garcia
—— —— Maria Luisa Garcia
—— —— Carmen Garcia

—— **Estefana Longoria** married **Crisanto Escobedo**
—— —— Matilde Escobedo
—— —— Marcolfa Escobedo
—— —— Alejandro Escobedo

Alejandro Longoria Sr.

When Alejandro Longoria (father of Estefana Longoria) was born in April 1859 in Mier, Tamaulipas, Mexico, his father, Abato, was 35 and his mother, Matilde, was 30. Alejandro married Estefana Martinez on April 26, 1883, in Matamoros, Tamaulipas, Mexico. They had eight children in 16 years (Guillermo, Luisa, Matilde, Benjamin, Estefana, Anselmo, Alejandro Jr., Cristobal). He died somewhere around 1926 at about the age of 67. His granddaughter, Carmen said that he was already dead when she was a young girl. Cause of death is unknown.

Estefana Martinez

Estefana Martinez (mother of Estefana Longoria) was born in 1861 in Monterrey, Nuevo León, Mexico, the daughter of Mariana and Esteban. She was baptized on December 30, 1858. Estefana Martinez married Alejandro Longoria on April 26, 1883, in Matamoros, Tamaulipas, Mexico. They had eight children in 16 years (Guillermo, Luisa, Matilde, Benjamin, Estefana, Anselmo, Alejandro Jr., Cristobal). She died sometime before 1926 at about the age of 65. Her granddaughter, Carmen said that he was already dead when she was a young girl. Cause of death is unknown.

Guillermo Longoria

When Guillermo Longoria was born on February 10, 1884, in Matamoros, Tamaulipas, Mexico, his father, Alejandro, was 24 and his mother, Estefana, was 23. Guillermo married Juana Anaya on February 19, 1910, in Cameron, Texas. They had four children during their marriage. He died on December 20, 1941, at the age of 57. Cause of death is unknown.

Estefana Longoria

When Estefana Longoria (mother of Carmen Garcia) was born in Ranch Los Cuates, Matamoros, Mexico about March 1892, her father, Alejandro Longoria, was 32, and her mother, Estefana Martinez, was 31. In 1900, Estefana's family moved to Brownsville, Texas. Estefana had two children with Canuto Garcia. Although, It's possible the eldest had a different father. Canuto Garcia disappeared from her life soon afterward. Estefana married Crisanto Escobedo about 1917 and had three children with him. Her husband, Crisanto died on September 14, 1929. Her brother, Anselmo moved her family to his home in McAllen, Texas a few weeks later. She died on December 24, 1931, from pneumonia in McAllen, Texas, at the age of 39.

Crisanto Escobedo

When Crisanto Escobedo (step-father of Carmen Garcia) was born on October 27, 1890, in La Ascención in Aramberri, Nuevo León, Mexico, his father, Donaciano Escobedo (b. 1858), was 32 and his mother, Anastacia Valdez (b. 1860), was 30. By 1917, Crisanto married Estefana Longoria (b. 1892). He had one son and two daughters with Estefana Longoria between 1922 and 1927. He was a farmer and a day-laborer. He died on September 14, 1929, of Lobar Pneumonia in San Benito, Texas, at the age of 38.

Anselmo Longoria

When Anselmo M Longoria (brother of Estefana Longoria, father of Anselmo Jr., "Chemo") was born on April 21, 1894, in Matamoros, Tamaulipas, Mexico, his father, Alejandro, was 35 and his mother, Estefana, was 33. Anselmo married Ofelia Montalvo on December 19, 1918, in Hidalgo, Texas. They had seven children in 11 years. He died on November 27, 1936 in a car accident, at the age of 42.

Ofelia Longoria

When Ofelia Montalvo (mother of Anselmo Jr., "Chemo") was born on March 22, 1900, in Guerrero, Tamaulipas, Mexico, her father, Evaristo, was 41, and her mother, Beatriz, was 35. Ofelia married Anselmo M. Longoria on December 19, 1918, in Hidalgo, Texas. They had seven children in 11 years. She died on December 15, 1959, of Myocardial Infarction in Hidalgo, Texas, at the age of 59.

Alejandro Longoria Jr.

When Alejandro Longoria was born on July 5, 1896, in Mexico, his father, Alejandro Sr., was 37 and his mother, Estefana, was 35. Alejandro Jr. had one son with Rosa Jasso in 1925.

Cristobal Longoria

When Cristobal Longoria was born on January 18, 1901, in Brownsville, Texas, his father, Alejandro, was 41 and his mother, Estefana, was 40. Cristobal married Clementina Laveaga on May 26, 1940, in Mexico. They had one child during their marriage. He died on January 6, 1941, of Cancer of the Stomach in Guadalajara, Jalisco, Mexico, at the age of 39.

Anselmo "Chemo" Longoria, Jr.

When Anselmo "Chemo" Longoria was born on October 9, 1919, in McAllen, Texas, his father, Anselmo Longoria, Sr., was 25 and his mother, Ofelia Montalvo, was 19. Chemo married Palmira Lucia Pina and they had four children together. He later married Mary Alice Chapa.

Maria Luisa Garcia

When Maria Luisa Garcia was born on September 16, 1912, in Brownsville, Texas, her father, Canuto/ Manuel Garcia, was 32, and her mother, Estefana Longoria, was 20. Maria Luisa had one brother and three sisters. She died on October 8, 1941, in Texas at the age of 29, from Tuberculosis and was buried there.

Matilde Escobedo

When Matilde Escobedo was born on January 14, 1922, in Brownsville, Texas, her father, Crisanto Escobedo, was 31, and her mother, Estefana Longoria, was 29. Matilde had four sons and two daughters with Abel Cadena Gomez between 1939 and 1956.

Marcolfa Escobedo

When Marcolfa Escobedo was born on November 4, 1925, her father, Crisanto Escobedo, was 35, and her mother, Estefana Longoria, was 33. Marcolfa Escobedo married Claude V. Ordonez in Texas on April 16, 1939, when she was 13 years old. She remarried. She had nine sons and eight daughters.

Alejandro Escobedo

When Alejandro (Alex) Escobedo was born on December 28, 1927, in Brownsville, Texas, his father, Crisanto Escobedo, was 37 and his mother, Estefana Longoria, was 35. Alejandro Escobedo married Julia Vidal and had one child.

The Mendoza Family Tree

Jesus Ramirez married **Guadalupe Garcia**
—— Encarnacion Mendoza

Juan de la Garza married **Mariana Ybarbo**
—— Margarita Garza

—— **Encarnacion Mendoza** married **Margarita Garza**
—— —— Virgilio Mendoza (adopted)
—— —— Jose Enrique Mendoza (1909-1909)
—— —— Enrique Mendoza
—— —— Encarnacion "Canacho" Mendoza
—— —— Heriberto Mendoza
—— —— Jesus Mendoza
—— —— Jose Armando Mendoza (1917-1918)
—— —— Maria Consuelo Mendoza
—— —— Margarita Elva Mendoza
—— —— Ruby Luz Mendoza
—— —— Leslie Mendoza

—— —— **Enrique Mendoza** married **Carmen Garcia**
—— —— —— Enrique Jr. ("Henry")
—— —— —— Minerva ("Minnie")
—— —— —— Irma
—— —— —— Ricardo ("Richard")
—— —— —— Maria del Carmen ("Mary Carmen")
—— —— —— Rosa Maria ("Rose Mary")
—— —— —— Ramiro ("Ramie")
—— —— —— Rogelio ("Roger")
—— —— —— Roberto ("Bobby")
—— —— —— Margarita ("Margaret")

Jesus Ramirez Mendoza

Jesus Ramirez Mendoza (father of Encarnacion Sr.) was born in 1852 in León, Guanajuato, Mexico, the son of Maria Antonia Ramirez and Nicolas Mendoza. Jesus married Maria Guadalupe Garcia in Mexico. They had at least three children (including Encarnacion Mendoza) during their marriage. His grandson, Enrique Mendoza (son of Encarnacion) didn't remember meeting his grandfather. He was told that his grandfather was a train engineer in Mexico and was rarely home traveling through the railway lines. Jesus Mendoza died sometime before 1918. Cause of death is unknown.

Guadalupe Garcia

Maria Guadalupe Garcia (mother of Encarnacion Mendoza Sr.) was born on October 14, 1861, the daughter of Maria Margarita Garcia and Gregorio Garcia. Guadalupe was baptized on October 18, 1861 in Santiago, Nuevo Leon, Mexico. She married Jesus Ramirez Mendoza (b. 1852) and they had at least two children during their marriage. Her father passed away in March 1889 at the age of 49. Her mother died about the same time. Guadalupe's husband passed away sometime before 1918. She had traveled to the United States on May 14, 1918 to accompany her daughter-in-law, Margarita Garza Mendoza to Seguin, Texas. Guadalupe died on August 26, 1920, in General Terán, Nuevo Leon, Mexico, at the age of 58 from "Tuberculosis Pulmonia."

Juan de la Garza

When Juan Jose De La Garza (father of Margarita Garza) was born about 1843 in Mexico, his father, José, was 32, and their mother, Maria, was 22. He had three sons (Eugenio, Juan, Salomon) and two daughters (Virginia, Margarita) with Margarita Lopez. Juan then married Mariana Ybarbo and they had a daughter (Margarita). He died on April 26, 1904, in Ciudad General Terán, Nuevo León, Mexico, at the age of about 61. Cause of death is unknown.

Mariana Ybarbo

When Mariana Ybarbo (mother of Margarita Garza) was born in 1848 in Nacogdoches, Texas, her father, Juan Jose Ybarbo, was 33, and her mother, Maria Alafonsa Flores, was 27. Mariana married Juan Jose De La Garza in 1883. They had a daughter (Margarita) during their marriage. In 1901 Mariana, her husband, and her daughter moved to General Terán. Mariana died on November 19, 1930 from Influenza and Pneumonia, in McAllen, Texas, at the age of 82.

Encarnacion "Chonito" Mendoza

When Encarnacion Mendoza (father of Enrique Mendoza) was born on March 25, 1882, in Ciudad General Terán, Nuevo León, Mexico, his father, Jesus Ramirez Mendoza, was 30 and his mother, Maria Guadalupe, was 20. At 26, Encarnacion married Margarita De La Garza on April 28, 1908, in Montemorelos, Nuevo León, Mexico. They had 12 children in 17 years. He and his wife immigrated to the United States before March 2, 1927 and lived with his family in Donna and then McAllen, Texas. He died on September 3, 1954, from a gunshot wound in San Antonio, Texas at the age of 72, and was buried there at the San Fernando cemetery No. 2.

Margarita de la Garza

When Margarita de La Garza (mother of Enrique Mendoza) was born on February 22, 1885, in Floresville, Texas, her father, Juan de la Garza (b. 1843), was 42, and her mother, Mariana Ybarbo (b. 1848), was 37. By 1904, Margarita's father had died at the age of 61 in General Terán. She and her mother lived together there until, Margarita married Encarnacion Mendoza on April 28, 1908, in Montemorelos, Nuevo León, Mexico. They had 11 children in 17 years and 1 adopted boy. She moved with her family and mother, Mariana, to the United States before March 2, 1927 and lived in Donna, Texas and then McAllen, Texas. Her mother, Mariana passed away on November 19, 1930 in McAllen, Texas at the age of 82. By the end of 1932, Margarita and her family were living in San Antonio, Texas. She died on January 7, 1948, in San Antonio, Texas at the age of 62, from carcinoma of the lung and was buried at the San Fernando cemetery No.2 in San Antonio.

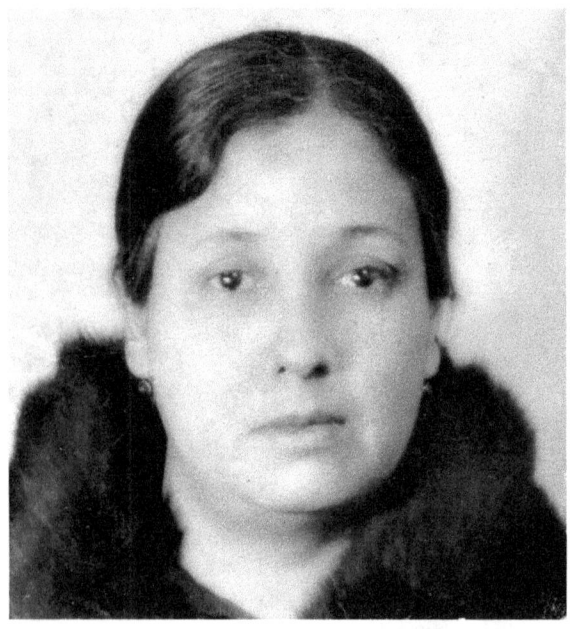

Encarnacion "Canacho" Mendoza, Jr.

When Encarnacion Mendoza was born on December 9, 1911, in Ciudad General Terán, Nuevo León, Mexico, his father, Encarnacion, was 29 and his mother, Margarita, was 26. Canacho had three sons and one daughter with Enriqueta Chapa between 1939 and 1951.

Heriberto Mendoza

When Heriberto Mendoza was born on February 10, 1913, in Ciudad General Terán, Nuevo León, Mexico, his father, Encarnacion Mendoza, was 30 and his mother, Margarita Garza, was 27. Heriberto had four daughters with Imelda Cantu between 1942 and 1952.

Jesus Mendoza

When Jesus Mendoza was born on April 2, 1916, in Ciudad General Terán, Nuevo León, Mexico, his father, Encarnacion, was 34 and his mother, Margarita, was 31. Jesus had three sons and two daughters with Delia Garza between 1938 and 1952.

Consuelo Mendoza

When Maria Consuelo Mendoza was born on August 2, 1918, in Ciudad General Terán, Nuevo León, Mexico, her father, Encarnacion Mendoza, was 36, and her mother, Margarita Garza, was 33. Consuelo had seven brothers and four sisters. She died as a teenager on June 4, 1937, from Broncho pnuemonia (complicated by epilepsy) in Texas.

Margarita Elva Mendoza

When Margarita Elva Mendoza was born on September 25, 1919, in Ciudad General Terán, Nuevo León, Mexico, her father, Encarnacion Mendoza, was 37, and her mother, Margarita Garza, was 34. Margarita Elva had three sons and five daughters with Francisco Trevino.

Ruby Luz Mendoza

When Ruby Luz Mendoza was born on June 17, 1921, in Texas, her father, Encarnacion Mendoza, was 39, and her mother, Margarita Garza, was 36. Ruby had two sons and two daughters with Ernesto Reygadas between 1941 and 1949.

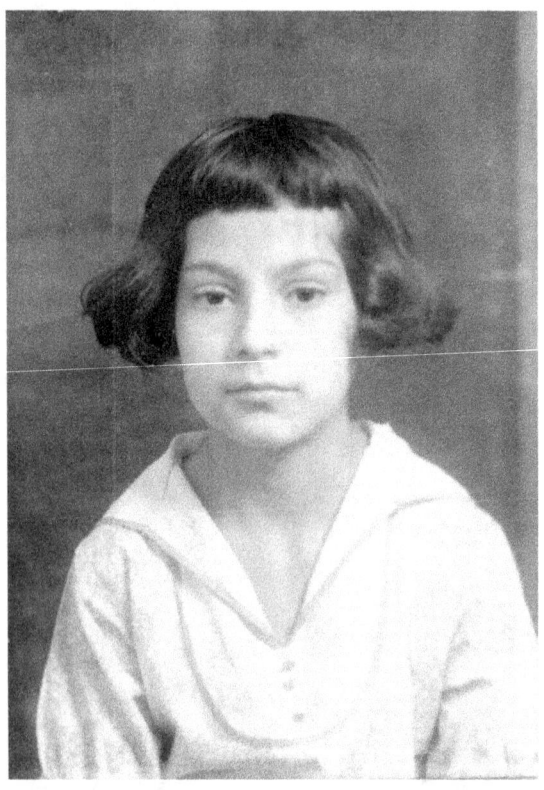

Leslie Mendoza

When Leslie Mendoza was born on September 25, 1923, in Ciudad General Terán, Nuevo León, Mexico, her father, Encarnacion Mendoza, was 41, and her mother, Margarita Garza, was 38. Leslie had one son with Carlos del Moral. She then married Pedro Manguba Rivera on May 1, 1954, in Seguin, Texas.

Enrique Mendoza

When Enrique Mendoza was born on July 8, 1910, in Seguin, Texas, his father, Encarnacion, was 28 and his mother, Margarita, was 25. Enrique married Carmen Garcia on July 24, 1932, in McAllen, Texas. They had ten children in 23 years.

Carmen Garcia

When Carmen Garcia was born on September 19, 1914, in Robstown, Texas, her father, Canuto, was 34, and her mother, Estefana, was 22. Carmen married Enrique Mendoza on July 24, 1932, in McAllen, Texas and soon after moved to San Antonio. They had ten children in 23 years. Carmen was born and baptized as Maria del Carmen, but everyone called her Carmen.

About the Author

Roger Mendoza lives in San Antonio, Texas, the seventh-largest city in the United States. In 2014, he moved back to his birth town of San Antonio from Parker, Colorado, where he had lived for fifteen years. Living on the outskirts of San Antonio, he still enjoys the taste of the rural life that he loves so much and the conveniences that the big city provides.

He worked most of his life as a Software Engineer in the defense industry, where he cultivated his passion for computer programming but is now retired. Along with writing novels, Roger is also a professional photographer and can often be seen toting his camera looking for photo opportunities in and around town. He loves to capture nature photography and beautiful scenery.

He was born eighth in a family of ten children. There were five boys and five girls with an age span of about twenty-three years. With a fascination for his family history, he has spent years gathering his parent's family photographs and documents. He has cataloged the family's collections and digitized them all. He loves keeping the family tree database updated with new family members as they are born. Roger loves to review the thousands of family photographs and documents while imagining what these people – these relatives and their stories were like.

Roger has always had an interest in understanding the philosophy of life, why people behave the way they do, and how we all fit into the grander scheme of life itself. He still believes in "happily ever after endings" even though life, on occasion, gets in the way of that outcome.

He's always had a fascination with unusual phenomena – the most being the drama of life itself. It still amazes him why so much drama fills the life of his friends and family. Perhaps it is observing that drama that sparks his imagination and gives his characters life.

Notes

1 - Estefana up to 1910

1. Rio Grande river was known as Río Bravo del Norte in Mexico
2. 500176; June 11, 1900; 12th Census of U.S. 1900 Census, Cameron County, City Precinct no. 3, Enumeration District No. 20, Street no. 9
3. 500176; June 11, 1900; 12th Census of U.S. 1900 Census, Cameron County, City Precinct no. 3, Enumeration District No. 20, Street no. 9
4. 500470; September 17, 1890; Birth certificate for Benjamin Longoria.
5. 500469; April 19, 1981; Baptismal certificate for Benjamin Longoria; Ancestry.com
6. 500348; November 19, 1903; Death certificate for Benjamin Longoria
7. 500472; October 14, 1904; The Brownsville Herald, Brownsville, Texas,3; "Called-for" letters list
8. 500473; October 28, 1904; The Brownsville Herald, Brownsville, Texas,1; "Called-for" letters list
9. 500475; November 18, 1905; The Brownsville Herald, Brownsville, Texas,3; "Called-for" letters list
10. 500471; March 25, 1907; The Brownsville Herald, Brownsville, Texas,1; "Called-for" letters list
11. 500474; July 13, 1909; The Brownsville Herald, Brownsville, Texas,3; "Called-for" letters list for Mrs. Estefana Longoria de Garcia
12. 500476; February 19, 1910; Wedding license from State of Texas for Guillermo Longoria and Juana Anaya.
13. 500416; March 23, 1910; State Board of Health Death Certificate for Luisa Longoria in Texas
14. 500477; June 9, 1910; 13th Census of U.S. 1910 Census, Cameron County, City Precinct no. 3, Enumeration District No. 29, Street no. 28A

2 - Encarnacion & Margarita up to 1910

1. 500478; June 17, 1880; U.S. 1880 Census, Wilson County, Texas, Justice Precinct no 8, Enumeration District No. 147, page 24.
2. Many books have been written about Antonio Gil Ybarbo, and a statue of him stands on the east side of the square in downtown Nacogdoches.
3. 301161; Abt. 1899, picture of Clarita (6), Guadalupe (2), and Margarita (4)
4. 500137; Music composition by Fernando Medina, Reynosa, Tamaulipas, Mexico.
5. 500146; May 1, 1918; Birth affidavit for Encarnacion Mendoza Sr., b. March 25, 1882.
6. 1907; Journal containing notes and recipes for pastries, and accounting of Loteria prizes for Encarnacion's businesses.
7. 500348; June 1907; Request to acquire more property for Encarnacion's business.
8. 500379; February 13, 1907; Manuel "Meme" Garza's baptismal certificates.
9. 500377; October 16, 1940; U.S. Draft registration card for Manuel Garza.

¹⁰ 500357; April 4, 1908; Wedding certificate for Encarnacion and Margarita Garza in Montemorelos.

3 - Encarnacion & Margarita 1910 to 1919

1. 500390; June 19, 1910; Border Crossing for Encarnacion Mendoza
2. 500386; June 19, 1910; Border Crossing for Margarita Garza
3. 500398; June 19, 1910; Border Crossing for Mariana Ybarbo
4. 500388; June 19, 1910; Border Crossing for Juan Saenz
5. 500063; July 15, 1942; Birth affidavit for Enrique Mendoza, b. July 8, 1910.
6. 500184; November 22, 1910; Baptismal certificate for Enrique Mendoza
7. 500061; June 1, 1910; Registration of birth of Enrique Mendoza in General Terán, Nuevo Leon, Mexico
8. 500352; December 9, 1911; Birth certificate for Encarnacion ("Canacho") Mendoza Jr.
9. 500063; February 10, 1913, Birth certificate for Heriberto Mendoza
10. 500351; November 6, 1913; The Evening Chronicle, November 6, 1913,9
11. 500355; March 25, 1914; Birth certificate for Consuelo Guadalupe Mendoza, Nuevo Leon, Civil Registration Births.
12. 500483; June 29, 1914; Death certificate for Consuelo Guadalupe Mendoza in General Terán
13. 500354; April 15, 1916; Birth announcement for Jesus Mendoza in Mexican Registry
14. 500363; October 16, 1940; U.S. Draft Registration for Jesus Mendoza for WW II.
15. Michael C. Meyer and William L. Sherman, *The Course of Mexican History*, [New York: Oxford University Press, 1995], iv
16. Michael C. Meyer and William L. Sherman, *The Course of Mexican History*, [New York: Oxford University Press, 1995], 545
17. 500394; February 4, 1917; Laredo Weekly Times, February 4, 1917,3
18. 500395; April 19, 1917; Laredo Weekly Times, April 29, 1917,10
19. 500138; August 6, 1917; Birth certificate for Jose Armando; also 500349 records from Mexican registry
20. 500082; January 19, 1918; Baptism of Jose Armando Mendoza
21. 500084; May 6, 1918; Declaration of alien to depart for the U.S. for Margarita Mendoza
22. 500414; May 14, 1918; Border crossing into the U.S. for Margarita Mendoza.
23. 500417; May 14, 1918; Border crossing into the U.S. for Guadalupe Mendoza
24. 500086; June 6, 1918; Funeral notice for Jose Armando. (d. June 5, 1918).
25. 500050; August 14, 1918; Birth registration in General Terán for Maria Consuelo Mendoza (b. August 2, 1918)
26. September 25, 1919; Birth certificate for Margarita Elva Mendoza
27. January 8, 1921; Baptismal record for Margarita Elva Mendoza

* * *

4 - Estefana 1910 to 1919

1. 500477; June 9, 1910; 1930 U.S. Census, Cameron County, Justice precinct 3, Enum District 29, Sheet 28A
2. September 25, 1912, Birth certificate not found, date provided by her sisters Carmen Garcia and Matilde Gomez. 500481; October 8, 1941; Death Certificate for Maria del Luisa Garcia
3. 500474; July 13, 1909; The Brownsville Herald, Brownsville, Texas,3; "Called-for" letters list for Mrs. Estefana Longoria de Garcia, and Manuel Garcia
4. Cecilia Escobedo was Estefana's sister-in-law after 1917 when Estefana married Crisanto Escobedo.
5. 500490; December 12. 1050; United States Petition for Naturalization, June 1, 1953, for Canuto Garcia. U.S. Citizen, December 12, 1959. Married on October 18, 1908.
6. 500376; August 29, 1917; Border Crossing Manifest from Mexico to the U.S. for Estefana Longoria accompanied by husband, Crisanto Escobedo.
7. 500489; July 11, 1921; Border Crossings: From Mexico to the U.S., 1895-1964 for Alejandro Longoria (25), Anselmo (26);
8. 500482; December 19, 1918; Marriage certificate for Anselmo Longoria and Ofelia Montalvo. State of Texas, Hidalgo County, #2150
9. 500175; November 26, 1919; Baptismal certificate for Anslemo Longoria Jr., b. October 9, 1919.

5 - Estefana & Carmen 1920 to 1928

1. 500486; February 27, 1920; 1920 U.S. Census, Nueces County, Justice of the Peace Precinct 2 - Nueces County, Texas, Sheet 11
2. Ancestry.com, 1930 United States Federal Census (Provo, UT, USA, Ancestry.com Operations Inc, 2002), Ancestry.com, Year: 1930; Census Place: McAllen, Hidalgo, Texas; Page: 10B; Enumeration District: 0023.
3. January 14, 2000; Biography of Matilde Escobedo Gomez, prepared by her daughters, Olga and Mary Lou
4. 1924; Newspaper article about the reconstruction of Sacred Heart Church
5. November 4, 1925; Birth of Marcolfa Escobedo
6. 500167; March 27, 1990; Anselmo Longoria, Jr., "Biography Data of Anselmo M. Longoria, Sr."
7. 500167; March 27, 1990; Anselmo Longoria, Jr., "Biography Data of Anselmo M. Longoria, Sr."
8. 500418; December 28, 1927; Draft card for Alejandro "Alex" Escobedo
9. Death of Anastacia Valdez; December 1927
10. Crisanto's father, Donaciano Escobedo (70), a widow since 1927, was a furniture maker. Crisanto's sister, Cecilia Escobedo Contreras (36), and her family lived in San Benito, Texas
11. Death of Cecilia Escobedo; April 27, 1948;

* * *

6 - Encarnacion & Margarita 1920 to 1924

1. Frank McLynn, Villa and Zapata, [New York; Basic Books, 2000], 383-385
2. Michael C. Meyer and William L. Sherman, The Course of Mexican History, [New York; Oxford University Press, 1995], 569
3. 500392; May 1, 1922; Marengo Republic News (Marengo, Illinois), May 5, 1922, Thu, 7
4. June 17, 1921; Birth of Rube de Luz Mendoza; Nuevo Leon, Mexico, Civil Registration Births, 1859-1947, Archivo General del Registro Civil del Estado (Civil Registry State Archives); Nuevo Leon, Mexico
5. Her name appears as Rube, Rubi, and Ruby in various documents. Most called her Rube.
6. Jürgen Buchenau, Plutarco Elias Calles and the Mexican Revolution, [Maryland: Rowman & Littlefield Publishers, 2007], 102-103
7. September 25, 1923; Birth certificate for Leslie del Roble Mendoza
8. 500391; November 2, 1923; Death certificate for Eugenio de la Garza
9. April 5,1924; Letter from Arturo Garcia to Teodoro Elizondo was on his property
10. 500189; August 26, 1932; Letter from Teodoro Elizondo to Encarnacion about a property dispute
11. 500407; July 3, 1926, Border crossing for Manuel (Méme) Garza.
12. 500083; June 30, 1924; Completion of "Escuela Oficial Para Niño's" in General Terán by Enrique Mendoza
13. Jürgen Buchenau, Plutarco Elias Calles and the Mexican Revolution, [Maryland: Rowman & Littlefield Publishers, 2007], 108
14. Heriberto's nickname was Beto
15. August 8, 1924; Baptism document of Leslie Mendoza
16. Jürgen Buchenau, Plutarco Elias Calles and the Mexican Revolution, [Maryland: Rowman & Littlefield Publishers, 2007], 112-113

7 - Encarnacion & Margarita 1925 to 1927

1. 500347; February 25, 1925; Legal document to form a partnership for Encarnacion's business.
2. 500146; May 1, 1918; Birth affidavit for Encarnacion Mendoza Sr., b. March 25, 1882.
3. Jurgen Buchenau, Plutarco Elias Calles and the Mexican Revolution, [Maryland: Rowman & Littlefield Publishers, 2007], 123
4. Michael C. Meyer and William L. Sherman, The Course of Mexican History, [New York: Oxford University Press, 1995], 584,585
5. Michael C. Meyer and William L. Sherman, The Course of Mexican History, [New York: Oxford University Press, 1995], 587
6. Andres Rendon, "The Cristero War and Mexican History," HistoricalMX, accessed August 2, 2020, https://historicalmx.org/items/show/128.
7. Jurgen Buchenau, Plutarco Elias Calles and the Mexican Revolution, [Maryland: Rowman & Littlefield Publishers, 2007], 161

8   500399; September 1, 1928; Record of Voluntary Departures, Encarnacion Mendoza Jr., age 17. Indicates Canacho living for two years, since December 15, 1926
500402; December 15, 1926; Border crossing for Encarnacion Mendoza Jr. ("Canacho").
9   Family Tree:
Encarnacion was married to Margarita Garza
    Margarita Garza was the daughter of Marianna Ybarbo
    Marianna Ybarbo's sister was Regina Ybarbo
    Juan Cordova (1835 - 1926) was married to Regina Ybarbo (1840 to 1926)
    Juan and Regina's son was Leandro Cordova (1858 to 1943)
    Leandro's son was Hernan Cordova (1904 to 1946)
10 500401; March 2, 1927; Border crossing for Encarnacion Mendoza Sr.; Encarnacion had black hair, brown eyes, and had a mole on his left cheek.

8 - Mendoza's Reunited 1927 to 1928

1   500146; May 12, 1927; Letter from Enrique Mendoza asking Gaspar Cantú Garza for money. Translated from Spanish.
2   Michael C. Meyer and William L. Sherman, The Course of Mexican History, [New York: Oxford University Press, 1995], 588
3   500183; December 10, 1927; Tax bill from General Terán the State Tax collection office
4   500368; March 20, 1928; Border crossing for Encarnacion Mendoza Sr.
5   500344; March 20, 1928; Letter from Gaspar Cantu (General Terán) to Encarnacion Mendoza in McAllen, Texas

9 - McAllen 1928 to 1929

1   500343; June 20, 1928; Loan document (Fox Motor Company) for purchase of Ford Model T(T)
2   500399; September 1, 1928; Record of Voluntary Departures, Encarnacion Mendoza Jr. ("Canacho"), age 17.
3   500400; September 4, 1928; Border crossing for Encarnacion Mendoza Jr. ("Canacho")
4   500092; September 25, 1928; Registration certificate for the Mexican Consulate in Hidalgo, Texas, for Encarnacion Mendoza Sr.
5   500113; November 3, 1959; The Juan Jose Ybarbo Grant in Rusk and Anderson Counties. It was filed by Jesus Mendoza to reclaim Ybarbo property.
6   Margarita's half-brothers were living in General Terán, and Mariana had a house in General Teran in 1908.
7   June 21, 1929; End of the Cristero Rebellion in Mexico
8   "Mexico Ending Church Restraints After 70 Years of Official Hostility" New York Times, December 20, 1991, Section A, Page 1
9   The Great Depression, which began in the United States in 1929 and spread worldwide, was the most prolonged and most severe economic downturn in modern

history. It was marked by steep declines in industrial production and prices (deflation), mass unemployment, banking panics, and sharp increases in rates of poverty and homelessness.

10 - Anselmo the Hero 9/1929

1. April 21, 1894; Birth of Anselmo Longoria
2. October 25, 1924; Fire destroys Sacred Heart Church.
3. 500426; November 20, 1926; McAllen Daily Press, November 20, 1926
4. 500167; March 27, 1990, Anselmo Longoria, Biography of Anselmo Longoria Sr., March 27, 1990

11 - Budding Romance 1929

1. Carmen spelled Leonor's last name as Padaz; the 1930 Census spelled her last name as Paras.
2. October 19, 1929; United States Stock Market crash
3. 500488; November 1, 1929; McAllen Daily Press, McAllen, Texas, 1 Nov 1929, 1
4. 2007, Video Interview with Margarita Elva Mendoza Trevino, La Familia Archives
5. 500036; November 18, 1929; Letter no. 1 from Enrique to Carmen.
6. 500035; December 4, 1929; Letter no. 2 from Enrique to Carmen
7. Guadalupe - unofficially adopted daughter of Encarnacion Mendoza.
8. 500093; December 24, 1929; Gift tag from Enrique to Carmen Mendoza
9. 500167; March 27, 1990; Anselmo "Chemo" Longoria, Biography Data of Anselmo M. Longoria, Sr.
10. 500155; January 12, 1930; U.S. Identification card for Enrique Mendoza

13 - The Census - 4/1930 to 8/1930

1. 500034; April 8, 1930; Letter no. 3 from Enrique to Carmen.
2. https://www.loc.gov/teachers/classroommaterials/presentationsandactivities/presentations/immigration/alt/mexican6.html
3. 500177; April 10, 1930; 15th census of the U.S. for McAllen, Hidalgo County, District No. 118-28, Sheet No. 10-B
4. 1930 population of McAllen, Texas
5. 1930 United States Census for District 013, Precinct 2, Nueces County, Texas
6. 500032; May 19, 1930; Letter no. 4 from Enrique to Carmen.
7. 500366; March 2, 1927; Border crossing record for Encarnacion Mendoza accompanied by son, Enrique Mendoza
8. 500029; June 18, 1930; Letter no. 5 from Enrique to Carmen.
9. 500095, August 5, 1930; Postcard sent by Estefana Longoria to her daughter Carmen.
10. 500094; August 2, 1930; Postcard sent by Maria Luisa Garcia to Margarita G. Mendoza

★ ★ ★

14 - Mamacita Danced - 9/1930 to 11/1930

1. 500021; September 27, 1930; Letter no. 6 from Enrique to Carmen.
2. 500020; October 3, 1930; Letter no. 7 from Enrique to Carmen.
3. McAllen Daily Press, McAllen, Texas, Sunday, October 5, 1930
4. 500019; October 9, 1930; Letter no. 8 from Enrique to Carmen.
5. 500021; October 22, 1930; Letter no. 9 from Enrique to Carmen.
6. 500016; November 12, 1930; Letter no. 10 from Enrique to Carmen.

15 - Mendoza Shakeup - 11/1930 to 12/1930

1. 500053; November 19, 1930; Death certificate for Mariana Ybarbo, widow of Juan de la Garza, mother of Margarita Garza
2. 500113; November 3, 1959; The Juan Jose Ybarbo Grant in Rusk County.
3. There are several books and articles written about Juan Jose Ybarbo that tell of this dark history that stained his family's history.
4. 500113.1; November 4, 1959; The Juan Jose Ybarbo Grant in Anderson County.
5. 500015; November 27, 1930; Letter no. 11 from Enrique to Carmen.
6. 500013; December 20, 1930; Letter no. 12 from Enrique to Carmen.
7. 500185; December 26, 1930; Receipt for Mosler safe

16 - Making Moves - 1/1931 to 3/1931

1. 500180; January 4, 1931; Letter from R. Martinez in Monterrey
2. 500152; January 9, 1931; Letter from Oscar T. Vale as reference for Margarita
3. 500011; January 10, 1931; Letter no. 13 from Enrique to Carmen.
4. 500011; February 8, 1931; Letter no. 14 from Enrique to Carmen.
5. 500008; March 1, 1931; Letter no. 15 from Enrique to Carmen.
6. 500008; March 13, 1931; Letter no. 16 from Enrique to Carmen.
7. Banks encouraged borrowers to repay loans in Great Depression 1929

17 - We Need Money - 5/1931 to 10/1931

1. 500004; March 12, 1931; Letter no. 17 from Enrique to Carmen.
2. 500002; May 24, 1931; Letter no. 18 from Enrique to Carmen.
3. 500000; June 2, 1931; Letter no. 19 from Enrique to Carmen.
4. 500048; June 9, 1931; Letter no. 20 from Enrique to Carmen.
5. 500131; July 2, 1931; Letter from McAllen Public Schools stating the good character of Margarita and her children
6. 500424; September 15, 1931; McAllen Daily Press
7. 500047; September 16, 1931; Letter no. 21 from Enrique to Carmen.
8. 500045; October 2, 1931; Letter no. 22 from Enrique to Carmen.

* * *

18 - One Door Closes - 10/1931 to 12/1931

1. 500152; January 9, 1931; Picture of Oscar T. Vale.
2. 500043; November 5, 1931; Letter no. 23 from Enrique to Carmen.

20 - Two Become One - 1/1932 to 7/1932

1. 500048; January 20, 1932; Letter no. 24 from Enrique to Carmen.
2. 500173.2; February 1932; Anselmo Longoria's Business Card, Monterrey, Mexico
3. 500167; March 27, 1990; Anselmo ("Chemo") Longoria, Biography of Anselmo Longoria Sr.
4. 500067; February 19, 1932; Letter no. 25 from Enrique to Carmen.
5. 500069; February 22, 1932; Only letter from Carmen to Enrique
6. 500071; March 18, 1932; Letter no. 26 from Enrique to Carmen.
7. 500073; April 28, 1932; Letter no. 27 from Enrique to Carmen.
8. 500075; June 2, 1932; Letter no. 28 from Enrique to Carmen.
9. Jurgen Buchenau, Plutarco Elias Calles and the Mexican Revolution, [Maryland: Rowman & Littlefield Publishers, 2007], 93
10. 500048; June 26, 1932; Letter no. 29 from Enrique to Carmen.

21 - Goodbye, McAllen - 8/1932 to 9/1932

1. 500189; August 26, 1932; Letter from Teodoro Elizondo the Encarnacion regarding a property dispute

22 - San Antonio - 9/1932 to 12/1934

1. 500190; September 20, 1932; Receipt for Baker's Oven.
2. 1933; Reynosa-McAllen international bridge replaced
3. 500155.2; January 18, 1933; Quarantine Identification card for Enrique Mendoza
4. 500096; March 25, 1933; postcard from Maria Luisa to her sister Carmen
5. 500147; April 28, 1933; Wedding toast for Encarnacion and Margarita Mendoza's 25 wedding anniversary
6. 500393; July 8, 1933; Associated Press; Abilene Reporter News; Two States in Mexico are Hard Hit by Gale
7. 500237; July 23, 1933; Wedding invitation for Meme Garza and Maria de la Luz Sanchez
8. 500340; July 26, 1933; Birth affidavit for Margarita Garza Mendoza
9. January 14, 2000; Biography of Matilde Escobedo Gomez, San Antonio, Texas, January 14, 2000
10. Jürgen Buchenau, Plutarco Elias Calles and the Mexican Revolution, [Maryland: Rowman & Littlefield Publishers, 2007], 169

* * *

23 - Family Life - 1/1935 to 10/1936

1. 500191; May 13, 1935; letter from The Physicians Health and Accident Insurance Company to Encarnacion Mendoza
2. 500192; June 12, 1935; postcard from Enrique in San Angelo, Texas to Carmen
3. 500309; September 26, 1935; Purchase of Chevrolet Truck by Encarnacion Mendoza
4. April 9, 1936; Calles deported to U.S.
5. 500240; May 6, 1936; promissory note to Frost National Bank by Encarnacion Mendoza Jr. ("Canacho")
6. https://www.dollartimes.com/inflation/?
7. 500291; September 16, 1936; Last payment to Ormsby Chevrolet by Encarnacion Mendoza
8. 500238; September 23, 1936; Declaration of last entry to the U.S. by Encarnacion Mendoza
9. 500193; September 24, 1936; Favorable consideration letter to Margarita Mendoza from Frost National Bank.
10. 500120; October 8, 1936; Letter from San Antonio Chief of Police stating no criminal record for Encarnacion and Margarita's family.

24 - Sacrifices - 11/1936

1. 500172; March 16, 1936; Letter from Anselmo M. Longoria to his daughter, Delia
2. 500167; March 27, 1990; Anselmo "Chemo" Longoria, Biography Data of Anselmo M. Longoria, Sr., McAllen, Texas

25 - More Family - 4/1937 to 12/1939

1. 500098; April 25, 1937; wedding invitation to Jesus and Delia Mendoza wedding
2. 500099, 500320; June 4, 1937; Death certificate for Maria Consuelo Mendoza
3. 500100; August 6, 1937; Purchase of 1937 Chevrolet Truck
4. 500119.1; January 7, 1942; Registration with war department for 1937 Chevrolet Truck
5. 500194; August 7, 1937; Cleared check for payment of Chevy Truck
6. 500369; November 16, 1937; Border crossing for Margarita Garza Mendoza
7. 500370; November 16, 1937; Border crossing for Heriberto Mendoza
8. 500371; November 16, 1937; Border crossing for Jesus Mendoza
9. 500372; November 16, 1937; Border crossing for Margarita Mendoza
10. 500373; November 16, 1937; Border crossing for Rubi Luz Mendoza
11. 500374; November 16, 1937; Border crossing for Leslie Mendoza
12. 500255; April 5, 1938; Receipt for eyeglasses
13. Santos Coy Gomez was born on March 29, 1862
14. Maria de Jesus Caden Gomes was born December 25, 1867
15. Eva Slightom was born on October 8, 1903
16. Her full name was Guadalupe Villalogin
17. 500301; April 12, 1939; Receipt for 1935 Chevrolet Sedan

18 500101; August 27, 1939; Marriage of Ruby de la Luz Mendoza and Ernesto Reygadas Reygadas.
19 500183; December 10, 1927; Tax bill from Mexico for Encarnacion's property

26 - Old Soul - 4/1940 to 12/1941

1 April 1, 1940; 1940 U.S. Census, Precinct 1, Block No. 689.
2 500102; August 19, 1940; Letter from Enrique to son, Enrique Jr.
3 500362; October 16, 1940; draft registration for Virgilio Mendoza
4 500360; October 16, 1940; draft registration for Enrique Mendoza
5 500356; October 16, 1940; draft registration for Encarnacion Mendoza Jr.
6 500361; October 16, 1940; draft registration for Heriberto Mendoza
7 500363; October 16, 1940; draft registration for Jesus Garza Mendoza
8 500377; October 16, 1940; draft registration for Manuel Saenz Garza ("Meme")
9 500468; October 16, 1940; draft registration for Abel Gomez
10 October 16, 1940; draft registration for Claude Ordonez Sr.
11 The Alazan Courts constructed in 1939 Low-income public housing.
12 Father Carmelo Tranchese, the pastor of Our Lady of Guadalupe Church
13 500396; May 14, 1941; The Brownsville Herald (Brownsville, Texas), May 14, 1941, Wed, Page 6
14 500244; August 18, 1941; Application for a job at Texas State Employment by Margarita Garza Mendoza
15 500196; January 12, 1942; Reference letter for Margarita Mendoza as Power Machine Operator
16 500436; March 25, 1904; Death certificate for Pedro (Pete) E. Herrera.

27 - New Home - 1/1942 to 5/1945

1 500196; January 12, 1942; Letter of recommendation for Margarita
2 500244; January 19, 1942; Margarita applied for another job
3 500292; January 22, 1942; Receipt from Bell Furniture for Margarita Mendoza
4 500119; January 27, 1942; Declaration of 1937 Chevrolet truck to War Department by Encarnacion Mendoza
5 500323; May 27, 1942; Civil Service Examination results for Enrique Mendoza, eligible for hire as Storekeeper.
6 Jurgen Buchenau, Plutarco Elias Calles and the Mexican Revolution, [Maryland: Rowman & Littlefield Publishers, 2007],193-192
7 500103; December 22, 1942; Wedding invitation for Leslie's wedding
8 500293; January 10, 1943; Rent receipts for Hill Street rent
9 500294; April 8, 1943; Rent receipts for Hill Street rent
10 500435; December 15, 1943; Deed transfer for 719 Camada Street from Abel and Matilde Gomez to Carmen and Enrique Mendoza
11 500325; February 1, 1944; Pay adjustment letter for Enrique Mendoza from San Antonio, Air service command

Migrants: Exploring the Colors of my Family History

12   500256, 500456, 500339; April 7, 1944; Paperwork for purchase of 659 W. Elmira house by Margarita Mendoza
13   500163; April 7, 1944; loan for Elmira house
14   500338; April 7, 1944; House repainted and repairs declaration
15   500310, 500339; September 25, 1944; Payoff and release of lien for 659 W. Elmira, Margarita Mendoza
16   500338; October 30, 1944; repair and repaint the outside of the house.
17   500201; July 7, 1944; Margarita donated $5 to Red Cross
18   500202; November 14, 1944; Margarita donated $10 to Red Cross
19   500203; September 11, 1944; Margarita donated $5 to Red Cross for USO. The USO provided a wide range of programs for soldiers and their families.
20   500324; January 1945; W-2 for Enrique Mendoza
21   500204; January 16, 1945; Encarnacion donated $10 to Brooks County Chapter of Red Cross
22   500205; Margarita donated $8.67 to Brooks County Chapter of Red Cross
23   500163; January 26, 1945; Margarita wrote a letter for rent control adjustment
24   500325.1; January 27, 1945; Pay adjustment letter for Enrique Mendoza from San Antonio, Air service command
25   500149; May 9, 1945; Children of Encarnacion letter to reclaim General Terán property

28 - Living 6/1945 to 2/1947

1   500457; August 4, 1945; Enrique sold Camada house at 719 Camada
2   500435; December 15, 1943; Purchase of Camada house from Abel and Matilde Gomez by Enrique.
3   500105; September 9, 1945; Donation to Red Cross by Margarita Mendoza
4   500207; October 4, 1945, Southwestern Bell Telephone letter to Margarita
5   500208; October 27, 1945; Purchase/credit agreement from Joske Brothers for Encarnacion and Margarita
6   500325.2; November 16, 1944; Pay adjustment letter for Enrique Mendoza from San Antonio, Air service command
7   500257; November 26, 1945; Statement from Flowers Furniture Company by Margarita Mendoza
8   500209; January 26, 1946; Personal letter from Maria N. Narvaez to Margarita with Cumulative donations
9   500206; February 1946; Notice from the government for stopped payment allowance
10 500325.3; April 8, 1946; Pay adjustment letter for Enrique Mendoza from San Antonio, Air service command
11 500263; January 18, 1947; Insurance payment to S.P.Walker & Company for Trailer for Enrique
12 500212; January 3, 1947; Thank you to Encarnacion from Sears for on-time payments.
13 500106; February 3, 1947; A statement from San Antonio Music Company for

washing machine

14 500380; February 6, 1947; Declaration of Intention to become a U.S. Citizen by Manuel Meme Garza

29 - It's Time - 4/1947 to 12/1948

1 500258; April 1947; Sale Tax licenses for Loteria for Encarnacion Mendoza
2 500140; October 1947; Letter from the doctor regarding Henry and TB
3 500213; December 29, 1947; Hospital Rental by Encarnacion.
4 500214; January 1, 1948; Store License for Encarnacion Mendoza
5 500259; January 5, 1948; Notice that Enrique had been certified to be Insurance Agent
6 500297; January 7, 1948; Receipt for funeral service, Joe Ortiz Funeral Home by Canacho.
7 500215; January 9, 1948; Death notice of Margarita Garza Mendoza
8 500303; January 10, 1948; Purchase two graves at San Fernando Cemetery No. 2
9 500260; April 20, 1948; Purchase grave headstone for Margarita
10 500261; May 27, 1948; Paid for Purchase grave headstone for Margarita
11 500459; June 17, 1948; Legal transfer of property by children to Encarnacion

30 - The Pace of Life - 2/1949 to 12/1953

1 500297; June 2, 1948; Renewed Commercial driver's license for Enrique Mendoza
2 500262; February 26, 1949; Receipt for Clary Electro Adding Machine
3 500218; January 16, 1950; receipt water heater from Encarnacion Mendoza
4 500248; January 22, 1950; receipt for Kirby Vacuum cleaner by Encarnacion Mendoza
5 500135; October 11, 1950; Mexican Identification card for Encarnacion Mendoza
6 50220; January 22, 1951; payment receipt from Jesus Mendoza at American National Insurance Co. for Leslie Mendoza
7 500250; July 30, 1951; Enrique sent $50 via U.S. Postal Money Order to Francisco Trevino in Roma
8 500266; September 14, 1951; receipt, Jesus purchase bedroom set from Encarnacion.
9 500267; December 11, 1951, receipt for property taxes paid by Encarnacion
10 500346; August 6, 1952; contract with IG&N Lumber co. for Enrique Mendoza
11 500224; November 6, 1952; receipt for property taxes paid by Encarnacion Mendoza
12 500225; March 26, 1953; Alien Registration ID card for Encarnacion Mendoza
13 500156; May 1, 1918; Birth affidavit for Encarnacion Mendoza
14 500154; March 28, 1953; Invoice for 1952 Chevrolet for Enrique Mendoza
15 500226; July 22, 1953; Property tax receipt of $75.60 paid by Encarnacion Mendoza
16 500160; July 25, 1953; Product tag for coffee pot gifted to Carmen Garcia Mendoza by Enrique Mendoza
17 500162; August 12, 1953; Final Will of Encarnacion Sr.
18 500252; September 19, 1953; Receipts for payoff of Encarnacion's will to Frank J.

Alvarado, Attorney at Law.
19   500157; October 21, 1953; postcard to Enrique Mendoza from Carmen Garcia Mendoza
20   500228; November 2, 1953; property tax overdue notice for Encarnacion Mendoza
21   500229; December 9, 1953; reassessment of Elmira house for Encarnacion Mendoza

31 - Peace at Last - 1/1954 to 9/1954

1   500270; February 12, 1954; 1953 Income Tax Return for Enrique Mendoza
2   500271; March 12, 1954; receipt from Sears for purchase of Lawnmower
3   500272; March 18, 1954; purchase of refrigerator by Encarnacion Mendoza from Pete Rivera.
4   Reposteria - a term used to refer to Mexican pastries in general. A family recipe handed down from Enrique's father, Encarnacion Mendoza, is also in the family cookbook (La Familia Mendoza Cookbook). The usage of Reposteria in the cookbook refers specifically to a shortbread-like cookie that Encarnacion used to make in his bakery.
5   500273; March 25, 1954; receipt for eye doctor office visit by Encarnacion Mendoza
6   500110; April 2, 1954; Letter from Antonio in Monterrey to Encarnacion Mendoza
7   500318; May 26, 1954; Air Force Personal Affairs statement for Enrique Mendoza (Henry).
8   May 1954; Operation Wetback
9   500311; July 6, 1954; Last Payment paid to Alamo National Bank by Encarnacion Mendoza
10   500145; September 3, 1954; Death Certificate for Encarnacion Mendoza

32 - Aftermath - 1954

1   500277; September 15, 1954; Invoice for $600 from funeral company for Encarnacion Mendoza funerals.
2   500307; September 20, 1954; Payment of $610 to funeral company for Encarnacion's Mendoza funeral.
3   500275, 500276; September 4, 1954; List of relatives to invite to funeral. Prepared by Enrique and/or Encarnacion Jr.
4   500308; September 4, 1954; Cherished Memories guest book for funeral service.
5   500156; May 1, 1918; Birth affidavit for Encarnacion Mendoza, born March 25, 1882.
6   500231; September 7, 1954; Telegram from Arthur C. Maldonado, Monterrey, Mexico
7   500232; September 7, 1954; Telegram from Jesus Garcia Guajardo, Monterrey, Mexico

33 - Rebuilding - 1954 to 1955

1   500295; September 23, 1954; Reconciliation of Encarnacion's estate by Enrique Mendoza
2   500295; October 7, 1954; Contract to pay Guadalupe Galvan and Virgilio.

3   500278; January 1955; 1954 Income Tax return for Enrique Mendoza
4   500151; January 14, 1955; Postcard from Carmen to her son, Henry
5   500164; February 5, 1955; Postcard from Henry to his mother, Carmen.
6   500315; July 22, 1955; Contract to sell Elmira house for $10,000
7   500296; August 30, 1955; Release of Lien for Aganier Construction addition
8   500280; December 31, 1955; Detailed report of the Estate of Encarnacion Mendoza

36 - Memorial - 1956

1   500281; February 20, 1956; Enrique filed Fiduciary Income Tax Return for the estate for Encarnacion Mendoza
2   500317; September 3, 1956; Memorial Mass for Encarnacion Mendoza
3   500159; December 2, 1956; Postcard from Enrique to Carmen

37 - Ghost of Plutarco - 1957

1   500282; February 1, 1957; 1956 Fiduciary Income Tax return for Encarnacion's estate prepared by Enrique Mendoza
2   August 9, 2020; Quote from Mary Carmen Mendoza Oblinger as posted on Social media
3   500306; September 3, 1954 to May 31, 1957; completed final reconciliation statement for Encarnacion's estate.
4   500234; July 24, 1957; Telegram for 25th Wedding anniversary for Enrique and Carmen
5   500285; December 26, 1957; loan of $3,500 from Texas Savings and Loan for a house addition.

38 - Family United - 1958

1   500111; July 5, 1958; Wedding certificate for Minnie Mendoza and Eddie Alejandro.
2   500235; July 15, 1958; Congratulations from Arturo G. Maldonado, Monterrey, to Minnie and Eddie's wedding.
3   500121; 1958; Graduation invitation for Irma Mendoza
4   500112; September 13, 1958; Wedding invitation for Fernando Mendoza and Beatrice Galindo.

39 - Future

1   500153; July 10, 1959; Purchase of Chevrolet Kingswood 8, four-door station wagon.
2   500113; November 3, 1959; Jesus attempts to reclaim Nacogdoches Ybarbo property
3   500087; December 16, 1959; Death of Ofelia Montalvo Vda. de Longoria.

www.ingramcontent.com/pod-product-compliance
Lightning Source LLC
Chambersburg PA
CBHW060101230426
43661CB00042B/1491/J